HIT MEN

IRONBARK

HIT MEN

A tribute to league's tough guys

By TONY ADAMS

IRONBARK

DEDICATION

To my family, for understanding and supporting my passion for sport over the years.

First published 1994, in Ironbark, by Pan Macmillan Publishers Australia, a division of Pan Macmillan Australia Pty Limited 63-71 Balfour Street, Chippendale
Copyright © Tony Adams
All rights reserved. No part of this book may be reproduced or transmitted in any form or by any means, electronic or mechanical, including photocopying, recording or by any information storage and retrieval system, without prior permission in writing from the publisher
National Library of Australia cataloguing-in-publication data:
Adams, Tony, 1959-Hit Men
ISBN 0 330 27356 6.
1. Rugby League football players - Australia - Biography. 2. Rugby League football - Australia - Anecdotes. I. Title.
796.3338
Typeset by Letter Perfect, 541 George St, Sydney
Printed in Australia by McPherson's Printing Group

ABOUT THE AUTHOR

Tony Adams is a senior sports journalist with the *Daily Telegraph-Mirror* in Sydney who has won awards for reporting both cricket and rugby league. He lives in Sydney's eastern suburbs with wife Dawn and children Dean and Cassie. This is his first book.

AUTHOR'S THANKS

First and foremost, I am indebted to the hard men of rugby league, who generously took time out to relive their careers in such colourful detail. The one point virtually every player interviewed made was how many hit men there have been down the years in league's "rank and file" — players who never get much ink in the newspapers but were tough, respected and talented nonetheless. I regret that space restrictions didn't enable me to tell the stories of more of these courageous players. In selecting the players featured in the book, I have strived for the game's most rugged players, but players of class as well. While some of the men in the pages that follow had brutal reputations, none were thugs — they were all talented players and all tasted some form of representative football. The book could also not have been completed without the help of many team-mates, coaches and media men who pitched in with fascinating tales about the men in the spotlight.

My thanks to the people of Ironbark — Ian Heads, Deborah Wood and Geoff Armstrong. Deborah encouraged and supported the project from its infancy, Ian helped in the task of selecting 25 hit men from the hundreds of candidates while Geoff was meticulous and patient as he edited close to 100,000 words.

I am also indebted to News Limited and the *Telegraph-Mirror* for allowing me to report on the game I love for over a decade.

PHOTOGRAPHS

Special thanks to Action Photographs, Rugby League Week and News Limited for their assistance in the production of the photo sections.

CONTENTS

Foreword	by Ken Arthurson A.M.	
Chapter 1	RAY STEHR *Retaliating First*	1
Chapter 2	FRANK FARRELL *The Bumper*	8
Chapter 3	HERB NARVO *Footballer and Fighter*	14
Chapter 4	DUNCAN HALL *The Grand Slam*	20
Chapter 5	BILLY WILSON *Captain Blood*	27
Chapter 6	NOEL KELLY *Fighting Fire With Fire*	36
Chapter 7	KEVIN RYAN *Playing without Pity*	45
Chapter 8	JOHN SATTLER *Broken Jaw Hero*	53
Chapter 9	JOHN O'NEILL *Playing For Keeps*	61
Chapter 10	ARTHUR BEETSON *King of Queensland*	69
Chapter 11	GEORGE PIGGINS *Rabbitoh Pride*	76
Chapter 12	BOB O'REILLY *The Bear*	85
Chapter 13	TERRY RANDALL *Aiming for the Rib-Cage*	93
Chapter 14	JOHN DONNELLY *King of the Fibros*	101
Chapter 15	ROD REDDY *The Rockhampton Rocket*	110
Chapter 16	LES BOYD *Toeing the Line*	122
Chapter 17	RON HILDITCH *Leading from the front*	129
Chapter 18	GEOFF ROBINSON *The Wild Colonial Boy*	136
Chapter 19	CRAIG YOUNG *As Tough as Concrete*	144
Chapter 20	PETER KELLY *Leader of the Gang*	151
Chapter 21	STEVE ROACH *Eye of the Tiger*	161
Chapter 22	GLENN LAZARUS *The Brick With Eyes*	169
Chapter 23	MARK GEYER *Rebel with a Cause*	178
Chapter 24	CRAIG SALVATORI *In the footsteps of Big Artie*	188
Chapter 25	PAUL HARRAGON *Towards the 21st Century*	199
Bibliography		209

FOREWORD

By Ken Arthurson A.M.
Chairman, NSW and Australian Rugby League

I'm going to kick off this book on the hard men of league with a confession that will surprise a lot of people — I once locked horns with the great 'Bumper' Farrell. I will never forget the day in 1951 when, as a raw Manly halfback fresh from the juniors, I lined up against Newtown. As a kid in the 1940s, I had followed Frank Farrell's career with awe, and I don't think I was ever as nervous in my life as when we ran onto the field that day. Bumper was a living legend, a 'knock 'em down, drag 'em up' type renowned for his ruthless play. Such was my fear of the man, I spent the next 80 minutes just trying to avoid coming into contact with him. As it turned out, he only collared me once — but it was a tackle that hurt for a week.

Rugby league's big men have always been one of the game's great sources of fascination. From the early knuckle men like Ray Stehr (who I saw in action, but *never* played against) to the modern warriors such as Glenn Lazarus and Paul Harragon, league's foot soldiers have held a special place in the game's folklore. While their styles have changed radically over the years, their influence has remained dominant. You can't win premierships without that special brand of footballer up front — just look at the great St George, Souths and Manly teams for proof of that.

A question that always comes up when discussing league's hit men is how the likes of Bumper Farrell and Ray Stehr would have gone in the modern game. Having spent 80 minutes on the field with Bumper, I'm certain that if he played in the same manner today he wouldn't appear in too many games — the judiciary would make sure of that. As the game has changed the enforcers have had to clean up their act. The traditional "softening-up" period, highlighted by the odd punch-up, has gone, as have the cheap shots and square-ups. But I'm not suggesting Bumper Farrell or Ray Stehr wouldn't have survived in the current climate. They were great competitors who would have adapted to the times. They could cut it in any company.

Take a look at every sport that is ruled by the stopwatch (like swimming or running) and you'll notice vast improvements over the years. I think it's safe to say we've seen the same improvements in league. With the benefits of better training methods and improved technology, league's hard men are now faster and stronger than ever. We had men who weighed over 100 kilos in my day, but they were never as mobile and fit as Lazarus and Harragon. The modern player trains harder, eats better and recovers quicker from injury than at any other time in the game's history.

But one thing remains constant for league's big men. They go into battle every weekend determined to get on top of their opposite number. That has never — and will never — change. *Hit Men* gives a fascinating insight into the lives of some of the game's most colourful characters. I'm sure you'll enjoy reliving their experiences.

HIT MEN

RAY STEHR

Retaliating First

Ray Stehr was the youngest, and many say the fiercest, front-rower ever to play rugby league in Sydney. He had just turned 15 when he made his debut for Eastern Suburbs in the engine room in 1928, playing against several opponents more than double his age.

For much of the next 18 years, Stehr ruled the premiership with an iron fist. The legendary hard man was the driving force behind Easts' premiership-winning sides of the mid-1930s and his battles with English Test prop John Arkwright have become part of the game's folklore. And after his retirement, Stehr became a larger-than-life character, an ardent critic of the league hierarchy and astute commentator on the game's development.

Legend has it young Ray Stehr was playing marbles with schoolmates in a back lane in the inner-city suburb of Paddington when he received his call-up to play for Easts for the first time. Stehr had already played a handful of reserve-grade games, quickly impressing club officials with his maturity and strength.

When the team found itself a player short for an away game in Newcastle, officials decided Stehr's time had come. The teenager was hustled away from his game of marbles, and rushed home, where he picked up his gear and then was driven north. Stehr handled his baptism of fire well and never looked back.

Yet only a few years earlier, Stehr's parents were resigned to having their son spend the rest of his life in a wheelchair. Born in Warialda in north-west NSW in 1913, Stehr had developed a blood clot on his hip when just eight years old. The clot paralysed his leg and doctors, unsure of what to do, encased the leg in plaster for over a year. At the end of that 12 months, the doctors saw no improvement, and pronounced him incurable, telling young Raymond to prepare for life as a cripple.

HIT MEN

As a last resort, Stehr's parents took him to a Chinese herbalist in Sydney. For six months the herbalist poured the foulest mixtures down the youngster's throat and forced him to wear a heavy corset to straighten his back. But, miraculously, the unorthodox treatment worked, dissolving the clot, and Stehr was able to walk again. However, the herbalist told him he would always have to avoid strenuous work or sport.

A decade later, just days after he was named in the 1933 Kangaroos, Stehr was walking down King Street, Newtown, with several team-mates when he spotted the old Chinaman.

"My mates thought I was crazy when I dashed across the street and shook that old man's hand," Stehr wrote in an essay for Jack Pollard's *Rugby League, The Australian Way* years later. "They had no way of knowing how much I owed him."

Stehr's family moved to Sydney where he attended Randwick High School, and began boxing to build up his strength. The skills Stehr learned with the gloves at that early age were to serve him well on both the football field and, occasionally, in the square ring in years to come. Stehr's first footballing ambition was to play rugby union for Randwick, the famous "Galloping Greens". The youngster turned up at Randwick with high expectations but lasted just two training sessions.

"Hardly a soul said hello to me so I packed in the union code and went to Eastern Suburbs league club," he explained.

Stehr immediately "clicked" at Easts, and after his debut in 1928, officials slowly but surely groomed the up-and-coming forward. He played seven first-grade games in 1929 and six in 1930, all the while patiently learning the front-rower's craft. By 1930, Stehr was a regular first grader and in 1931 played the first of his 19 interstate matches for NSW against Queensland. Two years later, at just 20 years of age, he won selection in the Kangaroos. That tour started a long-running battle between Stehr and the Englishmen that saw many violent clashes on both sides of the globe.

On the long boat trip to England, the more experienced members of the Kangaroo party warned Stehr of the tough road that lay ahead. It didn't take long for Stehr to see the wisdom of their words. In his Australian debut against St Helens, Stehr was knocked out cold by a stiff-arm tackle. He soon found retaliation was the best way to answer the treatment the Englishmen dished out.

"I was no Billy Graham myself and against Warrington on that tour was sent off for punching an opponent named Miller," Stehr later wrote. "By the time I got home I was well and truly versed in the mayhem that can occur in the name of football."

From his earliest days, Stehr was blessed with an eloquent tongue. The young prop so impressed the English judiciary with an impassioned speech after the Warrington game that he was let off with a caution. Despite being found guilty, Stehr convinced the panel he had been the victim of "extreme provocation" by the Warrington forwards. In years to come, many league officials back home would come to rue Stehr's expressive and persuasive words. Stehr couldn't escape being disciplined by his own comrades, however, and was stood down for two games by manager Wally Webb. While Stehr was fuming at the time, he held no grudge against the tour boss. Several years after the tour, the fiery forward married Webb's daughter.

Stehr made his Test debut in the first Test of that tour, at Manchester's Belle Vue ground. Because of injuries, the team wasn't picked until lunchtime on the day of the Test. The players sat down to a steak lunch. But it was a tour rule that the Test players were not allowed potatoes on match day, and as Stehr was about to tuck into a spud, Webb leaned across the table and told the young front-rower: "No potatoes for you today, lad." It was only then that Stehr knew he was in the side.

In a tough, hard match, Stehr played solidly but couldn't prevent the Englishmen taking the honours 4-0.

There were many highs and lows for Stehr and the Kangaroos in England in 1933. The tour started on a dreadful note with three key players, Easts' Ernie Norman, Balmain's George Bishop and Les Heidke from Brisbane, having to pull out through injury. Then when the 'Roos boat arrived in Malta, popular three-quarter Ray Morris was forced into hospital with a serious ear infection. The players sailed on without him and two days later received the news that Morris had died of meningitis.

On the field, the 'Roos faced fiery and determined opposition in nearly every match. In the same game at St Helens in which Stehr was KO'd, hooker Dan Dempsey was kicked in the face during a scrum. Dempsey was carried from the field with blood spurting from a wound over his eye but insisted on returning to the fray. He simply pushed the edges of the wound together and told an ambulanceman to insert a safety pin and let him get on with the game.

Against Hull Kingston Rovers, the Roos had to contend with a series of blatant home-town decisions from the local referee. After an Australian try was recalled for an alleged forward pass, Stehr had had enough. He stormed up to the referee and protested. But the man with the whistle shrugged his shoulders and replied: "Can't you hear that crowd roar, lad? Don't forget I've got to live here!"

Refereeing troubles struck again in the game against Cumberland, with the Aussies clinging to a 16-12 lead late in the game. Finally the signal came from the sideline that time was up but the referee waved play on.

Stehr and several team-mates pleaded for the referee to blow the final whistle but their words fell on deaf ears. The match went another four minutes — just enough time for Cumberland to score a converted try to snatch a 17-16 win.

Overall, the tour was a mixed one for the Aussies. Although they won 11 games straight at one stage, they found the British too strong in the Tests, losing the series 3-nil. But the Kangaroos finished the tour on a high note, introducing the code to France on New Year's Day, 1934. In an exhibition match against Great Britain on a frozen field in Paris, the Aussies scored a stunning 63-13 win. Stehr scored one of Australia's 15 tries, ending an impressive maiden tour for the young forward. Showing great stamina and strength, Stehr had played 26 of the 37 tour matches, including two Tests, picking up many tricks of the trade from the wily English forwards.

Stehr moved to the NSW country town of Mudgee in 1934, accepting an eight-pounds-per-week contract to coach the local side. But when Stehr was selected for NSW and had to miss several club matches, Mudgee officials promptly sacked him!

Stehr returned to Easts and became an integral part of one of the mightiest teams ever to grace the premiership scene. The Tri-colours won the title in 1935, 1936 and 1937, losing just one match in that three-year period. Containing legendary figures like Dave Brown, Joe Pearce, Andy Norval, Viv Thicknesse and Stehr, Easts were a class ahead of the rest. In 1935, Stehr played in all three Tests against New Zealand, helping the Aussies to a 2-1 series win. But Stehr saw the series as merely a warm-up to his date with destiny — another crack at the Englishmen the following season.

He wasted no time making an impact on the British forwards in the first Test of the 1936 series in Sydney. Stehr received his marching orders after just 10 minutes. He had retaliated after being belted by English forward Martin Hodgson in a scrum flare-up. Ironically, the referee picked the wrong man to accompany Stehr to the showers, dismissing Nat Silcock instead of Hodgson.

Silcock was a shattered man as the pair began the long walk back to the dressing rooms in the SCG Members Stand.

"Tis the first time I've ever been sent off," the Englishman moaned.

Stehr, trying to be sympathetic, replied: "You'll get used to it, Nat."

Australia won the Test 24-8, before Britain levelled the series with a 12-7 win in Brisbane. The teams returned to Sydney for the decider — a match that was to earn Stehr a slice of league infamy. He and arch rival Arkwright were goading each other from the start, as they had throughout the series. A known knuckleman, Arkwright had won the distinction of being sent off twice in the one tour game only weeks earlier. Playing against Southern NSW, Arkwright had been dismissed early in the game but was recalled by the local captain, Jack Kingston. But a few minutes later Arkwright was again banished — this time for punching Kingston!

Arkwright and Stehr made no secret of their dislike for each other and quickly tested the patience of referee Lal Deane. When Australia won a scrum in the first half, Deane followed the ball along the backline, while the two Goliaths were trading blows in the back play. Arkwright allegedly started the fight, splitting Stehr's lip and nose with a cruel uppercut. When Deane returned to the scene of the crime, he found Stehr lying bloodied on the turf. Arkwright was immediately dismissed, and Stehr sent off for good measure when he finally regained his feet.

Over the years, Stehr gave as many as four versions of the incident. In the best known, he insisted that he "took a dive" to convince the referee to send Arkwright off. But Stehr believed the move back-fired on him because earlier in the season, he had used a similar ploy to have a Souths player dismissed in a club match. Deane had controlled that game as well. "He must have recalled how I'd fooled him in that Souths game," Stehr said. "And I got sent off too."

But in another version years later, Stehr alleged he was an innocent victim knocked out by Arkwright's wicked blow.

Stehr became the first player sent off twice in an Ashes series and received plenty of flak after Britain took the match, and the Ashes. "I have always considered I was provoked beyond endurance and the charge that I lost a Test series really wounded me more than what I stopped from Arkwright," he wrote in *Rugby League, The Australian Way*.

Years later, Stehr and Arkwright had a beer together in England and agreed on one thing — that Deane couldn't have seen what happened as he was following the ball. At the post-Test inquiry at which Stehr was given a three-match suspension, Arkwright had claimed he was kicked by the Australian. But in his evidence, Deane said Stehr punched the Englishman in the ear and the side of the face.

At their later meeting, Stehr asked Arkwright what prompted the incident and the Englishman replied: "Ee, Ray, but thee were getting ball from side of scrum. And laad, thee mustn't forget I was playing for England. Something had to be done. So I did it, Ray, with no hard feelings."

With both combatants now dead, the real truth of the famous "Arkwright incident" will never be confirmed. But perhaps the best clue lies in rare archival film of the match uncovered by Sydney's Channel Seven in the late 1980s. The footage doesn't show the incident, but clearly shows Stehr in a dazed and distressed state after the dust-up. The Aussie hardman was obviously in trouble as he made his way off the field, suggesting he did more than merely "take a dive".

Stehr had one last crack at the Englishmen in 1937-8, making his second Kangaroo tour but again experiencing little joy against the old enemy. Great Britain won the series 2-1, taking the first two Tests in Leeds and Swinton before the Aussies struck back with a victory at Huddersfield.

Legendary commentator and former NSW team-mate Frank Hyde believes Stehr would have joined the handful of forwards to complete three Kangaroo tours but for the intervention of World War II.

"I played with and against Ray many times and he was one of the toughest players the game ever saw," Hyde recalls. "In all the time I knew him, he never took a backward step. But Ray wasn't all brawn — he had plenty of skill with the ball, and was a brilliant scrummager and a very constructive attacking forward.

"In my opinion he would have certainly been among the elite to make three Kangaroo tours. He terrorised the Poms in 1933 and 1937 and was still among our leading forwards in the early 1940s. The Poms had a very strong side at the time, and some rough, tough forwards, but they hated him. Ray loved mixing it with the best of them and his battles with Arkwright were legendary."

Hyde recalls some advice he gave a team-mate in a club match against Stehr in 1942.

"I was captain of Norths and we had a big game against Easts at the Sports Ground. We knew Stehr would try to take us on up front and we had a fine young forward called Gerry Scully who I was certain he'd target. So I pulled Gerry aside before the game and had a quiet word of warning in his ear. 'Stehr will try to put you off your game but don't pay any attention to him,' I told him. 'He'll talk to you about your mother, your father ... maybe even your sister. But it'll just be a ploy to make you lose your cool. Show him you're bigger than that and just get on with the game.'

"Gerry thanked me for the advice and vowed he wouldn't have a bar of Stehr's intimidatory tactics, which were well known in the game at the time. The game started and no sooner had the first scrum gone down than it erupted, with Gerry swinging wildly at Stehr. The referee had no hesitation in waving Gerry off, with Stehr playing the part of the innocent bystander to perfection. When I got back into the dressing room at halftime, there was Gerry sitting in a corner of the shed, shaking his head.

"'What happened out there, Gerry?' I asked, although I already knew the answer.

"Gerry gritted his teeth, still seething with anger, and said: 'Nobody has ever called me mother anything like THAT! ... Nobody!'"

RAY STEHR

Stehr had a distinguished career as Easts captain, leading the club to the title in 1940 and often inspiring his younger team-mates with his leadership from the front. He continued to play with Easts until 1946, racking up a then record 184 games for the club.

He also dabbled in professional boxing late in his football career. Stehr had 11 professional fights, the most famous against Herb Narvo, his former Kangaroo team-mate. Narvo, who went on to win the Australian heavyweight title, had too much power and class for Stehr, winning by knockout in the second round.

After his retirement, Stehr saved his best jabs for the NSW Rugby League. For many years, he feuded publicly with League President and Australian Rugby League Board of Control Chairman, Harry "Jersey" Flegg, dubbing him the "chairman of the Board of No Control". During Manly's first season in the premiership, in 1947, the club appointed Stehr as coach. The club finished second-last that year, and again (with Stehr as coach) in 1948, winning four games in each season. Stehr then stepped away, to become an ardent critic of the game's administration.

He exposed many incidents that had previously been swept under the carpet, and, as he had often done during his footballing days, left more than one official red-faced.

In one famous skirmish during his playing career, Flegg attempted to bring the then Prime Minister Arthur Fadden into the Easts game before a big semi-final. But Stehr refused to let them in, telling the doorman: "Say we'd be honoured to meet Mr Fadden later, but our job at the moment is to win the game."

When league came to television in 1961, Stehr was behind the microphone for the first telecast into lounge rooms around the state, giving a blow-by-blow description of the Balmain v Norths game at North Sydney Oval.

Stehr was afforded one of the biggest funerals ever seen in the eastern suburbs after he died in 1983 following a long illness. Easts players wore black armbands the following Sunday as the club mourned the passing of one of its favourite sons.

In his final words to his son in hospital, Stehr said: "I'll see you at the Pearly Gates, son. I'll teach Jesus how to hook and we'll need you for the front row."

HIT MEN

FRANK FARRELL

The Bumper

Colourful front-rower Frank "Bumper" Farrell was the central figure in the longest and most controversial judiciary case Australian rugby league has known. For almost 40 years until his death in 1985, Farrell found himself having to defend his good name against one of the game's most heinous crimes — the infamous ear-biting incident involving St George prop Bill McRitchie. The New South Wales Rugby League inquiry into the incident lasted a staggering seven months — an indication of just how seriously the affair was treated. The incident haunted Farrell throughout his life, somewhat unfairly overshadowing his deeds as Newtown skipper, Australian front-rower and highly-respected policeman.

World War II was in its final days when Farrell's Newtown side met St George on what started out as a quiet afternoon at Henson Park in 1945. But then a scrum went down some 15 minutes into the game, with Farrell and McRitchie, as opposing front-rowers, battling to gain the upper hand.

Suddenly the scrum exploded, and referee George Bishop had to jump in. When Bishop separated the pair, he was stunned by what he saw. McRitchie's face was a bloodied mess, with a large part of his ear almost severed. Farrell was also in distress, with the crusty front-rower claiming he had been gouged.

But most of the attention was on the bleeding Saints prop. "Look what he's done to my ear!" an enraged McRitchie complained to Bishop.

Bishop could take no firm action, as he hadn't seen the alleged crime. However, he apparently told Farrell: "I know what went on in there. If I'd caught you doing it, you would have been sent off for life."

Remarkably, McRitchie attempted to play on despite his shocking injury, before eventually taking the advice of both team-mates and opposing players to leave the field. "You'd better go and see about that ear, Mac,"

Farrell's Newtown team-mate Herb Narvo advised as they packed into another scrum. "It looks in bad shape."

When McRitchie finally went off for attention he was immediately rushed to hospital and given a tetanus shot. In fact, he was to spend an agonising 22 weeks in hospital as doctors attempted to rebuild his ear with skin grafts, while debate raged in league circles over Farrell's guilt or innocence. The affair became front-page news in Sydney, on several occasions knocking off the war as the lead story of the day. In an affidavit to the NSW Rugby League's investigation, McRitchie described how he clawed at Farrell, who bit him as he attempted to take the loose head in the scrum. "For God's sake, let me go," McRitchie had pleaded.

Farrell told the inquiry he didn't bite people — on or off the field — and had the evidence to prove it.

"I left my teeth in the dressing room," he said as he displayed his set of dentures to the league officials.

But McRitchie wasn't swayed. Examining Bumper's remaining teeth, he claimed: "They were enough for you to do the job, Mr Farrell."

With both his football and police future on the line, Farrell was strangely quiet at the hearing. He repeatedly declined opportunities to cross-examine McRitchie.

One league official said later he "had no doubt Farrell bit McRitchie"; another said "Farrell used his teeth under provocation". But when the general committee took its vote, Farrell was cleared by 15 votes to 12, while McRitchie was awarded a sum between 200 and 300 pounds as compensation.

But the matter didn't rest there. St George officials attempted to re-open the inquiry a month later, with club delegate Arthur Justice claiming: "It is the duty of the League to find the player who bit McRitchie's ear."

However, the League disagreed, voting by 21-2 against further investigation.

Even years after the incident, Farrell refused to give anything away. Many journalists, fans and officials over the years attempted to get Farrell to confess to committing the act. But Bumper, although he always handled the inquiries with his customary good-natured banter, refused to ever admit any responsibility.

"I know nothing about it," he told one reporter, grinning all the while.

"It couldn't have been me," he said in another interview, shortly before his death. "I was at home crook in bed."

With McRitchie also dying several years ago, the affair is destined to remain one of league's great unsolved mysteries.

Frank Farrell was born into a poor family in the inner-Sydney suburb of

HIT MEN

Surry Hills shortly before the Depression. Times were tough, and Farrell learned some valuable lessons for later life as his father battled to make a living on the railways.

"It was a real struggle and you knew you couldn't have what you wanted on your dinner plate," he said years later.

It was in those early days in the 1920s, and not on the football field as is commonly believed, that Farrell earned his nickname. As a schoolboy, a class-mate dubbed him "Bumper" because of his habit of picking up discarded cigarette bumpers and smoking them. The name stuck, following Farrell for the next 60 years.

As with many working-class kids, Farrell turned to football and quickly made a name for himself as a rugged front-rower in the Marrickville juniors. He was graded by Newtown in 1936, beginning a long and glorious career with the "Bluebags". In all, he would play 16 seasons in the club's famous blue jumper, becoming the first player to notch 250 matches for the one club.

Farrell served a two-year apprenticeship in the lower grades before finally being given his spurs in 1938. Fielding a young and relatively inexperienced side, the Bluebags acquitted themselves well that year, finishing in sixth spot. But the following season, Newtown crashed, collecting the wooden spoon. The club re-established itself in 1940, with the emerging talents of Farrell playing a key role as the club reached the finals for the first time since 1937. In fact, Newtown would enjoy one of its best eras during Farrell's first-grade career, which eventually ran for 14 winters, making the finals eight times, winning the title in 1943 and finishing runner-up in 1944.

Farrell and Frank Hyde were long-time adversaries, first playing against each other in their school days. Even then, Bumper was a feared front-rower, for Marist Brothers Kogarah, while Hyde was a classy centre at St Patrick's, Church Hill. The pair played together at Newtown before Hyde transferred to Balmain, and then North Sydney. In the 1943 Newtown-Norths grand final, the best mates found themselves as opposing captains, and it was Farrell who led his side to a crushing 34-7 win. The premiership proved to be Newtown's last (of three). Appropriately, it was Bumper who scored the last try in the Bluebags' finest win.

Hyde has bitter-sweet memories of his old pal.

"Bumper was a legend and took great pride in the fact he only played with one club throughout his career," he recalls. "He came to Newtown not long after me and we became lifelong friends — I even introduced him to his wife, Phyllis.

"Bumper had a lot of friends, but forgot them all the minute he took the

FRANK FARRELL

football field. He was the roughest, toughest player of his era. He looked at the rules as a minor distraction ... they never worried him. Yet beneath the rough exterior was a marshmallow heart. Bumper may have been tough and hard, but he was always fair, and I think everyone, even his enemies, respected him for that."

On the field, Farrell prided himself on his toughness and durability. After he quit the game, he pointed out many times that he never needed ambulance attention despite many bruising battles during his long career. One hapless ambulanceman could testify to Farrell's dislike of the "zambucks". With Farrell dazed on the ground after coming off the worse for wear in an altercation during a hectic battle, the unsuspecting ambulanceman ran onto the field to treat the big front-rower. The medico had just whipped out the smelling salts when Bumper came to his senses and lashed out with a massive boot, sending him scurrying back to the sideline.

"Nobody is going to make a cream puff out of me," Farrell yelled as he sent the stunned ambulanceman on his way.

"The Little Master" Clive Churchill was another who developed a grudging respect for Farrell over the years. Churchill, perhaps unfortunately, made his Sydney debut for Souths in 1947 against Farrell's Bluebags. In his autobiography years later, Churchill described that first meeting.

"I was getting up to play the ball," Churchill wrote, "when I heard a deep voice over me exclaim: 'Hello, son!' And almost at the same time I felt Bumper's big, powerful, clenched hands around my head, screwing it off. As I got to know him, I came to realise he was the most feared forward in football."

On the representative scene, Farrell was also a force to be reckoned with. He was a stand-out player for NSW in the '40s and made his Test debut in 1946, playing all three Tests against the touring Englishmen.

However, Farrell had anything but a smooth lead-up to his maiden Test. He was up much of the previous night in his job as a policeman, leading a raid on a notorious inner-city gambling house. After a few hours' sleep, he was back up at 5.30am for a daily swim, which he found relaxed the muscles and primed him for the battle ahead. In the dressing room before his Test debut, Farrell was a bundle of nerves.

"I just looked at the other faces and didn't even hear much," he recalled years later. "Then I heard the coach (the former international five-eighth, Albert 'Rick' Johnston) standing over me, giving the simple instruction: 'Give em hell, Bumper'. As we ran onto the SCG, suddenly I looked down and for the first time I really noticed the colour of the jumper I was wearing. I got a bit of a shock. I had half expected to see the Newtown colours I was so used to wearing. But the jumper was green and gold and I shivered with excitement. That was my greatest moment ... how could it have been anything else?"

Revelling in his first meeting with the rugged English pack at Test level, Farrell played with his customary aggression and vigour in a hard-fought 8-all draw. Surprisingly, this was the closest Farrell came to experiencing a Test win. Australia lost the remaining two Tests, with Britain taking home the Ashes.

In 1948, Farrell was selected in the first Test against New Zealand, in Sydney. The Kiwis won a see-sawing game 21-19, and after the loss Farrell was made a scapegoat. He was dropped for the return clash, which Australia won, and never wore the green and gold again.

Most old front-rowers fade into obscurity after they retire, but not Frank Farrell. The Bumper legend gained momentum after he hung up his boots, as he concentrated his unique talents on the formidable task of cleaning up the Kings Cross/Darlinghurst area of inner Sydney. Infamous characters, such as the "Vice King" Joe Borg, Dulcie Markham (the "Angel of Death", who reputedly had eight lovers murdered) and Tilly Devine, known as the "Queen of the 'Loo", regularly crossed swords with Bumper.

Veteran police roundsman Bill Jenkings, who wrote on Sydney's underworld for the now defunct *Daily Mirror*, held a special affection for Bumper.

"I've been reporting crime in this city for just on 40 years and Bumper Farrell was the most colourful cop I knew," Jenkings wrote shortly after Farrell's death in 1985. "His very appearance instilled respect and sometimes fear into hoodlums and criminals who infested Kings Cross, which was his domain for so many years. With his big cauliflower ears, rugged face and ham-like fists, Farrell was a formidable figure. If Bumper spotted hoodlums hanging about a street corner he would say: 'These mugs are up to no good. Let's attend to them.' Yet I never once heard of Bumper using his baton or gun. He enforced the law with his fists and was known to walk alone through the streets of Surry Hills, which was known as the Barbary Coast in Sydney."

Farrell became a celebrity with his very first arrest, a drunk lying in the gutter of a Darlinghurst street. Bumper decided to take the man into protective custody for the night and as he was checking him in at the station, the desk sergeant said: "Constable, how many eyes has your prisoner got?"

Bumper was taken aback. "Two, as far as I know," he replied.

But the wise old sergeant quickly corrected the new recruit.

"Have another look; he's only got one."

As Bumper escorted the prisoner to the cells, the man showed him a

FRANK FARRELL

false eye, which he produced from a matchbox in his coat pocket.

"One thing you must learn, son," the drunk explained. "Never take your eye off your prisoner."

Farrell rose to the rank of Inspector First Class in charge of the Darlinghurst station, with over 200 men under his command. Just before retiring in 1976, Farrell lamented the changing face of the criminal element in Sydney.

"The old crims were manly sort of blokes," he told well-known *Mirror* columnist Jack Darmody. "They took it and they gave it. Today they are slimy types with hearts as big as the buttons on their shirts. There's not too many men of action around now."

Farrell spent his final years as a security consultant for News Limited, located in his old stamping ground of Surry Hills, and was often entertaining the journos with tales from the good old days — on the field and on the beat. When he died peacefully in his sleep, at the age of 68, his long-time mate Bill Jenkings wrote in tribute: "Farrell's passing has ended an era in Sydney ...

"He was an institution."

HIT MEN

HERB NARVO

Footballer and Fighter

Respected league judge Frank Hyde doesn't sit on the fence when asked his opinion of Herb Narvo. "He was, simply put, the best second-rower I ever saw," says Hyde, a man who has been involved in league as a player, commentator or onlooker for over 60 years. "And also the fastest. Herb was a great athlete, a very dedicated player and a feared runner with the ball. He had great determination and strength and scored some memorable tries in his career."

The "Fighting" Narvo is most remembered as the rugby league player who mixed his football with boxing, winning the Australian heavyweight crown during his league career. But that, according to Hyde, doesn't do justice to his league talents.

"Narvo was one of the greats and would have been at home in any era," he says. "His fitness and dedication stamped him ahead of the rest."

Born Herman Nawo, of Polish parents, in the inner-Sydney suburb of Ultimo in 1912, Narvo was a sportsman from his earliest days. His family moved to Newcastle in his school years, changing his name to Herbert Narvo to fit in with his Australian surroundings. He began his league career at Wickham Technical Junior School, in the second row, and stayed in that spot for over 20 years, carving out a fearsome reputation. By the age of 18, he was playing first grade in the boots-and-all Newcastle competition, holding his own with battle-hardened veterans, some nearly double his age.

In 1937, with a Kangaroo tour as the major lure, Narvo decided the time was right to move to Sydney. Hyde still vividly recalls his first meeting with the young forward.

"I was playing at Newtown in 1937 and both he and Ron Bailey (who went on to captain Australia in 1946) came down to trial with us from

HERB NARVO

Newcastle. I was so delighted with what I saw that I took them home with me that night. We all went out on the town to the Palais Royale. I was confident we had found two very special players."

Narvo's many supporters in Newcastle expected him to take Sydney by storm and the big-hearted second-rower didn't disappoint. He won immediate respect for his no-nonsense style and gained a spot in the Sydney Seconds representative team, after only a handful of first-grade games with the Bluebags. But despite a whirlwind start to his career in the big time, Narvo controversially missed his goal — the Kangaroo tour.

However, just when he was poised to take up an offer from English club Huddersfield, fate smiled on Narvo. The Kangaroos, on their way to England and France, played a warm-up match in New Zealand where the classy Easts forward, Joe Pearce, suffered a broken leg, ruling him out of the tour before it had really started. Narvo received an urgent call-up to board the first boat for England, where he more than vindicated his selection, playing in four of the five Tests on tour, and producing a match-winning effort in the third Test against Great Britain, ironically at Huddersfield.

Although the home side had won the first two Tests to retain the Ashes, the Englishmen had no answer to Narvo's powerhouse running in the third. The hard-running forward scored one try and created another in Australia's 13-3 win.

Although a rugged, uncompromising forward, Narvo also had a soft side. A dedicated family man, Narvo was clearly uncomfortable at the thought of being so far from his family on Christmas day during the 1937-38 tour. Having to play a match that day only served to rub salt in the wounds. As the players lined up before kick-off, Narvo made it clear his heart just wasn't in the game.

"Harry, I reckon they're tough making us play football today," he told team-mate Harry Pierce. "It's the one day I don't want to play. I'd rather write home to mum and the kids."

Pierce sympathised but merely shrugged his shoulders, realising there was little anyone could do. But Narvo had other ideas. With the match just a few minutes old, he decked an opposition forward with a perfect uppercut ... right in front of the referee, who immediately gave the Aussie forward his marching orders. As he returned to the dressing room, Narvo, with a sly grin on his face, winked at Pierce.

Narvo won instant acclaim from the French fans with his hard-running style on the second leg of the Roo tour. In a match in Villeneuve, he split the defence time and again, with the crowd chanting "Bravo! ... Bravo!" every time the big second-rower strode through the opposition. Puzzled,

HIT MEN

Narvo turned to team-mates and said: "Struth ... how did they get to know my name over here?"

After the tour, Narvo returned to Newcastle, the town he always considered home, and in 1939 wrote his way into the record books as his Northern Suburbs side thrashed Morpeth by a world record 127-18. He returned to the Bluebags for a second stint in 1943, and helped the club reach the grand final against North Sydney, who they thrashed 34-7. The damage was all done up front, with Narvo and Bumper Farrell each scoring tries in the big win. Frank Hyde still has bitter memories of the match and the carnage caused by Narvo and company.

"They gave us a heck of a beating," he recalls. "After the match I looked a mess and the last two people I wanted to see were Herb and Bumper. But we were all great mates and they weren't about to let an opportunity to rub my nose in the dirt pass by. They made sure they came across to me in the Norths dressing room half an hour or so after the game and had a good laugh at my appearance. One of my eyes was hanging down near my chin and while I wasn't sure of exactly how it happened, I was pretty sure the perpetrator was one of the men standing in front of me. They looked as innocent as lambs as they asked me what happened. Bumper grinned and said: 'That couldn't have happened out there — you must have brought that injury with you.'"

By 1945, Narvo was the NSW captain and remained one of the most respected players in the country. His dedication to fitness and conditioning set him apart from his peers — Narvo was a Wayne Pearce-style character ahead of his time. Once he told colleagues: "The average footballers today trains a day less than he should. He should train at least three days a week. You must be in better condition than your opponents."

And like Wayne Pearce, Narvo was conscious of his image in an era when many league players thrived on the game's rough-and-tumble reputation. No better example can be found to support this than before an interstate clash at the SCG in 1945. This was an important occasion — the players were set to be introduced to the then Governor-General, the Duke of Gloucester, before the kick-off. As the NSW team left the dressing room, Bumper Farrell remarked to Narvo: "Hey, Herb, you've forgotten to take out your false teeth for the game."

Narvo looked at his long-time team-mate and replied patiently: "Frank, when you meet royalty, one must look one's best."

Years after he retired, Narvo revealed the NSW team had considered boycotting the above match against Queensland. Paid a paltry five pounds for representing their state, the players held a last-minute dressing-room meeting and refused to change into their football gear. Officials hastily

HERB NARVO

convened a meeting, increased the players' pay packets to 20 or 25 pounds (Narvo couldn't remember which) and the game went ahead, with the public oblivious to the drama.

Narvo also prided himself on his fair, albeit aggressive, style of play. Few players baited him because of his awesome reputation as a fighter and Narvo believed in a strict code of honour on the field: make it hard, but keep it fair. He felt so strongly about illegal play that once during his captain-coach days in Newcastle, he appeared before league officials to denounce the roughhouse tactics of an opposition team.

"My concern wasn't for myself, but the younger players in my team," he explained.

Controversy had a bad habit of dogging Narvo despite his good intentions. In 1943, the Newtown star was the subject of a scandal when offered a bribe by a black-market bookmaker to "throw" a match. Offers were also known to have been made to three of Narvo's team-mates, and to the champion Easts forward, Dick Dunn. Narvo said later: "If I wasn't heavyweight champion, I would have flattened the man."

The damaging forward was also a superstitious player. He had a lucky charm — the seal of a whisky bottle — which he wore around his neck whenever he played. In one game in 1946, he forgot to wear his 'necklace' and was convinced the bad leg injury he sustained during the match was a direct consequence. On another rare occasion when he left the charm in the dressing room, his St George team-mate Walter Mussing suffered a collarbone injury. Narvo told stunned players after the match: "It's my fault; I knew something would happen when I forgot to bring that whisky seal."

Narvo had shocked the league community in 1946 when he left the Bluebags to join the Saints. Rumours spread throughout the game that Narvo and three fellow Bluebags had left the club in the wake of the Bill McRitchie ear-bite scandal, which had involved Bumper Farrell in such controversy. However, Narvo denied the rumours, claiming he simply joined the Dragons because of an attractive captain-coach offer.

Narvo's move to St George proved a bonanza for the Saints. The big man's popularity saw home gates swell and even on training nights, it was common for hundreds of fans to come and watch Narvo's impressive fitness work with his squad. Saints won the club championship under Narvo's guidance in his lone year at the club. And they made the first-grade grand final, only to be pipped by Balmain 13-12.

The rampaging second-rower was renowned as the code's iron man of the '40s. He once played for St George on a Sunday, just 24 hours after defending his boxing title in the ring. On another occasion, during the War, he turned out for Combined Services in a rugby union match ... then rushed across town to play for Newtown an hour later in the league match of the day against Balmain.

Narvo was captain-coach in Cootamundra in 1947 (where in one game his side humiliated Junee 121-4) and Camden in 1948, before returning to Newtown for a comeback season in 1949. But the move proved one of the few poor choices of his impressive career. Troubled by injury, he appeared in just five games, before quitting Sydney to play out what proved to be his last season in Newcastle.

The hard-hitting Narvo's boxing credentials were every bit as successful as his football deeds. An excellent all-round athlete, Narvo excelled at many sports, including cycling and cricket. During World War II, he joined the RAAF as a physical fitness and boxing instructor and made such an impression he decided to try his hand in the square ring.

Before taking the plunge into a professional fighting career, Narvo consulted well-known trainer Tom Maguire, asking for a month's trial.

"I'll fight if you promise I won't make a fool of myself," Narvo told Maguire.

After the month's apprenticeship, Maguire was convinced his new pupil was ready. Narvo's first professional fight was in Newcastle in 1942, and resulted in a knockout win over Frank Price in the opening round. Just four fights later, Narvo found himself challenging Bill "Wocko" Britt for the Australian heavyweight title. Again, Narvo's power punching proved decisive as he KO'd Britt in a mere 23 seconds. Narvo often fought in challenge bouts, his most famous against another former Test great in Ray Stehr. The Kangaroo team-mates of '37-38 slugged it out for four action-packed rounds before Narvo emerged triumphant.

The "Fighting" Narvo held his national title for three years before losing his crown to Victoria's Jack Johnson. After that loss, he immediately announced his retirement. In his latter years, Narvo left no doubt as to which of the two sports in which he excelled he preferred.

"I did not like boxing ... so I got out," he said. "Some people in the game with whom I had to deal were not fair dinkum."

After finishing with football and boxing, Narvo tried his hand at managing several hotels in country areas without great success. When the first signs of the cancer that would eventually take his life began to show in 1957, Narvo was back in Newcastle, working on the wharves. Doctors told Narvo an operation would have a million-to-one chance of succeeding. Showing all the courage he displayed on the football field and in the ring, Narvo told the doctors to operate anyway. Unfortunately the surgery was unsuccessful, although it did manage to alleviate some of Narvo's suffering, enabling him to leave hospital, albeit briefly, to watch one last game of

HERB NARVO

football — the third Test between Great Britain and Australia at the SCG in July, 1958.

When his son Frank, who also played for Newtown, had visited him in hospital before that match, Narvo had said: "I want two tickets to the SCG on Saturday — one for the doctor and one for myself."

Narvo's determination to attend the match greatly heartened his friends, many of whom were convinced he would never leave hospital.

However, a little over a week later, Herb Narvo died, back in hospital. Shortly before his death, aged just 46, Narvo had said to the renowned sportswriter, W.F. Corbett: "What more could you want than to die in your sleep? I have enjoyed every minute of life and would do everything I have done all over again."

HIT MEN

DUNCAN HALL

The Grand Slam

Duncan Hall is considered by many to be the finest all-round forward Queensland rugby league has produced. A devastating ball-running second-rower in his early days, Hall smashed forward try-scoring records like they were going out of style. He was a man ahead of his time — a 1990s forward — tall and strong with awesome pace for a big man. Later Hall graduated to the front row, where he was a key man in Australia's Ashes successes in 1950 and 1954 against rugged Great Britain sides.

Hall's intelligent yet aggressive approach made him one of Australia's most valuable players in the immediate post-war era. Hard and uncompromising, he soon taught the Englishmen he was not to be trifled with and became number one on the Brits' "most wanted" list during his battles with the old enemy. Duncan Hall never took a backward step — from an opponent or a referee — in a colourful career that included 22 Test matches for Australia.

Born Douglas Hall at Rockhampton in 1925, as a youngster he spent most of his time with relatives whose surname was Duncan. That's what his young schoolmates called him and somehow the name stuck for life.

"I went to a small school on the outskirts of Rockhampton, near Yeppoon. There would have only been 12 kids in the whole school," he recalls today. "The locals were always looking for players for their senior side. By the time I was 13, I'd been playing for a few years and had a real passion for the game. So I'd sneak out and play for the seniors against Rockhampton. I got away with that until once I scored a try. My name was in the local paper the next day and my mother went crook at me. She couldn't believe her little boy was playing football against grown men. But there was no-one my own age to really play league against at Yeppoon. However, when I went to high school in Rockhampton things improved slightly."

DUNCAN HALL

Hall started playing in the second row for Christian Brothers and, when aged 14, his team won the Rockhampton secondary school junior competition. The following year he left school to become an apprentice fitter on the railways and began playing for the Brothers club. He was soon playing with the A-grade Brothers side, though one weekend he played minor, junior and senior grades.

"I loved the game that much I'd play every day if I could back then," he remembers. Hall was content to live and play in Queensland's far north, but a long and bitter railway strike in Rockhampton soon changed his destiny.

"The strike eventually saw my parents move to Brisbane in 1948," he recalls. "I decided to go with them. I had a try-out with Valleys and eventually made first grade with them.

"I went from there to play for Brisbane. My aim was to get into the Queensland side and I made it after a couple of strong showings for Brisbane. But it only occurred to me later on that had I not made the move to Brisbane, there was virtually no way I would have won that Queensland jumper. In those days, the state team was almost always made up of players from Brisbane, Toowoomba or Ipswich. The selectors couldn't see all the talent in faraway places like Rockhampton. If not for that railway strike, I may well have stayed an unknown for the rest of my career."

Always a phenomenal try scorer for a forward in Rockhampton, Hall maintained his impressive strike rate in the stronger Brisbane league, averaging a try a game in his first season

"In 1948," Hall tells, "I was a reserve for the Queensland side for the tour down south for the two matches against NSW and didn't get a run in the first game on the Sunday. When I was also left out of the second game on the Tuesday I was shattered. But I remember we pulled a trick on one of the forwards selected ahead of me. I went up to him the morning of the game and said: 'Gee, mate, you don't look too well.'

"In the next hour or so around three other blokes told him exactly the same thing. Before long, he really was feeling sick. He withdrew from the team and I came in to the front row. But when we packed in the first scrum I began to think I'd have been better off back in the grandstand. I came head-to-head — and I mean literally that — with Bumper Farrell. He was on the way out then, but was still a tough man. He butted me as we went down in the first few scrums and a few other things went on as well. But I refused to give an inch.

"After about the fourth scrum, Bumper growled to me: 'Well, son, I think we're starting to understand each other.'"

"I was a determined man in those days and fired back with: 'Please yourself, I'm younger than you and I'm prepared to keep going all day.'

I didn't know how Bumper would react but he just grinned and said: 'Now I know we understand each other.'

"That was the only time I played against old Bumper but he taught me a thing or two."

Hall's strong display opposite Farrell wasn't lost on the Australian selectors, and he made his Test debut that same season, against the Kiwis in Brisbane (a match Australia won 13-4). A week later, after the final interstate match of the season, Hall was named in the Kangaroo side to tour England at the end of that season.

"I was delighted to gain selection," Hall says. "They named me as a second-rower and it was one of the highlights of my life touring with such a great bunch of blokes.

"It was the last Kangaroo tour to go to England by boat and we loved it. While it was a long trip and our legs got pretty rubbery by the end of six weeks, it was the best way to get to know the blokes. By the time we got to England there was a real closeness between us which helped us during the campaign."

While the long voyage was ideal for team bonding, it counted against the Kangaroos in their opening match against Huddersfield. After trailing only 2-0 at halftime, the Roos were over-run 22-3 by a Huddersfield team spearheaded by Aussies Lionel Cooper and Pat Devery.

"Our legs just gave way in the second half and we couldn't keep up with the pace," Hall recalls. "We did a lot of training and scrummaging on the boat but it still wasn't the same as running around the football field; it took us a while to adjust to dry land again."

The match was a fiery affair in which another Aussie playing for Huddersfield, Johnny Hunter, was knocked unconscious by a high Kangaroo tackle. By the end of the match, the crowd was so incensed the Aussies feared for their safety as they left the field. Only some quick thinking by the local band-master, who began a chorus of *God Save the Queen*, defused an ugly situation.

Hall was a central figure in another spiteful match not long afterwards, at Castleford. Played just three days before the First Test, the game was described by *The Sydney Morning Herald's* Tom Goodman as "the most foul affair I have seen in 30 years of reporting football". The match featured an all-in brawl, high tackles, gouging and a series of off-the-ball incidents. Two players from each side, including Hall, were given their marching orders.

"Castleford were protecting an unbeaten home record that season and it was obvious they weren't going to surrender it without a fight," Hall remembers. "It was on from the start and I was sent off for retaliating after a bloke biffed me. The match went right down to the wire, with Johnny Graves scoring a try for us in the corner in the last minute to level the scores. The crowd were filthy, and were throwing lumps of coal and shouting abuse as Johnny lined up the conversion kick. They were all saying he was no chance, but Johnny, who was a cheeky blighter, yelled back: 'You don't think I'll kick it? Have a look in the newspapers tomorrow morning,"

"Sure enough, he booted a mighty kick right between the posts. As our boys ran off they were pelted with coal again. That was the mood of English crowds in those days. If their local side beat us, they'd heap praise on us and call us the best team to ever go on tour. But if by some chance we won, we'd be the sons of colonial convicts and that sort of thing."

Soon afterwards, at St Helens, crafty Australian five-eighth Wally O'Connell was targeted by the home team. Saints centre Doug Greenall, a noted hard man, swung a stiff arm at the little pivot. O'Connell was uninjured, but made the most of the incident, taking a "dive". Hall knew his team-mate was unhurt, but felled Greenall anyway, just for good measure.

Hall played in two of the three Tests in England on the '48 tour, missing the other through injury, as Great Britain retained the Ashes with a 3-nil whitewash. But while the final result may not have been what the Australians had been seeking, for Duncan Hall the tour was in many ways a great success. He captivated the English crowd with his speed and strength, and scored a remarkable 10 tries on tour.

Upon his return home, Hall played another season with Valleys before moving to Home Hill as captain-coach in 1950. The hard-running forward, now moved permanently up to the front row, experienced one of the highlights of his career that season, helping Australia win back the Ashes for the first time in 30 years. Hall played in the first Test of the series, but was axed after Australia's 6-2 loss. Australia won the second Test, yet despite the victory, selectors decided to recall Hall for the decider, a famous match won 5-2 by the home side in atrocious conditions, thanks to a try by winger Ron Roberts.

Pandemonium followed the drought-breaking win at the SCG. "Vic Hey was our coach and we celebrated for days," Hall remembers. "The win was a long time coming and we lived it up in style."

Hall spent the 1951 and '52 seasons at Toowoomba, where he came under the coaching of league legend Duncan Thompson. The pair formed a dynamic partnership, with Thompson rating Hall as one of the best players he had ever seen. He described him as "the dream forward".

Hall toured Britain and France again, with the 1952-53 Kangaroos, who proved tougher opposition for the Englishmen than their counterparts of four years before, but failed to retain the Ashes. The Aussies went down 2-1 in the Tests, with Hall again one of the most prominent figures in the torrid forward encounters.

By then he was established as the leader of the Australian pack, and consequently was frequently subjected to baiting and roughhouse tactics. In the first Test of the series at Leeds, Hall copped punches and fingers in the eyes in every scrum. After half an hour, he'd had enough, and grabbed his opposite by the collar, and declared how much he would love to punch him square on the jaw. "But I'm not going to do it," Hall said, "because I don't want to get sent off. So how about just playing football, mate, and forgetting the rough stuff?"

However, the Englishman refused to relent. "That's the idea — to get thee sent off. Then we'll play football."

On his return from England, Hall actually retired for a season due to a nagging nasal injury, the legacy of countless high tackles over the years. But an operation successfully repaired the problem, enabling him to breathe freely again, and extend his career.

One of Hall's major regrets is that he came within a whisker of joining a select band of players to complete three Kangaroo tours.

"We played a social game up at Murgon late in 1955 and I stuffed my knee up. Up until that stage, Wally Prigg (the great Newcastle lock forward of the 1930s, who led the 1937-38 Kangaroos) was the only Australian to make three Kangaroo tours. Clive Churchill, Kevin Schubert and myself both went in 1948 and 1952 and were very keen to equal Wally's record. But Clive was the only one of the three of us to make it. I played on in '56 with Wests in Brisbane but the knee kept giving me trouble. I hobbled around and was a hopeless case. I kept hoping it would come good but by the end of the year, it was time to give it away."

Hall never played in the Sydney competition, but revelled in the atmosphere of representative football. He played a staggering 82 representative matches during his 12-year career — 23 for Queensland and 59 for Australia. He captained Queensland during one of the Maroons' strongest eras, with star players like Kel O'Shea, Brian Davies and Bobby Banks under his charge.

"That was what you lived for in those days — the rep games," Hall says. "All the internationals were hard. I only played the Kiwis once but they had a very strong side. The Englishmen always gave you a real tussle and the French were very physical back then. In the late 1940s and early '50s, the French team was made up largely of former Resistance members. They'd fought the Nazis for years and survived — that's how tough they were.

"Their front-rower Lolo Mazon was a real competitor. He played against us in 1949 in France and again out here in 1951. He once told me about how he and several other underground men were being lured into a trap by the Germans during the war. Mazon suddenly realised what was happening and raised the alarm. They all got out alive, thanks to him. He had shown plenty of courage in life, and that carried over onto the football field."

Hall's uncompromising approach saw him sent off more than once during his career. In fact, he completed a "grand slam" by receiving his marching orders against all Australia's international opponents of that time — Great Britain, France and New Zealand.

"I went off a few times but I was never what you'd call a hot head," he explains. "They were hard times on the field and I had a real will to win. I never started anything, but if someone whacked me, I'd usually belt them back.

"Stiff-arms were part of the game back then, but, even though it was rugged, there was a code of conduct. I never gouged, put my knees into a bloke or kicked anyone on the ground. Those sort of things could maim a bloke for life and weren't on as far as I was concerned. There was plenty of spite, but there was still respect. It was give and take and you learned to live with that."

Hall toured Europe with Australia's unsuccessful 1954 World Cup side — a trip that contained its fair share of incidents.

"After a game in Marseilles we had to go to a function, and afterwards we called into a cafe to have a drink. (Australian coach) Vic Hey had this trick where he'd get a pin and prick his thumb, just enough to allow some blood to come out. He'd then tied a handkerchief around the wound and started waving a big knife around the thumb, which now looked soaked in blood. The Frenchmen thought he was crazy.

"'Stop him,' they cried. 'He's mad.'

"We got shown the door. Out on the street the boys started teasing Vic about his tackling ability. 'You're a pussycat ... you tackle like my grandmother,' a couple of them said to him. After a while, Vic was really riled. It was about four in the morning by this stage, and, as you could probably imagine, we'd had a bit to drink. We started walking back down the street towards our hotel when we saw a single headlight appear out of the darkness. It was a motorcyclist, probably on his way to work.

"'Can't tackle ... I'll bloody show you all,' Vic screamed.

"As the bike went past, Vic launched himself at it. You should have seen the result. The bike went one way, and the poor motorcyclist went the other; I think he got the shock of his life. Vic also went flying, but, as we all looked down at the sight of him and the poor Frenchman sprawled on the road, he barked at us: 'Now who said I can't bloody well tackle?'

HIT MEN

"We had a bit of explaining to do about that one. Then we moved on to America for some exhibition games and for some reason, Brian Davies decided to shave all the hair off his head. In Los Angeles we went to a party which ran out of beer. Brian, who we all called 'Bull', and I decided we'd fix that and drove down to the nearest liquor store, where we burst through the door, in a hurry to get back to the party. The sight of Bull, without a hair on his head, must have been too much for the owner. He threw his hands in the air and pleaded for us not to rob him. "Bull just grinned and said: 'We want your beer, but we don't want to rob you — we'll pay for it.'

After retirement from the playing field, Hall's life was just as colourful, if not more so, than during his footballing days. He tried his hand at administration, where his straight-talking approach made him a big hit with players many years his junior. Hall managed the Australian team that won the World Series in 1977. He was also well-known in Brisbane as one of the city's most prominent bookmakers, and for a period, in Tweed Heads, sold hot dogs — Duncan's Dinkum Dogs — made to his own special recipe.

One of Hall's proudest days came in the windy New Zealand city of Wellington in 1982, when both his sons, Duncan and Lindsay, wore the green and gold of Australia in rugby union. Duncan, a rangy back-rower who excelled in the line-outs, took on the mighty All Blacks in the senior Test, while Lindsay played for the Australian under-18s against the Junior Kiwis.

"It is every father's dream to see his son play for his country," he said. "To have both my lads playing on the same day was great ... I was in heaven. I travelled over there to see it and it was worth every mile.

"I would have walked if I had to."

HIT MEN

BILLY WILSON

Captain Blood

Team-mates dubbed Billy "Bluey" Wilson as rugby league's Captain Blood during his marathon career in the 1940s, '50s and '60s. Wilson played an incredible 20 seasons of top-grade football and during that time spilt more of his precious liquid in the heat of battle than just about any player in the game's history.

Although only a small man by front-row standards, Wilson overcame a series of shocking injuries during his career to rise to the very top. In one of league's most rugged eras, he tamed the best and toughest forwards in the game, won six premiership blazers with St George during the club's heyday, and, late in his career, was rewarded with the Australian Test captaincy. Wilson played 263 first-grade and representative matches before finally hanging up his boots in 1967, much to the relief of forwards throughout the rugby league world.

Born in 1930, Wilson served his apprenticeship in the St George juniors with the Kogarah Wanderers club. Playing in a variety of positions from centre to lock, Wilson was a sensational player at junior level — so good that Saints junior league secretary at the time, Gordon Lowrie, later described Wilson as "the best junior league player I've ever seen".

Wilson graduated into the Saints' President's Cup side as a raw-boned centre in 1947. He was graded at St George the following season, alternating between lock and centre as he attempted to break into a strong first-grade side. But, after two years with the Dragons, Wilson, who retained a love of travelling throughout his life, packed his bags for the bush. He accepted a handsome offer to play with Picton in the NSW southern highlands, captain-coaching the club at just 20 years of age.

After several seasons in the doldrums, Picton made the semi-finals under Wilson's guidance and the young utility star capped a fine year by

HIT MEN

playing for Southern Division against the touring Englishmen. He was on the move again the following year, shifting to Baradine in NSW's north-west. Again, it was Wilson's love of a challenge that took him to the small town; Baradine had been an also-ran for years and was looking to Wilson for guidance. Sure enough, the emerging youngster led Baradine to the premiership. But then he again moved on, this time returning to Sydney to rejoin the Saints for the 1952 season.

Wilson, now very much a back-rower, developed into a regular member of the Saints pack and was a key man in the club's charge into the 1953 final, against minor premiers Souths. But, not for the last time in his career, Wilson was sent off in the big game. He received his marching orders (along with Souths centre Martin Gallagher), for fighting, seven minutes after halftime, but by that point the match was already lost. With champion fullback Clive Churchill leading the way, the Rabbitohs were far too strong for the younger Saints side, and took the match 31-12, after leading 15-nil at the break.

The following season, Wilson gave team-mates an insight into his amazing courage and tenacity. In a semi-final against North Sydney, Wilson suffered a badly gashed eyebrow that saw him dash from the field covered in blood. With no replacements permitted for injured players, Wilson was back several minutes later, the wound held together by a series of stitches. Swathed in bandages, Wilson lasted the match, and helped Saints to a hard-fought 15-14 win. Back in the dressing-room, Saints official Frank Facer congratulated Wilson on his performance and asked him how the eye was feeling.

"It's not bad," Wilson said, adding casually, "but I broke my arm when I went back on and that's hurting a bit."

Despite that injury, Wilson was back playing at the commencement of the following season. It soon became clear that he had not given the arm time to mend completely. At halftime of one game, Facer asked him how he was bearing up. "I'm going okay ... but I've broken my arm again," Wilson replied.

However, needless to say, Wilson trooped back out for the second half moments later. The NSW Rugby League's official program, *The Rugby League News*, praised Wilson's courage after the extent of his injuries was revealed.

"Wilson followed the glorious tradition that demands that a player shall stay on the field while he is able to travel under his own steam," the program commented.

Once, early in a reserve grade game, Wilson had been kicked in the head and rushed to hospital where the wound was stitched up. Instead of re-

BILLY WILSON

maining in Casualty, he returned to the fray, covered in bandages which became more and more bloodied as the game went on. After the match, a weak and gaunt Wilson apologised to team-mates for "letting them down".

Wilson broke his arm for the third time in a famous club match against Balmain in 1956, but again stayed the distance, setting up the winning try with his bad arm strapped to his side.

He faced many rugged opponents in his day, but none troubled him more than noted English hard man Derek Turner.

"He was the hardest player I faced," Wilson said after his retirement. "One day he caught me around the throat with a stiff-arm and I thought he'd taken my head off."

Former Saints, NSW and Australian team-mate Johnny Raper still remembers *that* tackle.

"It was a killer and I think that was the only time I ever saw Bluey's legs buckle," Raper says. "He was really stung by the blow and was gone for a while. But, to his credit, he came back for more later in the game and gave Turner as good as he got."

With the likes of Norm Provan, Ken Kearney and Wilson leading the way up front, Saints were Sydney league's sleeping giant of the early 1950s. The Dragons finally broke through for the first of their incredible run of 11 straight premiership titles in 1956, with Wilson the key man.

Saints beat a determined Balmain side 18-12, despite playing with just 12 men for over an hour. Centre Merv Lees was helped from the field with a badly dislocated collarbone after only 13 minutes, leaving the Saints in disarray. But Wilson, always a calm man in a crisis, moved out into the centres. The remaining five forwards, led by Provan and Kearney, did the job as Saints secured the title in rousing style.

Despite Saints' success, Wilson went "walkabout" again in 1957, this time moving to Wagga. He returned to Saints in 1958 and slotted straight back into the pack as the Dragons won their third title on the trot, beating Wests 20-9 on grand final day. However, before the start of the '59 campaign, Saints decided to move Wilson to the front row. The hard-working forward, who thought he was barely big enough to play second row, was far from impressed. He offered to quit the game and had to be talked into remaining with Saints and trying his hand at the new position. It was only the insistence of Saints coach Ken Kearney that persuaded Wilson to try the new position.

"I didn't want any truck with the front row but Kearney finally won through," Wilson said years later. "Once I tried it, I found I loved the physical contact and, if I had my time over again, I wouldn't have wasted all those years in other positions."

HIT MEN

To say Wilson's reluctant move was a success would be one of league's great understatements. Within the first few months of his switch up front, Wilson found himself in the Australian team, making his Test debut in the home series against New Zealand. During 1959, Australia won that Test series 2-1, Saints again won the premiership (beating Manly 20-0 in the grand final) and Wilson capped an unforgettable year by winning selection on the Kangaroo tour.

In England, the tough, hard, slogging style on the heavy grounds suited Wilson and he played in five of the six Tests against Great Britain and France. In the first Test, at Swinton, Wilson gave the English a sample of his special brand of courage. Despite breaking his thumb early in the match, he stayed on the field as Australia swept to a 22-14 win. But all the plaudits that day went to Wilson's young St George team-mate Reg Gasnier, who scored a breathtaking hat-trick of tries in his first Test against the Englishmen. The British side regrouped after that initial loss, winning a highly controversial second Test, at Leeds, 11-10, before clinching the series with an 18-12 win in the mud at Wigan's Central Park in the decider. The victory gave the Lions' what remains today their most recent series victory on home soil, but Wilson and his team-mates gained some consolation by winning all three Tests against a powerful French side.

Back on the home front, Saints continued to sweep all before them. Premierships continued to flow — 31-6 over Easts in 1960, 22-nil over Wests in 1961 — and in 1962 Saints found themselves once more opposed to the Magpies in the season finale. This was a match in which Billy Wilson was involved in one of league's most infamous incidents. Saints five-eighth that day, Johnny Raper, takes up the story:

"Wests prop Jim Cody flattened our skipper Norm Provan and we were far from impressed as Norm was carried off on a stretcher. The mood was fairly ugly in the dressing room at halftime, as 'Sticks' lay there dazed in the corner. Plenty of the blokes were talking about get squares. But Billy, who had taken over as captain, suddenly jumped to his feet and made it clear there would be none of that.

"'I know you blokes are all fired up after what happened to 'Sticks' but I don't want you to go out there and look to get even with them. This is a grand final and we'll win it for sure if we keep level heads. I don't want to see any of you blokes throwing a punch — let's just go back out there and play football.'

"I was still a young bloke at the time and it sounded like good advice to me and besides, I learned early in life not to argue with a bloke like Bluey Wilson. We ran back on the field with our thoughts on nothing other than playing football and no sooner had we kicked off than I saw Jim Cody flat on his back, Apparently Bluey had hit him with the best left hook you'd ever want to see. Cody was carried off and Bluey was waved straight off by referee Jack Bradley. He gave us a wink and said: 'I'll see you all for victory drinks in the Members Bar after the game.'

"Luckily, we hung on to win 9-6."

Years later, Wilson claimed he only realised after he'd decked Cody that it was the same player who had earlier dispatched Provan. "It wasn't intentional," Wilson said. "I didn't know who it was but Saints still had to battle through with only 12 men."

Raper has fond memories of playing with Wilson during the Dragons' heyday.

"He was as hard a player as you'll ever see and I often remember him head-butting rival front-rowers for the loose head in the scrums," the champion lock recalls. "They'd butt each other like a pair of billy goats and would both look like a mess at the end of the game. I'd often see Billy an hour later sharing a beer with his rival, with both blokes sporting half a dozen stitches in their scones. They were a breed apart, front-rowers — blokes like Bluey were proof of that. He was always quite happy for the forwards to do the hard work and the backs to look good as a result. We had great backs as Saints like Gasnier, Eddie Lumsden and Johnny King, so his style suited us perfectly. He'd often tell them before a game: 'Us forwards will pave the way for you bastards out wide to score' — that was one his catchcrys."

Wilson never played for Saints again after his grand final send off. Although he was let off with a "severe caution" by the judiciary, there have been whispers over the years that Saints let him go as a result of his reckless act that almost cost the club its premiership run. Wilson contemplated retirement but eventually signed with North Sydney, after the Bears agreed to pay Saints a 900-pound transfer fee for his services.

Raper believes that, despite the great success Wilson went on to achieve at Norths, his heart remained firmly with the Dragons.

"I played with Bluey for four years and, like the rest of the players, was genuinely sorry to see him go," Raper says. "And I'm sure he felt the same way after being part of such a close-knit and successful team. I remember playing against him once and making a darting run down what I thought would be a gap on the blindside. I reckoned I was through but then I heard his gruff voice say 'Got ya, Chook' as he came across to nail me. I'd seen him hammer countless players in his day and braced myself for the impact of what I was certain would be a bone-rattler. But he just brought me down in a copybook tackle. That's when I came to realise how much Saints still meant to him."

HIT MEN

Reg Gasnier tells another story of the special bond between Wilson and his former Saints team-mates.

"We were playing Norths at Kogarah Jubilee Oval and just before we ran out onto the field, we got word that Bluey had a couple of badly broken ribs," Gasnier remembers. "There was no way he should have been playing but it was a game against Saints and he wasn't about to miss it. When we ran out onto the field to face them, we could clearly see he had rolls and rolls of elastoplast around his ribs for protection. The word was quickly passed among the Saints players to go easy on him. Every time we tackled him, it was like we were dropping Billy on eggshells.

"It didn't take long for Billy to work out what was going on and he was furious. He hated the thought of getting any special treatment, even though he was obviously playing in great difficulty. He really started getting stuck into us. 'You're a bunch of sissies,' he yelled at us. 'You wouldn't know how to tackle hard'.

"He was hoping his abuse would bring an end to our gentle treatment but we knew him too well. Our forwards looked after him all game and he lasted the 80 minutes without any problems, although his pride probably took a bit of a battering."

Gasnier believes Saints' hard men like Wilson, Kearney, Kevin Ryan and Provan made it easier for him to make such a spectacular impact on the game when he first entered the top grade in 1959.

"Billy stood for no nonsense — on or off the field," Gasnier explains. "It was always comforting knowing he was there and as a result of his presence, I'm sure a lot of rival players thought twice about picking on a young newcomer like me. They knew they'd have to answer to him if they did.

"On my first Kangaroo tour in 1959 he was a senior player and we all looked up to him. He liked having a good time as much as the next bloke, but if any of the young players were out of line, he'd be the first to clip them on the ear and tell them to wake up to themselves. He was a bit of an enigma in that he'd swear and carry on with the best of them when it was just the boys around. But when there were ladies in our company, he'd change completely. He was a real old-fashioned gentleman and would make sure there was no swearing or misbehaving in their presence. He told us to behave ourselves and when Billy Wilson told you to do something, you usually did it."

Gasnier can confirm Wilson was anything but a big man. "At one stage of the 1959 tour I actually weighed more than him," he says. "He was a lot smaller than many people realise and I think they have a mental picture of him as a big bloke because of his toughness and drive."

Wilson was always popular among team-mates and was blessed with a

BILLY WILSON

devilish sense of humour. He loved playing practical jokes — his favourite trick was biting the neck-ties of unsuspecting players at post-match functions.

"But he met his match finally," recalls Saints legend Ian Walsh. "Someone wore a tie with the new feature of metallic thread. Billy nearly wore his gums out trying to chew it off. He never tried that trick again."

Former Wests forward John "Chow" Hayes, an opponent in two grand finals, was one of the many victims of Wilson the prankster.

"I'm a big fan of the modern game but I believe the one thing that's missing is the camaraderie (that once existed) between players from rival clubs," Hayes says. "Saints and Wests were arch rivals in those days but we were always mates before and after the game. We used to hate playing Saints because they were a great side and often belted the crap out of us. But after the game we'd always get together for a drink.

"We played a lot at the SCG in those days and had many nights together, the two teams mingling and joking in the Members Bar. Billy was always a riot on those occasions. He was a real character and you'd have to keep your eye on him. If you didn't, odds were you'd lose your tie quick smart. More than one bloke had his tie severed when he wasn't paying attention to what Billy was up to. He loved playing that sort of prank but if someone played one back on him, he'd be just as happy — there was no lair in him. I don't think you could find anyone who'd say a bad word about him."

Hayes remembers his surprise at seeing Wilson many years after the pair had retired.

"I looked at him and thought to myself: 'Is this really the bloke we all feared and respected so much?' It was only then it struck me that he wasn't all that big. He couldn't have been much more than 14 stone (100kg) but he was tough and strong for his size and that's what stands out in my mind about him. He was no lethal weapon in defence but he'd keep coming and coming. He took a lot of punishment over the years — you only had to look at his melon to realise that. But he kept coming back for more and was always at you. He was hard, but not vicious and a decent bloke off the field."

Former supercoach Jack Gibson, a rugged front-rower himself in the 1950s and early '60s, also played in two losing grand finals against Saints — with Easts in 1960 and Wests in 1963. He had many battles with Wilson and has plenty of admiration for the man.

"There was never any doubt about his courage — that's what you could say about Billy," Gibson says. "He was probably scared a few times — we all were. The players who never had any fear in those days should have been locked away. But Billy could never be intimidated. He didn't say a lot on the field like some so-called tough guys. Billy just did what he had to do and went about it quietly and efficiently. He was never a cheap shot merchant — he'd take you on eye to eye. I respected him for that."

Wooden spooners in 1962, North Sydney were the big improvers of '63, with new signings Wilson and South African Fred Griffiths leading the way. The Bears were undefeated at North Sydney Oval and finally finished fifth, just missing out on a place in the then four-team finals series.

The representative selectors were highly impressed with Wilson's ability to get the best out of the young Norths pack. During the '63 season, he received the greatest honour of his career when selected as Australian captain for the first Test of the series against New Zealand in Australia.

The selection of Wilson as skipper was the seventh change in the Australian captaincy in as many Tests. At 33, Wilson was easily the oldest player in the Australian side — and the same age as referee Jack Bradley! He became the fourth Norths player to captain his country (after Dinny Lutge, Sid Deane and Brian Carlson) and his selection prompted a jubilant *Daily Mirror* to proclaim a revolution in the code. In a glowing editorial, the *Mirror* proclaimed:

"Australian rugby league has finally come of age with a new found tolerance of older players. In recent times, players have been considered on the scrap heap when they reached the age of 30. Clubs have insisted on discarding any player whose age topped 29. Last year Norths signed Billy Wilson who admits to being 33 but is suspected of a little subtraction. Wilson is only one of dozens of experienced men that clubs are now encouraging to teach their younger team-mates."

However, Wilson experienced only mixed success against the Kiwis. He led Australia to a 7-3 win in Sydney, before the Kiwis levelled the series with a 16-13 triumph in Brisbane. After that game, both skipper Wilson and his deputy, the Queensland halfback Barry Muir, were axed by the selectors, causing a furore on both sides of the border. But the move proved a successful one, with Australia taking the decider 14-0, and Wilson's 10-Test career had come to an abrupt end.

Norths reached the finals in 1964 but got there without Wilson, who broke his leg mid-season after playing just 10 matches. Of course, he failed to let the injury that ended his season prevent him from finishing the match in which it occurred. In fact, Wilson had an x-ray after the match which showed nothing more than deep bruising to the leg. So, he continued to play for the next three weeks. But the pain worsened and a second x-ray revealed a fracture which had not shown up in the earlier examination!

The following year the Bears had the distinction of finishing in second place behind St George in the minor premiership race. However, Norths

BILLY WILSON

failed to reach the grand final, falling 14-9 to a young and exciting South Sydney side in the preliminary final.

Wilson was thinking of retiring at the end of that season, but was coaxed into playing again by club officials. Long-serving Norths president Harry McKinnon was the prime mover behind the bid to keep Wilson playing.

"Bill can go on the field smoking a pipe if he likes," McKinnon said at the time.

In 1966 the Bears suffered a fall from grace and finished well down the ladder, with inconsistency plaguing the club. Wilson played 17 of the 18 premiership matches and was still a force to be reckoned with. However, when the club offered him the coaching position for the following season, he decided to retire. But, after only a handful of matches in the 1967 season, Wilson found himself playing again. Five losses in the Bears' first eight games made Wilson decide it was time to take drastic action. When legendary winger Ken Irvine relinquished the captaincy midway through the first round, Wilson decided returning to the field to lead his young side was the only remedy.

"If I don't have a go, I will always think I have done the wrong thing," Wilson told reporters. "I have been giving this move a lot of thought for the past couple of weeks. Some of the club members have mentioned it and there has been a lot of talk about it at the club. In this way I will find out one way or another just what is wrong out there. If it doesn't work out, then I can always hang up my boots again."

Wilson, now aged nearly 38, played three matches — and the Bears lost all three. He missed the following game through injury and Norths finally came good, downing Newtown 24-0 at Henson Park. That emphatic win satisfied Wilson his young side could survive without him and he hung up his boots ... for the last time. But, at season's end, Norths had finished well down the ladder and Wilson was replaced by controversial English coach Roy Francis for the following year.

Wilson remained in the coaching ranks for several more years at Cronulla, helping the new club's lower grades adapt to the Sydney premiership. After that mission was accomplished, Wilson again took to wandering. He went bush with his wife and three children, owning several pubs in country centres from Nambucca Heads on the NSW north coast to Gympie in Queensland before his death in 1993, aged 64.

On hearing of Wilson's death, Saints chief executive Geoff Carr echoed the thoughts of team-mates, opponents and fans:

"Billy Wilson was one of the game's great characters and lived life at 100 miles an hour. It's ironic that he died of a brain haemorrhage — he gave a lot of opponents those himself over the years."

HIT MEN

NOEL KELLY

Fighting Fire With Fire

Fifteen send-offs and 16 broken noses ... the statistics go a long way to telling the story of the career of Noel "Ned" Kelly. Those raw figures show Kelly copped plenty, but also dished out his own special brand of retribution. In the "wild west" atmosphere of the code in the 1960s, Kelly mixed it with the best of them. The former Queensland butcher was as tough as they come — a scheming forward who alternated between prop and hooker with devastating effect throughout his career.

The Kelly story began in Ipswich, 50 kilometres south-west of Brisbane, in 1936. However, the chubby youngster played his early football in the junior competitions of the tiny town of Goodna, about 25km east of Ipswich, before returning to Ipswich to begin making a footballing name for himself (Goodna was not big enough to field senior sides). Kelly played for Railways and then Brothers in the local Ipswich competition, and quickly earned a place in the district representative sides, under the coaching of former Kangaroo Dan Dempsey. In 1958, Kelly found himself in good company in the Ipswich front row that played in the Bulimba Cup. Alongside him, also earning $14 per game, were two other highly-rated prospects — Gary Parcell and Dud Beattie. In little more than 12 months, all three were playing for Queensland and, soon after, for Australia.

Kelly won Queensland selection at hooker in 1959, dominating the scrums against New South Wales and helping the Maroons take out the series 2-1. That proved Kelly's passport to Test selection and he won his green-and-gold spurs in the home series against New Zealand. The Aussies won a tight series 2-1, and Kelly did enough to earn a Kangaroo tour berth at the end of that Australian season.

"Looking back, that was one hell of a year for me in '59," Kelly recalls today. "I played for Ipswich, Queensland, and Australia and then went on the Kangaroo tour. You could say that was the year that put me on the map. I was young and keen and it all fell into place."

Unfortunately, the Kangaroo tour didn't go as happily as Kelly would have hoped. The rugged forward took a knee injury away with him and was rarely able to produce his best.

"It was one of those injuries you think you can get over but this one was too far gone," he remembers. "I used to strap it and strap it but the cartilage popped out in the third game against Warrington. And when it popped out, it really popped out."

Kelly played in just 14 of the 35 tour matches as Australia failed to regain the Ashes, and he had to look on as NSW's Ian Walsh claimed his hooking spot. However, the pair were to arm wrestle for the Test jumper throughout their careers.

"When I came back, I had a complete overhaul of the knee and the doctor removed three cartilages," Kelly explains. "It didn't totally fix the problem, but at least I was well enough to play again."

Kelly moved to Ayr in North Queensland in 1960, and managed to turn the tables on Walsh, regaining his spot for the World Cup tour to England at the end of the season. Kelly played throughout the Cup series, despite a bad leg injury that required hours of treatment before every game. Great Britain won the trophy after downing the Aussies 10-3 in the crucial final match, but Australia had managed to defeat the strong French side 13-12, and New Zealand 21-15. In these tough battles, Kelly took a pounding, his knees and ankles bruised and battered from being constantly kicked in scrums.

Sydney clubs had begun beating a path to Kelly's door, and a visit from popular Wests official Bill Beaver after the World Cup proved decisive.

"Dan Dempsey was keen for me to do well and helped me make up my mind to go," Kelly remembers. "Beaver came up to Ayr, which was something in itself as the place is 1000 miles past Brisbane. We had no money at the time and I realised I was going to be nothing more than a little butcher boy if I stayed in Queensland. Before I knew what had happened, I'd talked to my wife Chris and we had decided that to get a few bob we'd have to come to Sydney."

However, it didn't take the Kellys long to regret their decision to move south (in 1961). "My first year in Sydney was a bloody disaster," Kelly says. "Nothing went right and we had all sorts of troubles. I did a cartilage in an early game. That stuffed up the whole season ... I could never get fit and was playing on one leg. I finally had an operation mid-season. We were young, with a kid and trying to settle down. It was a hectic year for us ... but fortunately things improved."

HIT MEN

Kelly also ruffled a few feathers in the Magpie camp in a spiteful match against Parramatta in one of his first outings in the black-and-white jumper.

"A scrum blew up and punches were flying everywhere. I wasn't about to miss out on the action and started to let rip. But as I started to wind up for one big swat at a Parramatta bloke, our second-rower Kel O'Shea popped his head up and I caught him flush on the eye. He ended up having to leave the field with a gash that required six stitches. I couldn't believe it! He was a mess. He wasn't too happy at the time, but he forgave me."

Kelly recovered from his knee injury in time to play in the grand final, the first of three consecutive premiership Wests losses to the mighty St George machine. Those three defeats, the latter two by just three and then five points, still rankle with Kelly.

"That really hurt," he says. "They were a great side but we gave them a hard game every time. We had a good team. When I first came down, top players like Keith Holman, Harry Wells and Kel O'Shea were getting near the end of their careers. They were ready to get out when I came in. But we replaced them with some top players. Arthur Summons joined us, as well as Dennis Meaney, Jim Cody, Peter Dimond and Don Parish. We were young, eager and hungry and while we didn't have many stars, we were all goers. Saints had the edge on us in experience but we worried them. I still think we got a raw deal in the '63 grand final and could easily have won it. And plenty of people will agree with me. It was one of those days when some crucial calls went against us."

However, the record-breaking Kangaroo tour of 1963 helped erase the triple grand final disappointment for Kelly.

"I was chosen as a prop and that tour was one of the highlights of my life. It was just a magic blend we had ... a great team with no weak links. I think our secret was that we had the nucleus of players from both the 1959 Kangaroo side and the 1960 World Cup squad. Young blokes like Johnny Raper, Reg Gasnier and myself came through the ranks together and by 1963 we were hitting our peak.

"I believe it was the world's best football team. We were a gun side ... you wouldn't have got one better. Guys like Gasnier, Kenny Irvine and Chang (Graeme Langlands) were dynamic out wide ... if you threw the ball over your head, someone was there on the burst to pick it up. It just happened that way when you played in that side. You had to push blokes out of the way to get the ball, there was support everywhere and they all knew where each other were going."

Australia set the tone for the series by winning the first Test, at London's Wembley Stadium, 28-2, with the incomparable Gasnier scoring a hat-trick and Kelly, as a front-rower, starring despite suffering a badly-broken nose. The referee at one stage stopped play, using a handkerchief to stop the flow of blood from the damaged hooter. The referee, a Mr Davies, actually begged Kelly to leave the field but the big man wouldn't hear of it.

"It wasn't pleasant, but that broken nose was my trademark and I had to learn to live with it," Kelly says.

Mr Davies hadn't seen the head-high tackle from English prop Keith Bowman that caused the injury but Kelly had it filed away for future reference. The get-square came some 20 minutes later, with Kelly cracking Bowman across the head in a tackle. The Englishman lay prone for some three minutes on the Wembley turf before being carted off.

"It certainly got equalled up," Kelly says with a grin. "He had it coming. I always said if someone punches me, I'll punch them back. That was my nature."

The teams moved on to Swinton for the second Test, where Kelly played a starring role in one of Australian rugby league's finest moments. The Kangaroos thrashed the home side 50-12, scoring 12 tries in the process. Kelly's hard running had the Englishmen looking for places to hide and the Wests star scored his country's seventh try with a typical burst. Lurking out wide, Kelly picked up a pass meant for one of the outside backs and showed surprising pace to score.

Great Britain salvaged some pride with a 16-5 win in the third Test at Leeds, but the Australians moved onto the French leg of the tour with the Ashes firmly in their keep. As Walsh had broken his arm, Kelly moved back to hooker for the French games. Australia won the series 2-1, with Kelly again prominent ... sometimes for the wrong reasons.

Kelly's uncompromising style upset more than one French referee and led to his infamous double send-off in the match against Provence at Avignon. Kelly takes up the story with relish.

"It was unbelievable really and the sort of thing that could probably only happen in France. Over there you're liable to strike the same ref six or seven games in a row and that's what happened to me. I'd had this bloke, Monsieur Casson, time and again and we'd built up this great hatred for each other. It got to the stage where every time the ball went in the scrum and I won it, he'd recall it and make the ball go in again. I had cauliflower ears and a broken nose so I didn't fancy spending so long in the scrum, particularly as the ref was often just waiting for the other bloke to win the ball off me.

"Finally, in the Avignon game, I got fed up and asked (Australian utility back and later successful Manly and Australian coach) Frank Stanton, who spoke more French than the rest of us put together, how to call this bloke a 'so and so'. He told me and I gave the ref a mouthful. He sent me straight off but I just said I wasn't going. I sat down, and then I moved back to the second row. He tried to send me off again for something else but I just sat down again. Eventually he gave up and I finished the game."

Despite being sent off many times for scrum infringements, Kelly preferred playing hooker to prop.

"In those days it was a real contest against your opposite number and you could really get involved in it. Every scrum was a challenge and it was a battle from start to finish. I played about half my football at prop and half at hooker but I really preferred the latter."

The Englishmen returned to Australia with a new-look team in 1966 and, with Kelly out injured, won the first Test 17-13. That match gave Kelly his first look, albeit from the sideline, of a man who was to prove his nemesis for several years to come, the cheeky British halfback, Tommy Bishop.

"Bishop used to go on with all sorts of antics. He'd throw haymakers, jump on blokes' backs, kick them ... he'd do anything to upset you," Kelly recalls. "I remember seeing him for the first time when I was out injured that game and he was using every trick in the book. I'd never seen anything like it. I hated him immediately and thought if he tries this against me, I'll kill him."

Kelly got his chance in the second Test in Brisbane. "Play was only going a minute when he started carrying on so I gave him a back-hander. It was on from there. I gave him a boot up the arse a couple of times. He kept giving me cheek but we won the match 6-4."

Australia eventually retained the Ashes with a 19-14 win in the third Test, in Sydney. Bishop, however, was to have the last laugh on Kelly a little over a year later ...

A bad head injury in a club match in 1967 forced Kelly to miss 10 matches mid-season. But such was Kelly's standing in the game at the time that he only needed one game back to prove his fitness to the Test selectors, who rushed him into the front row for Australia's 22-13 win in the first Test of the series against New Zealand. Kelly was a star in that game, but in the second Test was sent off after just 90 seconds — a Test record.

Kelly contends he was merely retaliating after Kiwi prop Robin Orchard decked Aussie five-eighth Johnny Gleeson. "Poor old Johnny's eyes were going around like poker-machine reels. That really riled me."

Kelly became involved in a fracas with the Kiwis' other prop, Oscar Danielson, who later played for Newtown, and was promptly sent off.

He again toured England and France later that year, becoming the first man from the front row to complete three Kangaroo tours. Against

NOEL KELLY

Warrington in the opening tour game, Kelly copped a head-high tackle, suffering one of the worst of his 16 broken noses. The Australian doctor advised Kelly to rest for three weeks to give the wound time to heal. But Kelly, never one to listen to sensible medical advice, was back playing four days later. He was sent off twice on that tour, including once in the third Test, at Swinton. But, despite his absence, Australia won the game to retain the Ashes.

Kelly was fuming at the circumstances that led to his dismissal. His old foe, Bishop, had again been baiting him and at one stage, fell to the ground clutching his face and screaming as if he had been hit. Kelly was immediately shown the way back to the dressing room by the referee, despite swearing he never laid a hand on the "injured" halfback.

That match proved to be Kelly's last Test against the old enemy, a sour ending to a distinguished career against the Englishmen.

"It was a crazy thing," he recalls. "It was right at the end of the game and I didn't touch him. I should never have got sent off but the ref couldn't get rid of me quick enough. It was a sad way to end my career against the Poms."

Kelly again had more than his fair share of trouble on the French leg of the tour, in which the home side won the Tests 2-1. In one game, he received his marching orders in the first half and returned to the dressing room, only to find a local thief scrounging through the players' bags.

"I was filthy at being marched and obviously took him by surprise. The game hadn't been going long and he must have thought he wouldn't be seeing any players for a while. You should have seen the look on his face. I gave him a bit of a hiding and I don't think he ever got up to that again."

In 1969, Kelly left Wests to take up a captain-coach job with Wollongong, but wasn't happy with the move.

"I was over the hill and really didn't want to go but was talked into it," he says. "I couldn't finish the year quickly enough. The writing was on the wall and I hung up my boots after that."

Kelly then tried his hand at coaching and picked the most challenging club he could find — the North Sydney Bears.

"They were a challenge alright, but I really enjoyed it," he says. "I had them for four years and it was great until politics came into it late in the piece. There was a defeatist attitude throughout the club when I came and that was our biggest hurdle. We were just starting to get somewhere when there was a power struggle within the club and that set the place back years. We lost a lot of our best players and the spirit seemed to leave the joint. But things have all changed there now — the administration is good and the results are coming. I'm happy to see Norths doing well."

HIT MEN

Kelly scoffs at talk that players from the past wouldn't make it today.

"That's a load of bullshit," he says. "In fact, I believe the exact opposite is the truth. There's a hell of a lot of players running around now who wouldn't have survived in the '60s. It's a lot easier now, believe me. There were plenty of games where I'd have loved to put my hand up and spent 10 minutes in the blood bin and then come back refreshed. We never had that sort of thing in my day and it really was survival of the fittest. Of course, when you say this sort of thing people just reckon you're getting too long in the tooth or looking back through rose-coloured glasses.

"The fact is the game now is just so different to what it was then. It's been cleaned up a lot and is a better game for the players. I'd like to see some of the blokes from my era being allowed to play now. We had some great ball players even though we all had to run with our heads down. If we'd run with the head up like the current blokes, it would have been chopped off quick smart. They'd give you a coathanger straight across the beak."

"When I played, there wasn't a player in the forwards who couldn't handle himself," he says. "No-one would put the biff on and then worry about when he was going to get hit back. It was part of the game and you knew what to expect. If you could handle a stink and still play, you were a valuable player.

"When I was growing up, all the old blokes would say after a game: 'How'd ya play today? Did ya get a few cautions? There's never been a good front-rower yet who hasn't given away a few penalties.'

"That was the way things were in those days and it was almost expected of you. Front-rowers were the gladiators of the day and there weren't too many sides back then who won games without a bloody good prop forward or two leading the way. Now the front-rower's job is to make the 'hard yards'. There are plenty of blokes who take the ball up and don't even look to unload. They wouldn't have got a game in another era. But they are just doing what their coaches want, so I suppose you can't blame them.

"Nowadays they don't run sideways. In our time they did it all the time and while it didn't always come off, it often created something in attack."

Kelly rates several Englishmen as the toughest opponents he has faced.

"When we went over there with the 1959 Kangaroos there weren't too many forwards who weren't big and tough," he remembers. "They loved getting into us and gave us some trouble. The likes of Vince Karalius, Jack Wilkinson and Derek Turner. But some of the Aussies were right up there as well. For starters, Dud Beattie and Gary Parcell could mix it with the best of them and were as rugged as anyone I played with or against. In Sydney, Kevin Ryan and Billy Wilson from St George, John Sattler from

NOEL KELLY

Souths, Terry Randall at Manly ... they were all hard men. Brian Hambly, Ron Lynch, George Piper are others who come to mind. And Norm 'Sticks' Provan — he wasn't supposed to be such a tough man but he was built like a mountain. You could run into any part of him and knock yourself out.

"They were all big, strong hard guys. I hear people talk about Mark Geyer and Paul Harragon being monsters. If you line them up against Provan, Ryan or Rex Mossop, they'd be surprised. There were plenty of monsters in our day too."

Kelly cherished the camaraderie of the Australian side and touring with the likes of Graeme Langlands and Johnny Raper.

"We had some great times and there are some classic stories that have come out of those tours. I'm sworn to secrecy, other than to say that they are all true.

"I remember on several occasions we'd play little French teams that couldn't hold their hands up. We'd be beating them 50-0 so for a bit of fun we'd let one of their players look good. We'd yell out: 'Don't tackle him, don't tackle him'. We'd let him run and then knock him over before he scored. The locals would get all excited and think one of their blokes was a champion.

"Then big Peter Dimond would come in from the wing the next time the bloke got the ball and crash-tackle him, nearly breaking him in half. On one occasion the local band ran on and wanted to fight us; we were getting hit on the head with buckets and anything they could find."

Kelly has firm beliefs on violence in the game. "They've cleaned things up a lot but I advocate that a good punch in the nose never hurt anyone. When you see two guys on the field getting stuck into it hammer and tongs, these days players always rush in to break it up. But in the old days they'd keep going and eventually get sick of it.

"And when you're hot out there, you don't even feel it half the time. Once when I was playing for Wests I missed a game through injury and they put a hooker called Johnny Rogers in to play Parramatta. I thought they gave him a pounding. He was only a little bloke and they belted him in every tackle and hammered him in the scrums.

"He came in at halftime and I said to him: 'Jesus, John, how are you going? It looks like they're killing you.'

"He just smiled and said: 'Oh, gees, mate, it's nowhere near as hard as what you copped last week.'

"The game's a lot harder from the sideline ...

"Probably the worst things I've seen are the head butt and the elbow. The Poms used to love using them and you'd have to keep them at arm's length all the time because you never knew when they'd let one fly. But

HIT MEN

nowadays it's the big hit that's all the rage. The number of players wanting to do them is unbelievable. And there's no doubt when they come off they hurt — I'd rather get 10 punches in the nose than one of those."

Kelly admits he regarded getting sent off as an occupational hazard.

"I got marched a lot I suppose but I never lost any sleep over it. I played it hard and once you've got a reputation they go looking for you. There were plenty of games when the refs couldn't unload me quickly enough. I may have been sent off 15 times but maybe half of them were for alleged repeated scrum infringements. What a joke that was. When a ref got sick of you, he'd just "tip-toe" you and there was nothing you could do about it.

"There were times when the league told the refs to put a blitz on scrums and then we hookers knew we were in trouble. One day when we played Balmain I met their hooker Dick Wilson at the gate on the way onto the field. We'd both read in the paper that day that the blitz would be on.

"As we ran onto the field I said to Dickie: 'I think we're going to be having an early shower today if we're not careful. What are we going to do about this?'

"He replied: 'What about if we both keep our feet back (in the scrums) and let them sort it out for themselves.'

"It sounded a good plan. 'That'll do me,' I said as we took up our positions for the kick-off. We both stuck to our word but it didn't do us much good. After a handful of scrums the referee dismissed us both ... for repeated scrum infringements! We watched the game from the grandstand.

"I was exonerated two or three times and got let off with a caution on a few other occasions. The longest suspension I ever got was two or three weeks. You've got to understand I was a marked man and used to cop a lot from other sides. I was an international and captain-coach of Wests for a time so I'd get plenty of attention. You weren't expected to stand there and cop that — you had to fight fire with fire.

"The Poms enjoyed taking me on too and their refs got to me a few times as well ...

"For some reason they didn't like me!"

HIT MEN

KEVIN RYAN

Playing without Pity

Barrister Kevin Ryan used his intimate knowledge of football law to perfect one of the most lethal tackling styles rugby league has known. In league's blood-and-thunder days of the 1960s, Ryan was the toughest of the toughmen. Nicknamed 'Kandos', after the rock-hard cement, Ryan was a devastating defender, a man who combined law studies and football for much of his career. This combination enabled him to develop a legal, but awesome tackle.

"I took great notice of the rule regarding tackling back then which said 'when you tackle someone, you can encompass them within your outflung arms'" he recalls today. "And that's what I did. I used my arms to draw players in and then hit them with my shoulders. I found that an effective tackle along those lines would often do more damage than some nasty little incident."

Former team-mate Billy Smith was an ardent admirer of this defensive technique. "It was like a swinging-arm tackle," Smith once said. "He used to hit his arm diagonally across their chest as he grabbed them. You'd hear the wind come out of them as they'd collapse."

Ryan played in seven grand finals for St George but is probably best remembered as the man who helped end Saints' premiership run. As captain-coach of Canterbury in 1967, it was Ryan who masterminded the defeat of the Dragons one match short of a 12th consecutive grand final.

An opponent once said of Kevin Ryan: "He plays the game without pity." And the former St George ironman acknowledges this ruthless approach. "It was nothing intentional or pre-meditated but I'd grown up in tough surroundings in the country," he says. "I was brought up hard and wanted to win and didn't take kindly to blokes getting in the way of my objectives — it was as simple as that."

HIT MEN

Ryan spent his early years near Ipswich, at the head of the Brisbane river. "I never played an organised game until I was around 12 or 13 because I went to a small junior school," he recalls. "There were only 20 kids in the whole school and half of them were girls — we never had enough for a game. Then I went to boarding school at Nudgee College, which had a strong rugby union tradition. But I loved league, even though I'd never played it, and can still remember announcing to my father when I was 11 years old: 'I'm going to play rugby league for Australia'.

"Being a country bloke who didn't know or care a lot about sport, he was taken aback to say the least.

"Union was the staple diet at Nudgee College and, at 13, that became my game. I started to enjoy it, though, and played right through my school days and beyond."

Ryan's no-holds-barred approach saw him rise quickly to the top in the amateur code, with Queensland selection leading to a place in the Wallabies side that toured Britain in 1957.

"I toured twice with the Wallabies and I'll say this for union — you can't beat a rugby tour," he says. "In '57 we went over to England by boat, and it was a great trip through places like Colombo, Port Said and Bombay. It took seven weeks to get there and most of the blokes got off the boat a stone heavier than when they got on. There wasn't an awful lot to do on board apart from eating and most of us were having five meals a day. It wasn't a very successful tour — I only played one Test and we lost all the major internationals, even though they were all close."

Ryan mixed union with a successful boxing career and came within a whisker of representing Australia at the 1960 Olympics in Rome.

"I believe I could have gone to the Olympics if I'd really set my sights on it," he claims. "I got beaten in the Australian final, which was two months before the Olympic trials. In the meantime, I had to make up my mind whether to stick with it, because the sport was strictly amateur in those days. But I had my mind on a professional football career and headed down that path. It would have been nice going to the Olympics, but I was realistic enough to know I couldn't do that and play league."

It was on the Wallaby tour of New Zealand in 1958 that Ryan secured himself a future in rugby league.

"I had a good tour and was a part of the Test team by then," he remembers. "I got offers from several league teams when I returned home but St George had the initiative to send someone up to see me personally. I got a few other offers but always wanted to play for Saints. They didn't pay big money, but they were the top side and I saw trying to break into their team as a real challenge."

KEVIN RYAN

Ryan joined Saints in 1960 — mid-way through the Dragons' record-breaking run of 11 straight premierships. He went on to play in seven consecutive premiership-winning teams, but joining a champion club wasn't without its hiccups.

"I expected it to be hard to make the grade and it was certainly that," he says. "Saints had so much strength and depth that it wasn't uncommon to have a couple of international forwards in reserve grade in any given week. I had to fight to get into first grade and it took me half a season to do it. But I was a better player for it. Their policy was that players from outside had to prove themselves and I accepted that. It also took a while to get accepted by the Saints players. They didn't resent me, but I could sense a definite 'wait and see' attitude from them.

"Physically it wasn't a hard transition but it did take me a while to learn the game. I finally got my chance half way through my first season and had Billy Wilson to thank for that. Half the Saints side were playing for NSW in Queensland but they still wouldn't name me in the top grade, which riled me a bit. Saints played Norths that weekend and two strange things happened — Norths won the game and also won the fight. But Billy Wilson was the skipper and wasn't about to go down with the ship. In the final minutes of the game, he told Saints' kicker Brian Graham to boot the ball as high and as far as he could. As all eyes followed the ball, Billy handed out summary justice. BANG, BANG, BANG (Ryan slaps his massive right fist into the palm of his left hand). He knocked out three blokes. But that was his big mistake. If he'd only hammered two of them, he probably would have got away with it. But he decked a third, the referee saw it and he got sent off and suspended for two weeks. That gave me my chance and I came into the side to play Easts at the Sports Ground.

"Easts had a tough pack but I knew it was a make-or-break game for me. I handled myself well and never looked back. I never worried about opposition players or names — I just went out and tried to make them worry about me. After that game I came off and a couple of our blokes came up and said: 'Oh, do you know what you did to so-and-so.' But I honestly didn't worry. I just went out to play football and to win."

Ryan again met Easts in his first grand final for Saints later in 1960.

"I was keen for a big game because they were choosing the World Cup side (for the tournament in England) after that game. I remember a journalist writing at the time that I was the man to tame Vince Karalius and co. We won easily but I got sent off. It was some silly little incident. I was merely defending myself against some fellow (he laughs). We were winning easily and I think the referee saw it as an opportunity to even up the game."

Despite being one of the hardest men in a hard era, Ryan was only sent from the field a handful of times in his career.

"I wouldn't have gone more than five times and mostly it was for silly things," he says. "A couple of times I got marched when referees took exception to me, in my role as captain, questioning their decisions. I retaliated a couple of times but can't recall ever being sent off for anything particularly vicious."

It was at the end of that 1960 season that Ryan made what he regards as the biggest mistake of his football career.

"When I arranged my contract with Saints, I should have included a septic tank," he explains. "But I didn't think of it at the time and, as they cost 100 pounds (which I didn't have), I decided to put one in myself. I was digging through solid rock and messed up my back ... it was never the same again. It got worse over the years and I soon found I wasn't able to make those 30 or 40 yard bursts that I made in 1960. It limited my game and made me concentrate more on defence. But I played on another nine years with it. I played three grand finals with steel braces on and lost count of the number of needles I had over the years. The standard of orthopaedic medicine wasn't all that high in those days and there wasn't much the doctors could do for me. It was only years after I finished playing that I really learned to care for my back and it's not too bad now. If I'd looked after my back properly back then I could have been a much better player — it's my main regret that I had to play so much of my career in discomfort and never had the freedom to run that I enjoyed in my first season."

Despite his awesome strength, Ryan never worked out in a gym or pumped weights.

"I'd always been fairly strong from the hard manual work in the bush when I was a kid. I was cutting timber at the age of 14 and never found the need to use the gym," he reveals. "The thing I did do was work hard in the sand. I was a great believer in the techniques of Percy Cerutty, who trained Olympic champions like Herb Elliott and John Landy extensively in the sand. From about two months before the grand final every year, I'd hit the sand hills at Cronulla — they're all gone now — and by the time the match came around, I'd be jumping out of my skin. It was hard work but I found it very effective."

Ryan won Australian selection in 1962 against Great Britain but an injury robbed him of a green-and-gold jumper. The St George enforcer had to wait until the 1963 Kangaroo tour to join the select band of dual football internationals.

"That was a great tour for Australia but it was a personal disaster for me," he says. "I lasted just four games before suffering a major knee injury. I started well but the injury finished me and I needed an operation — I came home before the tour was even over. I had a full-length plaster on my leg and there was no point staying, especially as my wife was due to have a baby."

Ryan's injury came just before the first Test, in a clash with Hull. After playing the previous three games at second row, he had moved to prop and warned team-mate Ian Walsh before the kick-off: "I've been treating the Poms a bit too gently. From now on, if anyone lays a hand on me, he's gone."

But the Englishmen needn't have heeded the warning; early in the game team-mate Noel Kelly fell awkwardly on Ryan while the pair were completing a tackle, and caused major ligament damage that brought Ryan's tour to an abrupt end. Ironically, Ryan and Kelly, two of the toughest men in their era, had their own unique "non-aggression pact" when playing against each other in the spirited Saints-Wests clashes of the '60s.

"Ned and I were both Ipswich boys and always had an understanding," Ryan says. "We regarded ourselves as two boys from the bush trying to make it in the big city. As such, we never tried to give each other a hard time on the field."

Ryan returned to St George after recovering from knee surgery, but after Saints' victory in the 1966 grand final, rocked the Dragons by leaving the club for Canterbury.

"It was mainly a case of wanting to coach," he remembers, "and there was no opportunity for that at St George. Ian Walsh was coaching Saints at the time and there were a couple of blokes waiting in line for the job when he stepped down. The chance came up to take on the captain-coach job at Canterbury and I saw it as a good career move. Once again it was a challenge, as they were in the doldrums at the time. I found the captain-coach role a hard one but it was the tradition at the time and I had to follow it. You couldn't say 'Go on' — you had to say 'Come on' — and that wasn't always easy to do. You had to be playing well yourself before you could start criticising other players."

Using his St George experience, Ryan brought a professional approach to Canterbury that reaped immediate dividends. The Berries, as they were then known, reached the finals for the first time in 20 years and found themselves meeting St George in the final for the right to challenge Souths in the grand final. With the clock ticking away in that famous final, Canterbury were on the verge of doing the unthinkable — preventing Saints from reaching their 12th straight grand final. With less than a minute left, the Berries, leading 12-11, were in a dilemma when awarded a penalty.

"The one thing I'll always remember was thinking at the time that even though we had the ball and time was almost up, there was still plenty of fight left in St George," Ryan says. "I'd played with those blokes long enough to know they could get out of this situation if we weren't careful. We were deep in their end of the field but pretty wide out so I had the choice of going for goal or kicking for the touchline. I had visions of us missing the goal, and Gasnier picking up the ball and racing 90 metres downfield to score. In those days a scrum went down after a penalty kick for the line but we'd been winning the scrums all day and I was sure this was the right decision. So we went for line, the scrum went down, and you wouldn't believe it — Saints won the bloody ball. The next moment the ball was out the backline and Gasnier was away. I thought we were gone for sure but a brilliant tackle by our lock, Ron Raper, just got him. The hooter went and we were saved. I always thought Ron was a terrific player and if his last name hadn't have been Raper, he would have probably played for Australia. He definitely saved our bacon that day. It was a strange feeling for the Saints blokes but they accepted it manfully and didn't complain."

Ian Walsh has no doubt it was Ryan's influence that proved the Saints' undoing.

"He was the strength of the Canterbury pack and had he still been with us, I've no doubt we would have won," Walsh claims. "We had no-one to match him ... he was too strong for us."

While Saints players had to cope with sitting out the grand final, Ryan was also in an odd situation. "It felt very strange for me to play in my eighth straight grand final, but this time in a Canterbury jumper instead of a Saints one. We had Souths' measure for much of that grand final even though they were a very classy young side on the verge of a golden era. I thought we were the better side for much of the day but one piece of Bobby McCarthy brilliance proved the difference. He snapped up a 70-metre intercept and they won 12-10.

"We couldn't maintain our form in 1968 and I think that often happens to a team that comes so close to winning the title. You see it even now. We had our problems and finished well down the ladder. In 1969 we were having a top season and were leading the premiership at the halfway stage. But then I did my knee again and that was the end of my career — and we ended up missing the finals again."

While Ryan's injury proved the breaking point of Canterbury's season, the Berries' skipper at least had the satisfaction of going out in style.

"I have fond memories of my last game because it was in a match of the day at the Sydney Cricket Ground," he says. "It was against Balmain, and I finished the game even though the knee was in bad shape. And I got the man of the match award. I could have avoided another operation but the one I had in England was a success and I thought this one would be too. But it was a mistake. The knee was never the same again and every time I pushed myself at training, it blew up like a balloon. I wasn't ready to retire at 32, but the knee gave me no choice really."

Of the eight grand finals he played during his career in Sydney football, Ryan looks back most fondly on the 1965 premiership decider against Souths. Ryan was in his element as Saints outlasted the young Souths side 12-8 before a record crowd of over 78,000 at the SCG.

"I thought that was one of my finest games defensively," he says. "But my favourite memory of that match is that for the only time in my career I was able to push Johnny Raper aside and take the ball up. Raper had incredible energy and always wanted to be the man to do the hard work. I remember once he complained bitterly to us that we weren't giving him any work in defence behind the line. We weren't letting the other team through and he was dirty. He was all over the field and it was a delight to, just that once, say to him: 'Piss off, Rape, I'll take it up'."

Ryan had one year as non-playing coach at Canterbury and again steered the club into the finals before moving on to another challenge - administration. He spent a year helping to run the Canterbury club, before moving on to the other love of his professional life — the law.

"I went to the bar in 1970 and once I saw a career path there, I had to give the football away, although somewhat reluctantly," he says.

Ryan admits years of combining demanding legal studies and football took their toll on him.

"I studied from 1965 to 1969 and I regret those years in a lot of ways. I had no spare time and the combination of study and football exacted a very heavy toll on my family relationships. I was flat out all the time. To a large extent, playing and studying complement each other. But the captain-coach role is another story. The pressure is on you constantly and you're always being asked to spend more time on football matters. I had four kids at the time and I regret the toll it all brought on my relationship with them. Obviously I enjoy being a barrister, but it came at a cost."

Ryan's life after football has been just as hectic as during his playing days. Among the entries on his curriculum vitae are a stint as an ABC television commentator, a term as mayor of Hurstville, and two stays in State Parliament, firstly as a Labor MP and then as a fiercely-minded Independent. His most recent challenge has been as president of the players union, where he has locked horns with league's power base in Phillip Street. Ironically, Ryan's law chambers are directly across the road from League headquarters.

The players union had little impact until Ryan took control, but things soon changed. In 1991 he created national headlines when he took the

HIT MEN

league to court over the "Draft", a system in which players were not automatically entitled to sign with the club of their choice, and won. But despite his successes in that case, the role of players' union boss is one Ryan finds somewhat frustrating.

"It's difficult because you are fighting on behalf of people who aren't really organised," he says. "It's hard to organise league players because they are divided into 16 camps. Each of those 16 clubs is ruled by a chief executive who has power over any given player's future. Then you've got the media, which is largely in the camp of the league and has the old Australian mistrust of unions. So it's an uphill battle. As soon as I can get the players a new, better contract I'll move on."

Ryan has little time for many of the officials across Phillip Street. "To be honest, I expected more of them, particularly the ex-players who've been through it all and know what a raw deal the players get. I mean, apart from the few genuine superstars, most league players do it tough. Clubs can cancel players' contracts virtually at the drop of a hat; insurance is inadequate; there's no job security. A lot of players end up with bad injuries or having their family life and careers effected by football.

"There's still a lot to do, but, when I accepted the position, I had two objectives. Beating the draft was the first and we've achieved that. Now improving the standard contract is the second and once I've done that, I'll find other mountains to climb."

HIT MEN

JOHN SATTLER

Broken Jaw Hero

League critics were convinced South Sydney had unleashed a bull in a china shop with the shock appointment of wild man John Sattler as the Rabbitohs captain in 1967. Renowned as a player who stretched the rules to their limit and had major problems with referees, Sattler was thought to be beyond redemption. But the appointment proved a masterstroke, with Sattler leading the Rabbitohs to the title four times in the next five years.

Sattler led from the front, and the eager young Souths team were quick to follow. The former bad boy of league retained his natural aggression, but curbed his barbarian ways, to become an inspirational skipper. And his effort in the 1970 Grand Final, in which he led Souths to victory despite having his jaw broken in three places early in the match, has gone down in history among league's legendary performances.

Sattler will never forget the day early in 1967 that changed his life.

"Souths president, Denis Donoghue and coach Clive Churchill came to me one day and asked: 'How'd you like to be captain.'

"I immediately shit myself. I was still fairly young and we had a couple of experienced internationals in the club in Jimmy Lisle and Mike Cleary. But neither of them wanted the job and promised they'd help me out. It was something I never expected; I had a reputation ... been given a few holidays by the judiciary ... and had the habit of exploding every time something went wrong. That's where the captaincy really helped; instead of always acting on impulse I'd stop and think for a while and take a calmer approach. It was a responsibility I grew to enjoy."

However, Sattler almost drove a referee to distraction in his very first game as captain.

"We played a trial at Redfern Oval and I was determined to make a good impression first up in my new role. I thought it was the captain's duty to go up and question every decision so that's what I did. Every time we were pinged for offside or anything else I'd walk up to the ref — I think it was Laurie Bruyeres that night — and ask very politely: 'Excuse me sir, what was that for?'

"Finally after I'd done it about eight times, Laurie glared at me and said: 'Will you piss off and leave me alone.'

"Poor bloke, I think I was sending him around the bend. Later that week, a bloke called Joe Coffey, who was boss of the Referees Association in those days, came to training at Redfern. He came up and said Col Pearce, who was the number-one ref at the time, wanted me to go over to his place for dinner with his wife and daughter. I had no idea what he wanted. After we had a nice meal at his house, Col got out a magnetic board and told me: 'Now this is what you can do ... and this is what you can't do. But for God's sake, don't give the poor refs a hard time. Leave them alone and let them get on with the job."

As a child growing up in the outer Newcastle suburb of Kurri Kurri, Sattler didn't merely dislike league — he detested it.

"I was more interested in horses and stuff like that," he explains. "I used to look at league and think: 'Gosh, that's a rough game'. They tried to make me play it at school one afternoon a week but I was too smart for them. As soon as the lunch bell went, I'd bolt out the front gate, catch the bus home, and play around with the horses.

"One day when I was around 16 I was breaking-in a horse and my next-door neighbour Allan Williams was running some kids in a nearby paddock. He sang out for me to come and have a game of touch football. I tied the horse up and joined in — jeans, riding boots and all. I found I actually enjoyed it and when they asked me to play on the weekend, I said okay. I jumped back on the horse, rode home and told my dad, who couldn't believe it. But he said he'd buy me boots and the like, so long as I stuck to it; that's how it all started."

Sattler played in Kurri's under-16s in his maiden year of league. Within 18 months he was in first grade. In his second season of top-grade football, at the tender age of 19, he was thrown into an international match — for Newcastle against the touring Great Britain side.

"They'd won the first two Tests and were a crack side," Sattler recalls. "They picked a Test-strength side but we beat them in front of a huge crowd at the Newcastle Sports Ground. I was playing lock at that stage and must have gone okay because a few Sydney scouts approached me. Canterbury invited me down for a weekend and I went, and the same thing happened with Saints. But I knocked them both back — I just didn't think I was ready for Sydney. The big city terrified me. I was a real bush

Ray Stehr, a first-grade forward when aged just 15, and a bruising mainstay of Easts, NSW and Australian sides throughout the 1930s. Stehr remains the only man to be sent off twice in one Ashes Test series

Right: **Stehr**, playing out his enforcer role for Eastern Suburbs.

Left: **Herb Narvo**, the finest second-rower of his day, and an Australian heavyweight boxing champion.

Narvo playing for his first Sydney club, Newtown, where he won a premiership in 1943. Narvo also captain-coached St George to the 1946 final, where they lost to Balmain.

Frank *'Bumper'* Farrell, in the colours of his beloved Newtown, fights his way through the Souths forwards in a match at the Sydney Sports Ground in 1950.

Below: *Farrell,* on the beat in his days as a policeman in Sydney's infamous Kings Cross.

Right: **Billy Wilson,** who matched it with the best of Australian rugby league for two decades.

Queensland's **Douglas *'Duncan'* Hall** (right), and NSW's Fred de Belin (left) and Keith Holman training at the SCG No. 2 before the opening Test of the famous 1950 Ashes series.

Billy Wilson - Captain Blood.

Left: **Noel *'Ned'* Kelly**, bursting through the Balmain forward pack, which included Gary Leo (at top).

Below: ***Kelly*** on the charge against Great Britain in the second Test of the 1963 series, which Australia won 50-12. The Australian player in support is Ken Day.

Above: **Kevin Ryan** the feared, defender, arms spread wide, during the 1967 Souths-Canterbury Grand Final.

Left: **Noel Kelly** in earnest discussion with referee Laurie Bruyeres.

Below: Saints **Kevin Ryan**, about to smother another renowned front-rower, Souths Jim Morgan, in the '65 Grand Final.

Above: **Kevin Ryan**, chaired from the field by his Canterbury team-mates, after he had engineered the defeat of St George in the 1967 preliminary final. Saints, Ryan's former club, had won the previous eleven premierships. The other Canterbury players are second-rowers George Taylforth (number nine) and Kevin Goldspink.

Above: Souths captain **John Sattler**, his jaw horribly smashed, after the 1970 Grand Final.

The appointment of *Sattler* (above) as Souths captain in 1967 became one of the most inspired decisions in the club's history. The former Newcastle forward had developed a reputation for undisciplined play, but the skipper's role proved the making of him, and he went on to lead his club to four premierships in five years, and to captain Australia.

Souths *John O'Neill*, tackled by Balmain five-eighth Keith Outten, during the 1969 Grand Final.

O'Neill, fighting through the St George defence in a premiership match at the SCG in 1970. The Saints defenders are Dennis Brandley (number four) and second-rower Barry Beath.

Below: *O'Neill* (left) and Peter Peters, chairing off Manly captain Fred Jones after the 1973 Grand Final, perhaps the most violent premiership decider of all time.

Above: *O'Neill* playing for Australia against Wales in a World Series match in 1975.

Balmain's *Arthur Beetson* clashing with Souths Bob McCarthy (number 10) during the 1969 major semi-final. Beetson was later sent off. His subsequent suspension meant he missed the Tigers' shock victory in the grand final. The other players in the picture are Balmain's Len Killeen (behind Beetson) and captain Peter Provan, and Souths' Dennis Pittard (number six).

Left: **Beetson** (right) gets acquainted with Wales' toothless Jim Mills (far left) and John Mantle during a World Series international in 1975. Note the missing finger!

Left: **Beetson**, face to face with New Zealand referee John Percival.

Below: **Beetson** (right) with the great lock forward, Ron Coote (left), and master coach Jack Gibson, after Easts unprecedented 38-0 thrashing of St George in the 1975 Grand Final.

Souths tough hooker *George Piggins*, who battled through years of playing reserve grade to represent his country, to become captain, then coach and now president of the Souths club, and to establish a reputation for toughness that few first-grade forwards have matched.

Bob *'The Bear'* O'Reilly (right), battling with Souths Elwyn Walters in a premiership match at the old Cumberland Oval in 1971.

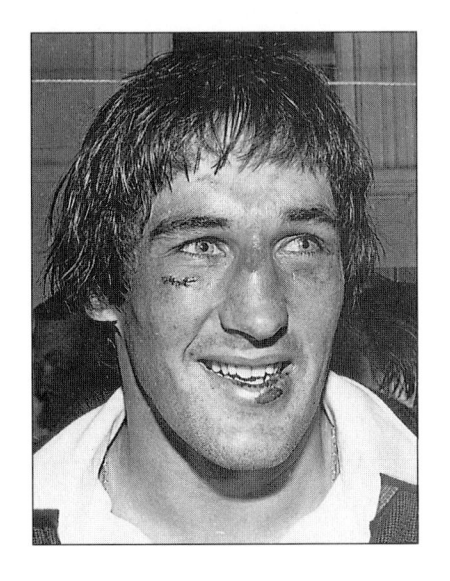

Two shots of Manly's *Terry Randall*, one of the hardest hitters to ever pull on a rugby league jumper.
The other Sea Eagles forward in the picture below is Bill 'Herman' Hamilton, who, with Randall, toured England and France with the 1973 Kangaroos.

boy and couldn't see myself surviving in Sydney.

"Then on New Year's day, 1963, a couple of old Souths officials, Joe Maloney and George Hanson arrived on my door and told me they wanted me to play for Souths. About three hours later I was in a car going to Sydney, and that night I signed a two-year contract in the basement of the old Souths Leagues club.

"I was just lost when I first arrived in town. I used to work in Mascot, live in Kingsford and train at Redfern. But I only stuck to the streets I knew and used to go from Mascot back home to Kingsford to get to Redfern. What should have been a five-minute trip took me nearly half an hour. One day, after a couple of months, Bobby McCarthy took me when I didn't have my car and that was the first time I realised how close everything was."

Souths were a struggling team of no-names when Sattler joined the club in 1963, and the young back-rower was immediately promoted to first grade.

"I was probably a bit fortunate because there were no real stars ahead of me. At that stage they were just looking for players ... Bob McCarthy and I both started that year. But it was a fairly hard initiation; we won just four games that season and copped a few hidings. I made my debut against Parramatta in the pre-season at Redfern. They had some top players like the Thornett brothers and Ronny Lynch. The main thing I remember about that day is finishing in South Sydney hospital getting eight stitches in a cut above my eye. My dad, who was normally a quiet bloke, saw the mess my face was in and said: 'You can't take this sort of thing every week; you're going to have to give some back to these blokes or they'll kill you.'

"So I followed his advice and probably did it to the extreme. I was sent off three times that first season but in those days that was the way the game was played. You dished it out, you copped it, and occasionally you'd fall foul of the referees as a result."

Sattler believes the turning point in Souths' fortunes in the '60s came with the appointment of Bernie Purcell as coach in 1964.

"Bernie was a real 'Plain Jane' coach who just stuck to the fundamentals. But he knew the game inside out and knew how to handle the players. He was without doubt the best coach I ever had. We had some cranky players and a few big heads, but he sorted them all out.

"Our fullback, Kevin Longbottom, who was a bit of a problem child, didn't take kindly to criticism. On a Tuesday night at training, Bernie would tell him what he did wrong on the weekend and, more than once, 'Lummy' would go off home and sulk. 'Go on, off you go,' Bernie would say. He didn't try stopping him or having it out and, 10 minutes later, Lummy would be back on the paddock training with the rest of us.

HIT MEN

"Good players like Ronnie Coote started to arrive in '64 and we had a fair year, just missing out on the finals. We really started to click in '65 and made the grand final but lost to St George. In '66, we started well but faded and Bernie had some arguments with the committee, which led to them sacking him. Clive Churchill took over and I found he was also a great coach, although very different to Bernie. While Bernie would do more technical work, Clive would keep everyone laughing and happy. There were times we'd be in big trouble at halftime and he'd come into the room and tell a joke. But in one match, after we'd played poorly in the first half, Clive walked in and yelled: 'I don't want to talk to youse after that. Youse work it out.' With that he walked out again. And it worked; we knew he was dirty and really lifted our effort in the second half."

Souths won the competition in Churchill's first season as coach in 1967, and forwards Sattler, Elwyn Walters and Coote all made that year's Kangaroo tour.

"That trip was probably the highlight of my career," Sattler says. "We were this bunch of young guys who'd all come up together and worked so hard. To win the comp was just about the ultimate. Then to be selected on the Roo tour capped it all off.

"We should have had Bob McCarthy on tour too, but somehow the selectors managed to leave him out. They picked a Canterbury bloke, Kevin Goldspink, who wasn't half the player Macca was.

"I remember I was rooming with Noel Kelly and Peter Gallagher — two great front-rowers. On tour they asked me to play a couple of games in the front row, which was all new to me as I'd been a back-rower all my life. 'Ned' asked me which side of the scrum I preferred and I asked innocently: 'Is there any difference?'

"The two of them couldn't stop laughing. Then in one game against Widnes, their hooker, Ray French, was giving us a real hard time. Ned told me to keep him busy during the next scrum so we came to blows. We were going hammer and tongs when Ned came in from the side and pole-axed him with a right hook. French went down in a crumpled heap — his legs were shaking and I thought he was dead. Ned just jogged away. When I caught up with him, I said: 'That was the cruellest thing I've ever seen in my life.' But Ned just shrugged and said: 'He was only a Pommy, mate — never hit them when they're looking at you.'"

In some ways. the '67 Roo tour wasn't all Sattler hoped it would be.

"I had a bad elbow that I carried through the tour and used to strap very heavily before every game. I wasn't supposed to play in the game against Swinton but one of the fellas, I think it was Elwyn Walters, slipped in the bus on the way to the ground. He did his shoulder and pulled out, and they

JOHN SATTLER

asked me to have a run. I didn't strap the elbow and, with a few minutes to go, I went in to do a high tackle. One of our blokes, Johnny Greaves, came in to help but all he did was knock my elbow. It was dislocated, turned inside out in fact, and the party was over. I was going all right, too, but never got to play a Test.

"I had to wait until 1969, when we played New Zealand, to make my Test debut. I also captained Australia in a Test against the Poms in 1970 and that was a great feeling."

Souths' shock grand final loss to underdogs Balmain in 1969 remains something of a sore point for the Rabbitohs then skipper.

"We were 100-to-one on that day," he remembers. "Everyone thought we were going to romp home. Before the game we were up in the grandstand, looking down at the Giltinan Shield. I was sitting next to John O'Neill and he just shook his head and growled: 'It's a bloody joke, playing this mob of cats. We're going to murder them. We should just pick up that shield and take it down to the Cauliflower Hotel and have a beer.'

"Anyway, it's history now that they were too good for us in the game. I'll never forget the stunned look on Lurch's face with about five minutes to go. 'You know something,' he muttered to me. 'This mob of cats is going to beat us!'

Great Britain defeated Australia 27-8 in Sattler's lone Test as captain in the 1970 series, but the Souths strongman won himself a place in league's Hall of Fame for his amazingly courageous performance in the grand final later that season. Playing against Manly, Sattler had his jaw horribly smashed in three places in an off-the-ball incident by Sea Eagle forward John Bucknall. The injury came early in the game, but Sattler refused to leave the field, and led the Rabbitohs to a memorable 23-12 win.

Moments after the incident, Sattler said to team-mate Mike Cleary "Mike, hold on to me ... don't let me fall. I don't want the bastards to know I'm crook." But, today, he plays down the courage he showed on that famous occasion.

"Bucknall was essentially a lower grader who only got into their team because a couple of other blokes were out injured," Sattler says. "I think he just went out there looking for some easy pickings. Their forward, Bill Hamilton, ran through and Bucknall came up beside him, screaming for the ball. But he didn't get it. Then, as he ran back onside, he hit me with the best forearm jolt you'd ever see. I was down on one knee, but got up, and he belted me again. He finished up breaking the jaw in three places — on either side and right through the centre.

The ref was Don Lancashire, who ended up being a mate of mine. Years later he said to me: 'Mate, I never knew who got you at the time.' But I didn't believe him. Everyone knew. It was a nasty injury, but I always thought that if you gave it out, you had to expect some back. Not that you ever wanted to cop something like that, but sooner or later you knew your number would come up.

"Six of my teeth were smashed — I knew immediately it was a bad injury. But I stayed on because I wasn't getting any mad, crazy pain. It was very uncomfortable, but I thought I could put up with it. At halftime, only a couple of blokes knew the extent of the damage. Bob McCarthy was one and he called Clive Churchill over. They asked if I wanted to stay off but I said I'd be right to go back; I could just keep jamming up into my mouthguard with my fingers.

"It wasn't until after I cooled down that the pain and shock of it all really set in. They took me straight to hospital and I was in there for two weeks ... and wired up for another 14. It was a horrible injury because I'd go to sleep then wake up with a start and break all the wires; that held up the healing process."

George Piggins, a man known for his toughness on the football field, cannot speak highly enough of Sattler's effort that day.

"The injury was a big handicap to carry around and the Manly blokes thought they were going to win the game because of it. And they were entitled to — no team carrying a bloke with a broken jaw should win a grand final. But guys like Elwyn Walters, Ron Coote, John O'Neill and Gary Stevens all rallied around Satts. He was the finest captain I ever played under and always got the best out of his players, even at a time of great difficulty like that."

Souths won the title again in 1971, downing St George in a game Sattler rates as the best game of his five consecutive grand finals. But after that success, the Rabbitoh empire began to crumble.

"Cootey left, so did John O'Neill, Ray Branighan, Elwyn Walters and Bobby Moses," Sattler recalls. "It left a fair hole and I thought I'd play one last year in 1972 and then call it a day. But, at the end of '72, I got a call from Ron McAuliffe, the old Queensland Rugby League chief. NSW used to flog the Maroons in those days, but Ron was determined to reverse the trend. I remember him ringing me up and just saying: 'John, it's Ron McAuliffe here; how'd you like to come up and play in Queensland?'

"I said: 'No, not really.' Even when he hit me with a good amount of money, I said: 'It'd take 10 grand more for me to be interested.'

"He said that was way too much and we said our goodbyes. I thought that was the end of it. I sat at the dinner table with my wife that night and we thought it was a pity such a good opportunity had come and gone so quickly. I'd never made much money at Souths — I think $10,000 was the

JOHN SATTLER

most I ever made in a year — and this would have been the chance to make some good dough before giving it away. 'Easy come, easy go,' I thought.

"Anyway, a couple of days later, solicitor Jim Comans, who was acting on behalf of the Queensland Rugby League, rang and said the request I'd put to the QRL for the extra $10,000 had been approved. 'Be there in a month,' were Jim's parting words.

"I was stunned. I had a steady job, we'd just bought a new house ... I hadn't even had time to discuss it seriously with my wife. But we were there a month later and we've been either in Brisbane or on the Gold Coast ever since."

On the football field, the move north had its early hiccups. Sattler led a raw Queensland outfit against a star-laced NSW side that cleaned up the 1973 interstate series 3-nil. Worse still, the Maroons didn't score a point in the entire three games.

"I warned them when I signed not to expect me to turn things around. I was never the type of player to run 50 yards to score tries, even in my prime. Then they put me in with the Wests club in Brisbane and it was just a disaster. To put it simply, they had no idea — on or off the field. The players were nice blokes but couldn't play and the officials weren't up to it. They were the two hardest years of my life and I'd love to just wipe them from my memory. But they were that bad I just know I can never forget them. I was glad when the second year was over and couldn't retire quick enough. But then Tommy Bishop, the little English halfback who'd taken over as coach of Norths in Brisbane, came over for a cup of tea one day. 'Come and have just one year with us,' he asked.

"Norths had a good young side and I could see they were going to go places that season. But I said no — I'd retired and that was that. They went on their way but I found myself saying to my wife: 'I'd love to have one last year to wipe out that awful mongrel time at Wests.' She said to go for it. They told me they couldn't pay me much money — I think they gave me $300 at the end of it all, but it was tremendously satisfying. We had some good young players and got as far as the final — I was happy to call it quits after that."

Like many of league's hard men, the John Sattler off the field was a complete contrast to the man the footballing public saw every weekend.

"Noel Kelly used to say that sort of thing; I roomed with him on the Kangaroo tour and he once said to me: 'For such a fiery bloke on the field, you're awful quiet off it. I think it's your mouthguard — when you put it in it's like a flicking switch and you go off your head.'

"Can you imagine that coming from Noel Kelly — he was a fine one to talk! We were chatting a while ago about the modern game and he said to me: 'With all this video citing business, it's just as well we're not playing nowadays — we'd only get a game every leap year.'

"But it was the way the game was played in those days. I was never a Gasnier or a Raper who could run and score tries, so I had to rely on other things to get by. We had other players in the Souths team who could do that. I did the heavy stuff and they scored the tries. I was a bit on the fiery side, but I enjoyed it."

Now firmly entrenched on the Gold Coast, where he runs the Helensvale Tavern, Sattler was a key member of the consortium that brought the Gold Coast Giants (now Seagulls) into the Winfield Cup in 1988. But the consortium relinquished ownership of the club after a couple of seasons, and Sattler's sole involvement with the game at the moment is following son Scott, who transferred from Gold Coast to Eastern Suburbs in 1994.

"When Scott came back home after first talking to Easts, I asked him what he thought, and he said: 'Gee, dad, I just couldn't live in Sydney'. Two weeks later he signed and now he loves it down there.

"Like father, like son, I guess."

HIT MEN

JOHN O'NEILL

Playing For Keeps

John O'Neill, the renowned enforcer of the late 1960s and early '70s, has the best grand final record of any front-rower in league's modern era. In an amazing nine-year run, O'Neill played in eight first-grade grand finals, and enjoyed the post-match victory lap no less then six times.

The man known as "Lurch" was the cornerstone of a South Sydney pack that dominated the premiership between 1967 and 1971, and formed a devastating partnership with the bruising Rabbitoh skipper, John Sattler. In 1972, O'Neill moved to Manly, and his switch proved the turning point in the Sea Eagles' history. After a series of near misses in semi-finals and grand finals, Manly finally broke through for its maiden premiership in O'Neill's first year with the club. The Sea Eagles were back again a year later, with O'Neill leading from the front against Cronulla in perhaps the bloodiest grand final of them all.

O'Neill hailed from Gunnedah, the first in an impressive line of front-rowers the town developed in the modern era. O'Neill, John Donnelly, and Lindsay Johnston all hailed from the same town before making their names in Sydney, as did the Test hooker Ron Turner.

O'Neill began playing league (in the centres) at the age of 11, in his first year of high school before graduating to the second row and then the front row. By 16, he was in Gunnedah's first-grade side and already starting to attract attention. He played for Northern Division while still a teenager and, at the age of 20, tried out for Sydney champions St George in 1964.

O'Neill was graded by Saints, but opted to return to Gunnedah after some fatherly advice from Saints' astute secretary Frank Facer.

"Frank told me I was better off going back home as I would have spent the year playing lower grades," O'Neill recalls. "Saints had plenty of good forwards at the time. Being a young bloke, I copped the tip. I played for

61

HIT MEN

Country against City later in 1964 and then got selected for NSW Colts against the touring French side. The joke was I didn't even know the game was on ... someone told me I had to be in Sydney to play the Frenchmen and I thought he was pulling my leg. That was my first meeting with guys like Ron Coote and Bob McCarthy. It was a great experience.

"Souths spotted me in that game and signed me up. That was the start of my Sydney career. I never worried about the money — I think I got around 600 pounds for the year, while the internationals in the club were on two thousands pounds. I signed on for three years and the plan was to go straight home to Gunnedah after that. And I'm still bloody well here!"

O'Neill had the hardest possible debut in 1965 — against Saints, the team that had shunned him the previous year.

"While they were a great side, Saints didn't worry me," he remembers. "I was a kid from the bush and didn't even know who Johnny Raper and Reg Gasnier were!

"But, it ended up being a tough initiation. I remember our veteran hooker Freddie Anderson telling me after the game: 'If Norm Provan had connected with that stiff arm he threw at you, your head would have been over the goalposts.'"

"I didn't even know which tackle he was talking about. It was a hard game in those days and you had to watch out for yourself in every tackle. It was a lot more physical than at the moment, that's for sure.

"The next game we played Balmain and they were a hard side too. Guys like Dicky Wilson, George Piper and Bob Boland were all established players so I had a couple of real hard games to test my mettle early on."

However, O'Neill passed his demanding initiation and went on to great heights in his debut season.

"I was the only bloke in the side to play every game and we finished the year by playing St George in the grand final before a record crowd of over 70,000 fans at the SCG. That was probably the hardest grand final I played in. We were a young side and they had guys like Kevin Ryan, Norm Provan and Johnny Raper in the pack. They beat us 12-8 and while the better side won, we gave them a run for their money.

"It still seems like yesterday — I remember how nervous we were running out before such a huge crowd. We kept at them but their experience and guile proved the difference in the end. The following year in 1966 was disastrous; we had internal troubles and didn't even make the grand final. But then Clive Churchill took over as coach and we began a great Souths era."

After spending time in reserve grade during 1967, the Rabbitohs grand final win that year proved a triumph for O'Neill. The big man played the

JOHN O'NEILL

game as if to prove a point to Churchill, who kept him in reserve grade for several weeks mid-season. He scored the first of Souths' two tries with a determined burst and constantly troubled Canterbury with his aggressive play. Souths were on a roll and the following year, defeated Manly to win another title. There were high hopes of a hat-trick of premierships when Souths met rank underdogs Balmain in the grand final of 1969. But things failed to go as expected. Like many Souths men from the era, O'Neill still cringes when recalling that game.

"It was a strange game ... a nothing game really," he said. "It wasn't tough like the other grand finals and everyone seemed to wait for someone else to do something. We thought we had their measure and there's no doubt we were over-confident. But, in the end, the longer the game went, the more they would have beaten us by.

"We had around three tries disallowed in the first 10 minutes and that good start was probably the worst thing that could have happened to us. We lost our way after that. Every time we got going they started lying down, but you can't take it away from Balmain. They had a better side than people gave them credit for. There weren't too many good players in our side that day ... we all just went through the motions and got beat 11-2.

"We got back on track and won the titles in 1970 and '71. When we won the grand final in 1970 against Manly we went back to the club and were all concerned about John Sattler and his broken jaw. Satts had played most of the game with the injury and was obviously in great discomfort.

"We were given sandwiches to eat, while the officials were all wining and dining themselves. We copped it sweet but the same thing happened the following year. By that stage I'd had it ... I blew my top and I belted a couple of the old officials right there in the club. Next thing I knew I was on the open market. Even though Canterbury offered me the most money, I decided to go to Manly. Ken Arthurson was running the show and I already knew him and former Souths players Ray Branighan and Bob Moses, who had transferred there. I felt welcome. I wasn't to know it at the time, but it was the best move I could have made.

"We won Manly's first comp in 1972 and then backed up again in 1973, beating Cronulla. We should have won in 1974, too, but Easts, under Jack Gibson, had our measure in the finals, even though I thought we had a better side than them."

O'Neill plays down his own contribution in his phenomenal run of grand final success.

"I just pulled the right rein all the way along ... I was lucky. It's easy to play in good company. There are some great players who never played in a grand final yet I played in eight.

HIT MEN

"Whenever I look back I think just how fortunate I was to play for two champion clubs."

O'Neill rates the 1973 grand final and the 1970 World Cup final between Australia against England as the two toughest matches he ever played in.

"Going on the tour of England (in 1970) was one of the highlights of my life," he says. "It was my first big tour and we won the Cup which was a real bonus.

"I remember when they picked the Australian team that year. We were back at Souths Leagues Club after winning the grand final. I was that keen to go I was scared to cross the street in case something happened — that's how much it meant to me."

O'Neill was one of Australia's form players throughout the tournament and loomed as a key man in the final. But after being cautioned four times in the lead-up game against England a fortnight earlier, O'Neill was under strict instructions from coach Harry Bath to keep his hands down in the decider. The Englishmen bashed and butted him, stomped and sledged him, but O'Neill never lost his cool and was a hero in Australia's 12-7 win.

"We were lucky to beat the Poms in the final, though," he says. "They had a top side and if we played them 10 times, they'd probably win eight, but this was our day. We decided the best way to win was to get stuck into them early and, while I was very careful what I did, it worked. Our aggressive play put them off their game. There was plenty of spite right until the end when Eric Simms was punched in the face by one of their players when he tried to shake hands. They had a tough side and fought fire with fire.

"The '73 grand final against Cronulla was boots and all. Of all the grand finals I played in, that's the one people always ask me about. It's the game they all remember. And it's not because of the quality of the football; it wasn't a great game as such. They remember it because it was such a rugged affair.

"At one stage their little halfback Tommy Bishop, who was a cheeky bludger, kicked me in the shins. I started chasing him but he ran off and hid behind big Cliff Watson. I nearly caught up with him a few times but he was too slippery. Games like that were hard, but they were great to play in. You knew what was required in those days — you had to get over your opposite front-rower. And, while it was tough, not too many players got badly hurt. The hard stuff was all part of the game and you accepted it."

The big front-rower found himself drawn back to Souths in 1975 but suffered a bad shoulder injury early in the season that was to ultimately prove his undoing.

"I was over the hill and the injury made it hard," he says. "I'd had a good innings and at the end of 1976, I knew there was no point going on. Souths tried to talk me into playing again, but I knew it wasn't the thing to do."

However, O'Neill's association with Souths continued in 1977, when he was appointed first-grade coach.

"I enjoyed the coaching, but could never do the job justice because of my work as a builder," he says. "I just couldn't put in the coaching hours and run the business as well. We had a young side that needed guidance which is why I knocked on Jack Gibson's door. He came and helped out and, while he didn't get great results, he never had the players. They weren't coming through. The money wasn't there to buy talent so we suffered. It's been the same story ever since."

O'Neill still lives in the Souths area and admits he finds the Rabbitohs' struggle to survive in recent years hard to take.

"The club has done it tough in the past few years and things have certainly changed since the old days," he says. "It's been a long time between drinks for Souths. I'd love to see them win another comp, but the club's had no money and has gone from bad to worse. But I'd like to think Souths can turn the corner and become a force again."

O'Neill has no hesitation in rating John Sattler as the toughest player he encountered in his career.

"I played with and against him and there was no harder man," he explains. "He was great to play with because you always knew he'd be there when you needed him. But playing against him wasn't much fun — he seemed to enjoy giving a mate a good whack on the jaw.

"And there were plenty of others. Noel Kelly, Kevin Ryan, Jimmy Morgan, Arthur Beetson and Bob O'Reilly were all a handful. Ryan was up there with the best of them. He wasn't a dirty player but a real granite-like defender. And if things got hot, he could mix it with anyone. There were plenty of others I can't even think of. We had some rugged encounters but I never used to worry about it before or after the match. I remember on occasion being told before a game 'You've got to watch this bloke or that bloke', but I never paid any attention. I didn't care who I was playing week to week. I just went out and did my best. You were judged on your toughness in those days and you knew the first 15 minutes, no matter who you were playing, was going to be a test."

One of O'Neill's few regrets is that he didn't play more Test Matches for Australia.

"There were a lot of World Cup games back then and I played plenty of those," he says. "But it was crazy that they didn't count them as Tests. It meant I only played two fair dinkum Tests ... I was always out injured or suspended when they came around. On the 1973 Kangaroo tour I was looking forward to the Test series but had my faced smashed in by a headbutt in an early club game. It was a beauty and that stuffed up a lot of my tour. Another year we were playing Norths at North Sydney Oval and I'd already been named in the Test team for the following week. Norths had a strong pack with guys like Jim Fiddler and Merv Hicks. It was fairly fiery and in one scrum Fiddler, a Pommie on a guest stint, hit the deck and I just walked over the top of him. The ref said I kicked him in the head, and ordered me straight off. I got six weeks for that and it cost me a few Test caps. Back in 1971, I received a six-week suspension — one of two I got in in quick succession — and that ruled me out of a Test tour to New Zealand.

"I got marched a few too many times; sometimes I deserved it, sometimes I didn't. Those two six-week stints really hurt though. That was as long as anyone ever got suspended in those days; it would be the equivalent of a six-month sentence now. The first time, I was sent off against St George for kneeing their second-rower, Barry Beath, and then, in my first game back against Parramatta, I was hoisted again on a similar charge. But I should never have been sent off that day.

"I trained my arse of with (legendary fitness trainer) George Daldry and came back for the final and then the grand final, when we beat Saints to take the title."

Long-time team-mate Bob McCarthy has vivid memories of O'Neill's suspensions which made headlines back in 1971.

"Whenever I think of Lurch, it's the first thing that comes to mind," McCarthy says. "Against St George, he kneed Beath in the face and was sent straight off. I can still see Beath lying there, unconscious on the ground, the blood dropping down from his forehead and forming little pools in his closed eyes. He was really gone; they had to cart him off.

"Then, against Parramatta, he flattened Bob O'Reilly the same way and couldn't believe it when the ref, Keith Holman, sent him off again.

"'You're kidding,' big Lurch protested.

"'Just look at what you've done to O'Reilly,' said Holman in reply, pointing to the prone figure of the giant Parramatta forward.

"Lurch just shook his head as he walked off, screaming: 'What's the game coming to?'

"That was typical Lurch; he's just about maimed two blokes but couldn't understand what all the fuss was about. He was a genuine hard man who dished out plenty on the field but never complained when it was handed back to him. It was a different era in the game and he played for keeps."

McCarthy also remembers team-mates always fearing for O'Neill whenever the Rabbitohs took out a premiership title.

"We all loved to celebrate, but Lurch really went over the top," he says.

JOHN O'NEILL

"He'd disappear for three days and how he kept awake for that long always had me buggered. But then he'd sleep for two days to make up for it, so he lost just about a whole week out of his life every time. The one who really felt it was Gary Stevens, who was his partner in the building game. He'd have to cover for Lurch every time and must have been dreading it every time we won the comp." Although he pulled off many bone-jarring hits during his football days, O'Neill rates one bootlace tackle among the highlights of his career.

"We were playing St George at the SCG and the ball was kicked to Graeme Langlands. I took him on one-on-one, he put his big step on but to everyone's amazement I brought him down with a copybook tackle. I got up with a huge grin on my face and I think even Chang could see the funny side.

"'What the hell are you doing tackling me?' he asked with a stunned look on his face.

"We used to have a lot of fun like that — on and off the field. Once we went up to New Guinea for our end-of-season trip and wanted to make some money for our drinking fund. So in a match against the locals, we rigged the first try scorers. We passed the word to let one of their blokes score but Gary Stevens had cauliflower ears and didn't hear the message. We all let this bloke past us before Gary hammered him with a beauty. But he finally got the message and the next time the Papuan got the ball, he ran 70 metres to score. There were Souths players missing tackles, left, right and centre, and this guy thought he was another Reg Gasnier.

"Touring with the 'Roos was great, even though they put us in low-class hotels back then. One section of the pub we stayed in we called 'Surry Hills'; you wouldn't go there after dark. Tim Pickup, Terry Randall, Tom Raudonikis and (journalist) Bill Mordey hung out there, and one night they had a water fight. Someone ended up bringing in a fire hose and the whole floor collapsed. The management nearly went crazy. Bob McCarthy went up the fire escape one day just for a laugh and it disintegrated under his weight; he was lucky he didn't kill himself. They were great days ... they just went too bloody quickly."

To say John O'Neill isn't a fan of rugby league in the '90s is an understatement.

"In my day you wouldn't go onto the field without shin-guards," he says. "If you did, you'd get your legs kicked off in the scrums. Scrums really disappoint me nowadays. They're not a contest anymore and are so predictable. They've taken the excitement out of them. It's not an entertaining game any more. You know what's going to happen. One team has the ball for five tackles, then kicks it downfield. Then the winger will let it go out ...

that really irks me. And then they put down a scrum and start all over again.

"It's too predictable. We weren't as fit or as strong as the current players are, but now there aren't enough good players to go around all the clubs. The overall standard of the game isn't high and there are plenty of kids in first grade now who wouldn't have got into third grade in our era.

"I find the way they replace players every five minutes hard to take. In my day, if a coach would have told me to come off, I wouldn't have gone. Even if I'd been playing the worst game of my life, I would have stuck it out. I started off under the no replacement rule and played for NSW against the Poms in 1970 for 40 minutes with a bung shoulder. I had to put my hand in my shorts but I stayed on the field and helped my mates out. If a bloke tapped me on the shoulder to come off, I'd tell him to go to the shithouse. When I ran onto the field, I was there for the 80 minutes.

"There was no place to hide back then and if you had a bad game, at least you had a chance to come good. It's still a great game, but if they keep changing the rules, we're heading for disaster."

O'Neill admits he enjoyed playing football in the pre-video era.

"What happened on the field stayed on the field in our day," he says. "There were times having no video evidence helped you and times it hindered you. But the refs made plenty of mistakes back then, just like they do now. Without the video, there was nothing you could do about it.

"I wouldn't have been a referee to save my life, and, with the advent of television, they became show ponies. I had a reputation and that counted against me with them. Other blokes would throw stiff-arms and nothing would happen, but I was in trouble when I lifted my little finger. And you had no recourse when you went down to the judiciary in those days. You sat there, the ref said what you did, and you copped two, three, four, five or six weeks."

Like many players from his era, O'Neill believes his love of the good life prevented him from reaching his peak.

"If I had my time over again, I think I'd be more dedicated," he says. "I used to love having a good time — we'd go to the pub at the drop of a hat. If I'd been a bit more conscientious, I may have played a few more Tests ... you never know."

HIT MEN

ARTHUR BEETSON

King of Queensland

When Arthur Beetson came into the game, prop forwards were regarded as league's beasts of burden. They would put their heads down and do the hard, grafting work that allowed the backs to cut loose. But Beetson's marvellous ball skills opened the way for modern forwards to play their part in attacking football, paving the way for props such as Bob O'Reilly, Darryl Brohman, Craig Young and Steve Roach.

No forward in the modern game has been able to stamp his influence on a match in the manner Beetson dominated league in the mid-1970s. In that era there was a simple rule of thumb — if big Artie had a good game, his team would win. "The most constructive or destructive player I have seen in over 30 years," former Kangaroo coach Don Furner declared — and few could argue.

Remarkably mobile for a big man, Beetson was the scourge of the Englishmen during the '70s and the cornerstone of the awesome Eastern Suburbs machine that took out the premiership double in 1974-5. Then, in the '80s, Beetson's enthusiasm and drive, first as a player and then as a coach, was largely responsible for the State of Origin concept proving such a tearaway success. Through his career, Beetson has been a controversial figure, a lovable rogue to some, a rebel to others. From his early days in Sydney when he was haunted by the tag of "half-a-game Artie", to his colourful coaching career and frequent battles with administrators, Beetson has been one of the game's most significant figures.

Young Arthur Beetson grew up in poor surroundings, in the central Queensland town of Roma. The son of a local bushworker, Beetson was one of seven children, three of whom died early in life, and, from his earliest days, saw football as his ticket to success.

"I made a decision at 16 years of age that I was going to be a professional footballer," he said years later. "Don't ask me how I knew, but it was something I just knew."

A five-eighth or centre in his early days, Beetson moved to Brisbane as a raw 20-year-old in 1965, linking with the Redcliffe club. However, after only a handful of games, astute Redcliffe coach Henry Holloway asked Beetson to move into the forwards and the big man never looked back. A year later, he was in Sydney, playing first grade with Balmain, and then, after just a handful of games for the Tigers, was lining up for Australia against Great Britain.

It was in his Test debut, at the SCG, that the Beetson legend began to sprout wings. Before a crowd of over 63,000 fans, Beetson tore apart the English defence in a magical first-half display. He created Australia's opening try for winger Ken Irvine and then, minutes later, burst downfield. Realising the defence was converging, Beetson sent down a perfectly-placed grubber-kick for his other winger, the alert Johnny King, who touched down.

At halftime, Australia led 8-2, but Beetson never returned for the second half, which led to the young champion being labelled, somewhat unfairly, with the tag 'Half-a-game Artie'. A popular theory that was put forward at the time was that he didn't come back after halftime because he was exhausted. Some cynics went further, and suggested he had only kicked the ball for the King try because he couldn't run any further. The truth, however, was that the kick for King was an example of Beetson's attacking wizardry at work, while it had been a severe shoulder injury that had prevented him playing the second half.

Beetson had a brief stint in England with Hull Kingston Rovers in 1967, fine tuning his ball skills in the British game. Later that year, Beetson was using his emerging ball-playing talents to destroy the Great Britain side in the World Cup in Australia, and he played a key role in Australia's eventual Cup triumph. In 1969, he enjoyed a fine season with Balmain but was sent off in the major semi-final, and missed the Tigers' stunning upset win over Souths in the grand final. The following year, Balmain finished well down the ladder in 1970, and Beetson began to get itchy feet.

When Eastern Suburbs coach at that time, Don Furner, approached Beetson at the end of that season, it didn't take big Artie long to make up his mind on what was to be the most significant career move of his life.

"We had a good look at Arthur when he was at Balmain and there was no doubt he was an undisciplined player," Furner remembers. "But the thing that impressed me was that he was successful with a minimum of effort. I knew if he ever produced his best, he could be a world beater. He was so mobile for a big bloke, had great hands, could read a game — in short he

ARTHUR BEETSON

was the complete footballer. Other blokes wanted to play with him, and he was effective when only 70 per cent fit; there aren't many players you can say that about.

"I remember going to see him and telling him that whatever he was on at Balmain, we'd double. We ended up signing him for $6000, and then the really hard work began."

Furner embarked on a task many league critics thought to be mission impossible — turning the then rolly-polly Beetson into a lean, mean football machine. He took Beetson on a daily torture course through Queens Park near Easts' headquarters in Bondi Junction — a routine Beetson loathed.

"The first few times we did the course, I beat him and I think that made him more determined," Furner says. "It didn't take long for him to get in front of me and while he didn't enjoy it, I think he knew it was doing him good. I also set about changing his image in the media. Photographers loved to take snaps of him getting stuck into a pie or a giant steak and I think that was part of Arthur's problem. Everyone expected him to be the big man with the big appetite and he was happy to play along. I said: 'No more of those shots for the papers — from now on whenever they want your photo taken, get them to take you lifting a keg or working out at training.'

"Slowly but surely we turned him around."

Beetson helped Easts reach the 1972 grand final against Manly, but the Roosters lost 19-14 in controversial circumstances. A year later, he made his only Kangaroo tour and revelled on the soft English grounds. Beetson played more games than any other forward and won an award as best forward on tour. Legend has it that through some of the tensest matches on tour, Beetson would carry the ball forward fearlessly, singing *Waltzing Matilda* as he did so.

The other turning point in Beetson's career was Jack Gibson's arrival at Eastern Suburbs in 1974. Although initially worried by Gibson's reputation as a strict taskmaster, Beetson soon became a disciple of the master coach. Gibson appointed Beetson as captain — a move that would have been considered unthinkable only a couple of years earlier — and the Roosters reaped the rewards.

"We got the players to fill in a survey when we came to Easts and sent it off to the United States to be analysed," Gibson's right-hand man Ron Massey reveals. "When it came back, it showed that Beetson was a born leader. He came out top of the class. So we gave him a shot at the captaincy, and he never looked back."

Easts won the grand final in 1974, their first premiership since 1945. For both Beetson and Gibson, it was their first title. The Roosters downed

HIT MEN

Canterbury 19-4 in the grand final, with Beetson scoring the opening try to put his team on the road to victory. But it was the following year that Easts gained the reputation as one of the finest club sides league has known. The Roosters won 20 of their 22 premiership matches and then thrashed St George 38-0 in the most one-sided grand final in history. Beetson was in his element against a shell-shocked side, again scoring a try, and continually popping passes to team-mates from seemingly impossible positions.

Gibson later said of Beetson: "He could do it all on a football field and he could sell season tickets. He was an entertainer and a great player. He was good to coach; he was co-operative and he could take tough coaching ... you didn't have to mince words or sweetheart him. He contributed — he was generous and he helped other people. He never blamed anyone else ... if he had a bad game, he'd admit it."

At the end of the 1975 season, Beetson made his last playing trip to Europe, once again sweeping all before him as he led Australia to victory in the World Series.

In 1976, Easts were knocked out at the minor preliminary semi-final stage. For '77, Beetson replaced Gibson as Easts coach, and the Roosters promptly won the pre-season competition, with big Artie accepting the trophy from the Queen, who was touring Australia. Later in the year, Easts reached the final of the Amco Cup (to be edged out, by a single point, by Wests) and the premiership semi-finals (where they were beaten in the preliminary final by Parramatta). However, Beetson made his biggest headlines that season when he was omitted from the Australian team for the opening game of the World Series, against New Zealand. Then ARL chief Kevin Humphreys refused to accept the team without Beetson's name in it, so the selectors reluctantly included him, and named him captain. But Beetson, never one to rely on the charity of others, withdrew from the team when told of the circumstances of his selection.

"It was a slap in the face," he said some time later. "I thought I had been playing the best football of my career. But there had been some deals done in the selection room and I was made the scapegoat. It was a matter of pride. I couldn't play knowing the selectors didn't think I was worthy of the job."

Beetson returned to the side for the remaining World Series matches, and led Australia to the title in a fitting finale to his distinguished international career.

After Easts missed the 1978 semi-finals, Beetson decided it was again time to move on, and joined Parramatta. Although now past his best, Beetson still gave the Eels plenty of value and helped develop the team that was to take the premiership by storm in the '80s.

ARTHUR BEETSON

In his final season in Sydney football, 1980, Beetson, now all of 35-years-old and a reserve grader with Parramatta, experienced one of the high points of his career. Although a veteran of many interstate and international campaigns, Beetson had never worn the famous maroon jumper of Queensland. However, on the night of July 8, 1980, in what was to be quickly recognised as one of modern league's most memorable nights, he received his chance.

The venue was Lang Park; the event league's maiden State of Origin match. Neither the capacity crowd, nor the players for that matter, were quite sure how the new "State against State — Mate against Mate" concept would work. But when a fired-up Beetson landed a punch squarely on the jaw of Parramatta team-mate, NSW centre Michael Cronin, all doubts quickly disappeared. With one blow, Beetson had ensured that State of Origin football was "fair dinkum" — and that it was here to stay.

The Maroons won that first game 20-10, with the Lang Park crowd chanting "Artie! ... Artie!" through much of the second half.

Over the next decade, Beetson towered over the State of Origin scene like a colossus. He coached Queensland to victory in the one-off match in 1981, and to series wins in 1982, 1983, 1984 and 1989. But the board-room men were unkind to Beetson — he was dumped after losing a series for the first time, in 1990.

It was not the first time that Beetson's outwardly relaxed approach to coaching had cost him dearly. In 1984, Beetson lost the Australian coaching job after New Zealand had scored a shock win over the Aussies the previous year. No official reason for his sacking was given, but administrators were known to have been unimpressed by Beetson's laid-back style. And in 1993, the Cronulla club sacked big Arthur after the Sharks failed to make an impression on the race for the finals.

Injuries prevented Parramatta seeing the best of Beetson during his two-year stint with the Eels in 1979 and 1980. In his first season, he suffered a knee injury early on. When he returned, he was beginning to hit top form when he came up against his former Easts team-mates for the first time. In a mistimed tackle, Beetson's head hit the knee of an Easts forward and he suffered a badly-broken jaw. Complications set in, Beetson developed osteomyelitis, and had four operations in eight days. "I nearly died," he said later of the experience.

The finish to Beetson's Sydney career was emotional, but not quite the fairy tale he had hoped for. His final appearance was in the 1980 reserve-grade grand final, where the Eels went down to Canterbury 18-16. While the Bulldogs received generous applause after their win, the biggest cheer came when Beetson was chaired off the SCG by his team-mates.

HIT MEN

Beetson continued his career back in Brisbane, steering his old club, Redcliffe, to the grand final in 1981. Redcliffe led for much of that game but in a heartbreaking finish, went down in the last 45 seconds to Souths. He then continued to play the occasional social match for Moreton Bay until he was nearly 40, before returning to Sydney for stints as coach of Easts and then Cronulla, as well as spending time as an ABC television commentator.

Tales of Beetson's appetite have taken on a legendary status in rugby league folklore. Fellow front-rower Bob O'Reilly, another big man with a voracious appetite, recalls with relish some of the the pair's culinary adventures in Britain:

"On the 1973 Kangaroo tour, Arthur and I were room-mates and had Paul Sait and Gary Stevens next door to us. Arthur could never get enough to eat over there and some of the food wasn't all that crash hot. So we all put in some money and bought a stove, which Arthur insisted go in our room, next to his bed. Every day we went out to stock up on supplies of eggs and meat. After matches, or on days off, we'd have a few beers and then something like eggs on toast. Arthur would always allow us to go first, so we'd have an egg or two; then when we were finished he'd take around 18 eggs and have the world's biggest omelette. I don't know how he did it, particularly as it was often one or two in the morning, but he managed to finish it all.

"(Test hooker) Elwyn Walters was a pastry cook at the time so we invited him in to cook on occasion. But Arthur was the king of the stove, and we took it everywhere we went."

When he joined the Leagues club staff of Eastern Suburbs in the mid '70s, Beetson was offered a lavish office upstairs in the tower of the club, with superb views of the harbour. But he rejected it ... for far more modest accommodation downstairs.

"Arthur much preferred the office downstairs, and for good reason," recalls Ron Massey. "It was right next to the kitchen, and that was far more important to him than having a view or fancy furniture. The chef used to tell us how he'd never have to worry about burning any of the cookies or pastries he was making. There was a bell on the oven that used to go off when they were ready and as soon as it rang, Arthur would always be there, ahead of the cooking staff, giving the goodies all his tender loving care. And, of course, he'd have to sample the merchandise to make sure it was cooked just right."

Massey, one of modern football's shrewdest observers, passes a surprising judgement on Beetson's football talents.

"Everyone used to say Arthur was a terrific attacking player with good ball skills," declares Massey, "and you'd get no argument from me. But if

ARTHUR BEETSON

you asked me what his biggest attribute was I'd have to say it was the way he was able to read defence. He may not have always been able to get there, but he always knew exactly which way the opposition was moving the ball and where the danger lay. He would talk to his team-mates and tell them where to move and that must have saved countless tries over the years.

"Arthur just knew the game so well that he was able to predict where the ball was going to be at any time."

Former Kangaroo halfback Johnny Gibbs backs up Massey's view of Beetson as a strong defender.

"Like most people, I always thought of Arthur as just a great attacking player. But I learned through bitter experience he was a lot more than that," Gibbs comments. "In fact, while I was playing the game, Beetson was the one forward I found you always had to look out for. While other forwards would just fling you to the ground if they got hold of you, Arthur had the mobility to do more damage. He'd get a good hold of you and then smash you into the ground. The tackles he used were legal, but boy, you'd feel them all right."

Bob O'Reilly recalls an occasion when the call of nature became too much for Beetson on the 1973 Kangaroo tour.

"One night we were playing Bradford Northern at Odsal Stadium," he tells. "The field was down a massive set of stairs from the dressing room and it was a real climb. At halftime, you didn't even go back up — it was that far — they had a little hut for us to rest in.

"Early in the second half, Arthur told the referee he was busting for a leak, but the referee said he couldn't hold the game up for Arthur to climb up all those steps to the dressing room and come back. The big fella had a solution. 'Don't worry about that,' he told the referee. 'Just give me a few of my boys around me for protection and I'll do it right here.' So we formed a ring around Arthur so the crowd couldn't see anything and he did it right there in the middle of the field. Luckily for him it was a foggy night and the crowd couldn't see too much at the best of times. But the poor Pommy ref couldn't believe it; he just stood there and shook his head."

O'Reilly remains an ardent admirer of Beetson, both as a player, coach and sportsman.

"Besides being a tough player, Arthur also had the skills," he says. "He could unload a ball from anywhere, he could take a hit and was always a handful. There wasn't a sport he couldn't play. Tennis, golf, squash ...

"He was just a natural."

HIT MEN

GEORGE PIGGINS

Rabbitoh Pride

George Piggins is rugby league's version of the little Aussie battler come good. Born one of five kids in a tiny weatherboard house in Mascot, right in the middle of South Sydney territory, the cards were always stacked against him — in football and in life. But the man who, through his loyalty to Souths, for years played second fiddle to Test stalwart Elwyn Walters eventually received his just reward, becoming one of the club's favourite sons and wearing the green and gold. And in business, Piggins the truck driver developed a loading system that revolutionised the trucking game. A corporate giant would eventually buy him out, and earn Piggins early retirement in a luxury house overlooking Coogee bay.

Piggins cut his football teeth in the Souths district in the late '50s and early '60s, when a group of young Rabbitohs were developing skills that would lead to one of the club's golden eras. Every weekend he matched it with the likes of Ron Coote, Gary Stevens, Bob McCarthy and company. And while there were plenty of players with more skill and flair than Piggins, the little hooker had a tenacity that kept him up there with the best of them.

"It wasn't easy for mum and dad with such a big family, but they got us three meals a day and a bed to sleep in," Piggins recalls. "We lived in a 100-year-old house built by my grandfather but we didn't really miss out on much. Football was just a way of life at the time for any Mascot kid and I started playing at school in the under 4 stone 7s."

Piggins couldn't remember how old he was when he first ran onto a football field — it was "around 12 stone ago". The nuggetty young George started his career in the second row and, as with many major career moves, his shift to hooker came quite by accident.

"I always played in the second row and never really thought of playing

GEORGE PIGGINS

elsewhere," he says. "But then at around 12 or 13 I was playing E grade and our hooker got hurt coming into the semi-finals. They moved me into his spot — we went okay in the finals — and I was there from then on."

Piggins won selection in the Rabbitohs' President's Cup side in 1963. Remarkably, he had never seen South Sydney play when called up to grade the following year.

"It might sound strange, but I'd honestly never watched them go around," he explains. "As a kid, I wasn't really a spectator. I enjoyed doing things and I liked playing. In my teens I was playing C, B and A grade. That was three games of football a weekend, which didn't give me time for much else. I've had a lot of time to be a spectator since then — at the time it wasn't a priority."

Piggins hardly had a fairytale start to his grade career. In his debut, in third grade, against Wests at Pratten Park, he turned to pass the ball and collected the top of an opponent's head square in the middle of his back. The impact broke five vertebrae in his spine and kept him out of football for the rest of the season. In fact, his football career almost ended with that one brief appearance in Souths' colours.

"At that stage, I was only a young bloke, recently married and trying to get established. I wanted to play, but they offered me lousy money for '65 and in the meantime I was offered a job on the Sydney waterfront. That was a big break and I thought there wasn't enough money in football to knock back Sunday work on the wharves. So I told Souths I wasn't going to play any more. It wasn't an attempt to get a better offer out of them; I really meant it ... my football career wasn't that important to me then. But they did come back with an offer for more money and I decided to give it another go."

Although highly regarded by the Rabbitohs, Piggins found himself on the outside, looking in, for long periods of his early career. The established Freddie Anderson had the number-one hooking spot in 1965 and resisted a challenge from Piggins to remove him from the spot. A third competitor emerged in '66 — Elwyn "Aub" Walters — who would eventually become a regular fixture in the South Sydney, NSW and Australian teams.

"I was in and out a bit. But even with both Anderson and Walters there in '67, I still played 16 of the 22 preliminary games," Piggins remembers. "But I injured myself in the last round before the finals. I never got the position back after that. Walters played the last game, the semi-final and grand final and went to England with the Kangaroos. From then on it was his position and they only used me occasionally when he was injured or in rep camp."

But the tables were turned in 1971, when incumbent hooker Walters missed the grand final through injury and Piggins stepped in. The game proved among the most significant in Piggins' career. Souths won a hard-fought encounter against St George 16-10, and the under-rated replacement hooker played a vital role. On at least half-a-dozen occasions, at key points in the match, Piggins, standing at marker, raked the ball back from unsuspecting Saints opponents in the play-the-ball. In a tight match between two top-class sides, Piggins' ploy proved a major factor in Souths' favour. Realising the importance of the game to his future career, Piggins also excelled around the rucks, giving good service to his fellow forwards and tackling anything that came near him.

Playing such a significant role in Souths' win gave Piggins tremendous satisfaction for another reason. In the lead-up to the game, former top referee turned commentator Col Pearce was highly critical of the stand-in hooker's aggressive style. Piggins had the opportunity to dish out a king-sized helping of humble pie in the biggest game of the year.

"Pearce gave me a terrible time right through my career and gave me a tremendous bagging before the game. One of the highlights of that game was making him eat his words. He was not a fan of mine, but I had the opportunity to hit back. To his credit, he retracted what he said in the Sunday papers and that made it all that much sweeter.

"That game helped my profile within the club and changed things a little as far as getting another crack at the top hooking spot."

However, until Walters left to join Easts in 1974, Piggins was more often than not back in the familiar role of reserve-grade hooker. Yet curiously, at the time, it didn't worry him.

"Elwyn had a more illustrious career than mine and he was in first grade and I was in seconds ... it was as simple as that," he says. "If you'd asked me would I swap positions with him, I would have done it in an instant, but I never got too upset at being number two. Souths were paying me fair money to play reserve grade and I was enjoying it."

Piggins was not short of offers to quit the Rabbitohs, with then arch rivals St George persistent bidders for his services. Even in 1964, before his career had really started, Saints, through highly-astute club secretary Frank Facer, sounded out the young hooker.

"That was a great compliment as at the time Saints were in the midst of their 11 premiership run," Piggins says. "It might sound strange as I knocked them back more than once, but I rated being approached by St George as a career highlight. I've often wondered why I said no to them. Looking back now, I do regret not playing more first grade and I might have given them a different answer if I had my time again. But back then I was a Souths man. I played for the district

GEORGE PIGGINS

all my life, I was happy and I decided to stay where I was."

Always known as a fierce competitor, Piggins' reputation as one of league's hardest men was cemented one afternoon in 1973 at the SCG, when he clashed head on with Manly and their rugged English import, Malcolm Reilly. Neither player was accustomed to taking a backward step and in a vital match to both team's finals chances, the pair were at each other from the start.

Piggins recalls the "meeting" with a wry grin. "I hold no grudges. He was a tough player and he certainly gave as good as he got. He might see it differently but I remember it all started when I tackled him early on. As he got up he lashed out with his boot and caught me in the mouth. I've still got the lumps on my lip 20 years later to remind me. I didn't think it was any accident and next chance I got, I gave him a clout. He didn't fancy that and we were into one another. (Referee) Laurie Bruyeres said: 'You'se two clash again and you'll be off.'

"Well, his words obviously made no impression on Malcolm. Next time we met he head butted me, I butted him back and it was on."

The two men grappled on the ground for several minutes, punching, kicking, butting and gouging in the shadow of the famous SCG Members' Stand. Legend has it that Piggins told team-mates after the dust had settled: "I had my finger in the bastard's eye ... I should have flicked it out."

Both players were given their marching orders. Twenty years on, Piggins sat uncomfortably in his chair as he talked of the incident.

"We got a couple of weeks each down at the judiciary which was par for the course at that stage. It was a pretty nasty sort of incident. I didn't say a word to him as we trudged off the field. I was tempted, but I figured enough was enough."

The trip to the judiciary was a familiar one to Piggins. He was sent off 14 times in his career with the Rabbitohs, a "strike rate" few players in any era could match.

"I got to know the blokes on the panel fairly well," he grins. "As a matter of fact, I was sent off in my first game in first grade. I remember it well — it was Anzac Day in 1967 and we were playing against Newtown at Redfern. I was up against a bloke called Clarrie Jeffreys, who ended up coaching Newtown later, and wasn't about to let him get on top of me in my debut. We were at each other from the start and finally the ref (by coincidence again Bruyeres) got sick of us and sent us both off. I'm not overly proud of that judiciary record but the way I looked at it, if anyone belted me, I belted them back.

"Unfortunately, I think I wouldn't get a game today with that sort of record. Even when I was coaching (in the late '80s), when a player became a luxury you had to leave him out. But back then, when two big packs came together, people knew what to expect in the first few scrums and it was exciting. If I thought I could hurt someone, I'd hurt them. Not maim them, I never went out to do anything like that. But if a little halfback was making plenty of darting runs and giving us trouble, I'd see what effect a thumping would have on him. Maybe he wouldn't run as hard the next time. It was part of the game and nobody minded."

Firmly established at Souths following Walters' move to Easts, Piggins soon attracted the attention of the representative selectors. Despite the fact that Souths played so poorly that they would eventually finish last in the 1975 premiership, Piggins won selection in Australia's World Cup team that played New Zealand mid-season and so impressed the selectors he was named in the squad to tour Britain and France for the second leg of the tournament at the end of the season.

Years later, Piggins admits he was set to feign injury to pull out of the tour.

"It was only really for my wife and my father that I decided to go. I'd been to New Zealand earlier in the year — I thought I'd played for Australia once and I was contented to say that was enough. When I got picked to go to Britain I made up my mind I was going to pull out with an injury, but dad eventually talked me into going. I wasn't keen to go for such a long time because my business was just starting to go well and I'm not any great traveller. I don't drink and never fancied being away from the home and the family for that period of time. I won't say I didn't enjoy it when I got there; the experience of playing and travelling around was great. But I'm still no great tourist. It was alright for the guys who liked to party, but I was never one of those and we also trained two and three times a day, which I didn't really fancy."

Another highlight of Piggins' career was an amazing try he scored against Western Suburbs at a packed Lidcombe Oval in 1976. Wests won the match, 17-13, but few in the crowd of over 17,000 could forget Piggins' memorable charge through the teeth of the Magpie defence to score. He began 15 metres from the Wests line and swatted off half-a-dozen defenders as he bulldozed his way to the line. The try was a classic of its genre, similar in power and determination to Canberra forward Steve Jackson's epic four-pointer that sealed the Raiders' maiden grand final win over Balmain in 1989. The try so impressed TV commentator Rex Mossop he incorporated it in his opening sequence on Channel Seven's Big League show for years afterwards.

"I didn't score many tries and it was probably my best," Piggins comments. "I just put my head down and charged ... somehow I got there. I haven't even got it on video but got a kick out of it recently when a mate showed me his tape of it. I hadn't seen it for years."

A football purist, Piggins sees many problems in the modern game.

"They've taken all the fun out of it. It used to be a tremendous game to play and you'd have fun ... even the rough part of it was fun. No-one held any grudges against you.

"Now, coaches play with the video all day and the media covers every aspect of the game, which leads to more pressure. The poor bastards who run onto the field every week now can't make a mistake without it being plastered all over the TV or the newspaper. Twenty years ago, you had the personality players who carried the game. All of them couldn't do 40 tackles and take the ball up 44 times, but they could play football. The personalities are gone. Nowadays, personality players, even brilliant players ... if they don't do their share of the tackling, the coaches don't carry them.

"Take Arthur Beetson — they say he was lazy. Gee whiz, if you look at his contribution to the game of football it had nothing to do with laziness. Today, he could find it tough to get a game. Players such as myself, who probably gave away a few penalties in scrum situations, we might not get carried today. I lost a few games by giving away penalties or getting marched and you'd just get a pat on the back and someone would say: 'Bad luck, mate.' Nowadays players are made to suffer for a week for making a mistake ... that's why I wouldn't probably even get a start.

"I've even got my doubts I'd want to play today. You've got to like what you're doing. It's all too professional for my liking. The way coaches are handling it, they don't leave any room for mistakes. I think that would've bugged me to a degree.

"Maybe, when I was older, I might've been able to handle that situation, but, when I was younger, I wouldn't have had the discipline to play the modern-day game. I would have walked away and done something else.

"Coaches also demand professionalism from their players but forget it's still a semi-professional game. You're only in there for a short time and few players make enough money to retire from football. You've got to be able to keep some sort of employment going for your future. Coaches want you to devote your life to the game and train five days a week. But if you're trying to establish a career or run your own business, there's not enough hours in a day. You'd go mad. That pressure alone would be enough for me to say work's more important to me. And even today, I think the player's future and his job after football should be the most important thing in his life.

"I remember when I bought my first truck. It was damn hard work, long hours, and fitting the football in was hard. I was playing second grade at the time and luckily our coach, Fred Nelson, understood. I was a bit late to training at times and there was never any drama. Even in first grade, (coach) Clive Churchill was good and gave me some lee-way. You couldn't not show up, but so long as I got there and put in an effort they were happy. There were plenty of times I parked the loaded truck outside Redfern Oval, trained, and then hopped back in the driver's seat and kept working. It was never easy, but I wanted to better myself and it was the only way I knew how at the time."

Piggins bettered himself, and how. Originally a driver for Meadow Lea, he went from driving one truck to owning 10. And he developed a loading system on his trucks which turned the trucking business on its ear. Eventually, the massive TNT corporation bought the business, setting Piggins up for life.

"It gave me the kick along I needed and life's been comfortable ever since," he says. "Nowadays I'm semi-retired. I've got a nursery that does well and I go in there a couple of days a week just to make sure it's all running smoothly. I like horses and took out a training licence a few years back so I could run around with them. Being in this position gave me time to coach Souths and now I'm president (of the football club) I'm able to put the time into the joint."

Piggins categorised the tough players of his era into several areas.

"To me, there are different forms of toughness," he explains. "I remember blokes who were callous — they'd kick you in the head or king hit you as quick as they'd say hello.

"But then there were those who would belt you and a minute later they'd be carting the ball up giving you the opportunity to put it back on them — to my mind they were the real hard men. When they hit you, they hit you. There were plenty of those around in the '70s. There are the ones everyone knows about, the Sattlers and O'Neills. But there were plenty of others you didn't read about in the papers.

"Rod Gorman, who played only a handful of games for Souths in first grade, was as tough as anyone. Charlie Frith, who played with us at Souths was a huge hitter, but played at a time when he didn't have many good players around him. He hit Bill Cloughessy of Wests one night at Redfern ... belted him so hard his teeth just came out of their sockets. They didn't break — they just came clean out and it was a hard a hit as I've seen in my life. He was tough without ever throwing a punch. Geoff Connell, who played for Balmain and Canterbury, squeezed my head so hard I thought it was going to pop off. He was around for years and as hard as nails. Jim Cody was another. Never hit the Sunday papers, but boy was he a handful. I remember Norths hooker Ross Warner in one match in 1967. He nearly kicked my shins off. I didn't know what to do so

GEORGE PIGGINS

I kicked him back. In the end, we both got sent off.

"One man who really scared me was big Saints forward Robin Gourley. He was a mean, giant Irishman; someone took him on in a scrum once and he yelled out: 'I'll kill you!' I tell you, the whole scrum shook. I thought he'd murder us one by one. He was such a fearsome man and at the time we were just a bunch of kids.

"Back then it was all just part of the game. You'd hit and be hit. There aren't too many cowards playing first grade football. Most players, even nowadays, can handle themselves in a stink.

"I remember the days when you could argue with a coach or club secretary and it didn't seem to worry anyone like it does today. When there are 50 odd individuals in a club, a few are bound to rub you the wrong way from time to time and it's natural that you're going to say some harsh words occasionally. Today, you'd be up before the board, and fined. I had that many blow ups that if I was playing nowadays, I'd end up owing them money.

"One coach once told me he didn't want me in his side. I said something, and he told me to piss off. I invited him to settle the matter behind the toilet. I was probably sporting him a few too many years and he declined the offer. But we got over it — today we're pretty fair mates."

Piggins finally retired from football after the 1978 season — an easy decision in the end.

"I knew it was time when I couldn't get out of bed until Wednesday," he says. "Jack Gibson coached Souths at the time and he really made us work hard. I remember telling him: 'Gee, Jack, if you want me to train this hard, I'll do it, but I won't be able to play.' I was 34 and my body was just about gone from all the knocks over the years. We finished the season in '78 and Jack asked if I had another year in me. I said to him: 'Jack, I couldn't play for the Lord himself.'

"It was time to give it away. In the end, I probably went on too long and now I'm suffering from playing football; my ankles and knees are killing me all the time. I can barely play golf or tennis or any other sport.

"But I'd be lying if I said I never enjoyed it. It was a lot of fun and I'm in debt to league. It has given me the opportunity to have a fair sort of life."

Despite having only a brief player/coach association with Jack Gibson, Piggins and the man known as league's master-coach have become life-long friends.

"I first met him playing for 'The Rest' versus the '73 Kangaroos early in '74," Piggins says. "When the 'Roos came back, they picked a team to play them which I was in and Jack was coach. I took an immediate liking to him — he was certainly different from most coaches and knew what he was on about. When Jack came to Souths in '78, I was delighted. It was a bit unfortunate we didn't do as well as expected that year as far as winning games, but in my book you measure success by a lot more than where you finish on the premiership table. Jack ran a tight ship, the players learned a lot, and, considering what he had to work with, I thought we did well. Jack may have been one of the best, but any coach is only as good as the material he's got to work with."

Even in retirement, Souths have never been far from Piggins' heart. He coached the Rabbitohs for five years, from 1986 to 1990 — "four good seasons and one bad" — and is now proud president of league's most traditional club.

Being president of one of the game's most famous teams is no easy task. Sydney's urban sprawl, and the expansion of the game, both geographically and financially, have left inner-city clubs in a difficult position in the 1990s. The Souths district is no longer the focal point of Australian rugby league, and consequently the football club's future in the big league is currently under something of a cloud.

But, with the tenacious Piggins at the helm, fans can rest assured the Rabbitohs won't go down without a fight.

HIT MEN

BOB O'REILLY

The Bear

When Bob O'Reilly began his first-grade football career in 1967, some critics predicted he'd burn out before he had the chance to reach the top of the rugby league mountain. But O'Reilly confounded the smarties by becoming one of the longest-serving front-rowers Australian league has known. His career may have had its low points, but O'Reilly fought back from adversity time and again, and finally went out a winner, as a key part of the mighty Parramatta machine that won that club its first top-grade premierships, in the early 1980s.

In all, O'Reilly played a mammoth 313 grade games over 15 seasons, including a then record 284 in first grade. That mark was subsequently overhauled by one-time Parramatta team-mate Geoff Gerard, who also finished in the front row, but played in a variety of positions including centre and second row during his career. O'Reilly, however, played all his games in the cauldron that is rugby league's engine room — taking the bumps and bruises up front week after week. And, while the critics dined out on O'Reilly over his fitness and physique for long periods of his career, it was the "Bear", as he was universally known, who had the last word.

His record says it all. No player could have come close to O'Reilly's achievements in the game without the required fitness and dedication. "I'd be lying if I said the jibes didn't get to me from time to time." O'Reilly says today. "I always thought people had the impression I was fat and lazy. Granted, I had a couple of slack years, but as far as I'm concerned, that wasn't the way it was. For me, to last that long, I had to be doing something right and, apart from the couple of years I spent at Penrith in the mid '70s, I thought I looked after myself well. I did the hard work and did extra training when required.

"At Penrith, I was saying to myself the same sort of things the critics were saying in the papers — I *was* overweight and not training to my best. And I paid the penalty. My game suffered, I wasn't happy, and I played some reserve grade. But I got myself out of the rut and apart from those two lost years, I was very happy with what I achieved in my career.

"I started in the mid '60s when training was just a pastime, and finished in the early '80s playing against blokes like Wayne Pearce who drank carrot juice all day. I had to change my game to adapt with the times and I did plenty of hard work. Early on I had some pace and could hit the line hard but later on, with good players around me, I was able to concentrate more on ball distribution. In the last couple of years at Parramatta, Jack Gibson wanted me to direct traffic and that was fine by me."

Although he played all his football as a proud New South Welshman, it's a little-known fact that Bob O'Reilly was, in fact, a Queenslander. The Bear was born in Rocklea in 1949 — just two years after the Parramatta club was admitted into the NSW Rugby League premiership after years of trying.

Young Robert spent his first five years in the northern state, before his father's job saw the family move south of the border. The O'Reillys shifted temporarily to the Sutherland shire, before settling more permanently in Mount Pritchard in Sydney's western suburbs. It was at age 11 that Bob first played for the local B-grade side ... as a winger!

"People may find it hard to believe but I played a fair bit on the wing in those days," he says. "I had a bit of pace back then and also played a bit at lock. At 15 I went over to Guildford and that's when I switched to the front row. I'd put on a bit of beef and they decided to move me up front. I played there in the Flegg and President's Cup for Parramatta and was there to stay.

"I was graded in 1966. Third grade was pretty hard then — there were some older players running around and they seemed to enjoy breaking in the new boy. In my debut against Manly I got a lesson from a crafty old bloke opposite me in the front row. I'd never worried too much about scrummaging until that day, but he quickly showed me the error of my ways. In the first scrum I wasn't quick enough putting my head down and he smashed the top of his head into my face as we packed. The impact splattered my nose all over my face ... it was my first broken nose and I wasn't a pretty sight. After that I led with my head instead of my face; it was a quick learning process.

"I finished that season in reserve grade and when Brian Hambly took over from Ken Thornett as coach for 1967, he picked me in first grade for the trials. My debut was against Penrith, in their first game when they entered the comp in 1967, and we did okay. I thought to myself: 'This first

BOB O'REILLY

grade business can't be too hard.' But it took only a week to change my mind. In my second game we met up with St George and that was a real shock to the system. I'll never forget the sick feeling I had in my stomach as they all ran out onto the field. Raper ... Gasnier ... Smith ... Langlands ... it was like a nightmare.

"We didn't have a bad pack in those days with guys like Hambly, Dick Thornett, Ron Lynch and Billy Rayner, but were no match for them. It was a great experience, though; seeing a master like Billy Smith putting his team-mates through holes and Raper weaving his magic.

"Parramatta were a fairly successful side in the mid-1960s, even though we never made the grand final. There were guys like Barry Rushworth and Ivor Lingard out wide and that strong pack of forwards. Things went downhill in the early '70s, but luckily when I came in there was plenty of talent and experience in the side. I was a big Dick Thornett fan and he looked after me in my first few games. He was a class forward; big and strong and able to slip a nice pass. I liked the way he played the game, even though he might have been a bit lazy in defence. It gave me a lot of confidence playing alongside him and Ronny Lynch."

O'Reilly has bitter-sweet memories of his first send-off in grade football, against Cronulla in an early premiership game in 1967.

"Cronulla had just come into the competition and we went down there to play them," he recalls. "As a new side, they were intent on taking us on to show they weren't easybeats and it wasn't long before the rough stuff started. There was an all-in brawl, I belted a bloke, and next thing I knew I was off. But the part that really hurt was that the referee was Phil McCarroll — a mate of mine. He'd been my coach in third grade the previous year! He was a good coach, too and a tremendous influence on my career, but had decided to turn his talents to refereeing. And here he was giving me my marching orders ... I couldn't believe it. As he pointed to the dressing room I pleaded: 'Phil, I'm your boy ... your old mate .. how could you do this to me?'

"He just shrugged his shoulders, kept pointing and said: 'Robert, there's nothing I can do for you, son.'

"Phil was the first bloke to ever send me off. It was quite a blow coming from him, even though we laugh about it now." O'Reilly won his representative spurs for City Seconds in 1970 and progressed from there to the NSW side. Then, after an impressive performance against Queensland, O'Reilly gained selection in the Australian team for the World Cup at the end of the year, earning him the honour of being the first Parramatta junior to wear the green and gold.

"Plenty of other blokes came close, but I was fortunate enough to be the first," he says. "The seeds were planted earlier that year when the Englishmen beat us in the Test series in Australia. The selectors obviously decided it was time for new blood and guys like Paul Sait, Ron Turner, Ray Branighan and myself all got picked in the World Cup squad. Even Arthur Beetson got chopped from the Test team that year.

"The World Cup was played in England and, after the preliminary rounds, Britain had finished undefeated on top of the table. We scraped into the final on for-and-against, but knew we were up against it.

"I still can't believe the final at Leeds and the way the Pommy referee lost control. The game was simply brutal — there was no other word for it. People nowadays wouldn't believe what went on. There were blokes getting kicked in the head, butted, gouged ... you name it, there's a fair chance they did it.

"We had had trouble winning the ball off the Poms when we met them in the lead-up game, so (coach) Harry Bath brought in a mate of his who was a hooker from the old days. He said we'd have to make sacrifices to put them off their game and allow us to get the ball. He said someone would have to niggle them, and I immediately volunteered Lurch (John O'Neill).

"'He's the best man for that job,' I said.

"Lurch's task was to upset big Dennis Hartley, their front-rower, and he ripped into Hartley's gut every time in the scrums. It wasn't long before Hartley started to retaliate. The punches were flying but we were told to leave Lurch alone because we couldn't afford to have other blokes away from the game in the blue. I remember feeling terrible at the time; there were two and three Poms ripping into big Lurch but we were under strict orders not to get involved. I had to follow the play downfield and leave him to fend for himself.

"In another incident I saw Bob Fulton get kicked in the head; other blokes were getting stiff-armed and king hit, but we kept our cool and won the game, 12-7. By today's standards, I don't think there would have been too many players left on the field."

O'Reilly visited Britain again for the World Cup in 1972 but played his best football on his third — and final — tour, with the 1973 Kangaroos.

"I enjoyed the Roo tour a lot because I regarded the World Cup campaigns as 'hit-and-miss' affairs," he says. "You'd go over there, play a few quick games, and then come home. But on the Kangaroo tour you had a long time to settle down, get up some form in the lead-up games, and then put your all into the Tests. I played all three Tests in England, even though I had a badly busted mouth in the second. The front-row spots were always going to be a battle between Lurch, Arthur Beetson and myself. But when Lurch copped a head butt in one of the lead-up games, it opened the way for Arthur and I to grab the two spots."

In one legendary incident during the '73 tour, the Aussies were involved in a dogfight with the strong Widnes club. Midway through the first half, Widnes prop John Warlow carried the ball forward, only to be hit in a devastating tackle from O'Reilly. The Aussie prop barrelled his opposite number ball-and-all in what journalists later described as the hit of the tour. But Warlow, one of the hardest men in Britain at the time, bounced straight back to his feet, glared at O'Reilly and snarled: "Now it's your turn, lad. Come on — you run at me." O'Reilly accommodated the British prop minutes later, and copped a bruising square-up. But, overall, the The Bear finished a clear points winner nonetheless.

Like many of his team-mates, O'Reilly revelled in the off-field activities on tour as well as the football.

"We used to train at Huddersfield, where they had a running track around the back," O'Reilly remembers. "We all had old bomb cars we bought over there and found this track to be the perfect place to hold some drag races. One day the team manager, Charlie Gibson, was on the football ground when he heard all this screeching of tyres and grinding of gears from the track. He ran up the hill to see what was going on and nearly had a heart attack ... half his Test team were flying around in these rickety old cars, at 90 kilometres-an-hour, trying to run each other off the track. If we'd had a big stack we would barely have been able to field a team there were that many blokes involved. On the final week of the tour, we lined the cars up in front of a big brick wall and all headed straight for it at great speed. One by one the boys accelerated towards the wall and then jumped out at the last second, wrecking every car. It was our way of finishing a great tour with a bang."

O'Reilly returned from the Roo tour a hero. He played the next two seasons with Parramatta before making the biggest mistake of his life.

"I was up for contract at the end of 1975, and it was then that things went horribly wrong," he explains. "It was the real start of Parramatta's golden era; they made the grand final the next year and there was I, watching from the sidelines. In retrospect, I joined Penrith for all the wrong reasons. I'd been well looked after at Parra, but I'd been there for years and felt like a change. Penrith offered me double what I was on, and a five-year contract helped me get a house. The money swayed me — it was too hard for me to knock it back. But if I'd looked at it objectively I would have realised that Penrith were struggling, while we were on the way up. But, as I said, the money was too good and I switched.

"My form dropped once I got there and it seemed nothing was going right. There was no hunger — I lost the desire and put on weight. The atmosphere within the Penrith club didn't help. They weren't as professional as Parra; they seemed to constantly have a power struggle within the joint. And every two years or so they'd be shuffling coaches. I had some injuries which didn't help either but, by the end of the second season, I could see the writing on the wall. I had three years left on my contract, but knew I wouldn't make it to the end. I approached the board and told them if there was any chance of buying my way out, I'd be prepared to do it. Penrith were quite happy to end the association too; I paid them $6000 and was a free man again.

"I got a couple of phone calls while I was on the open market — one from (Eels coach) Terry Fearnley inviting me back to Parramatta and another from my old mate Arthur Beetson at Easts. The Parra offer was tempting but I thought another change would do me good and joined Arthur at Easts. The change was just what I needed; I played some of my best football at Easts in 1978 and '79. It helped get my career right back on track after the lost years at Penrith.

"I started to work really hard on fitness and on the weights, and it paid dividends. Easts were a progressive outfit and had some real professionals like Mark Harris, Ron Coote, Bob Fulton and Bill Mullins. We went well both seasons I was there but, at the end of the two years, I knew I didn't have long to go. So this time I rang Parra. I told them that if there was an opening, I'd like to come back and finish my career there.

"They had a lot of forwards there in 1980, but I played a bit of first grade before doing the medial ligament in my knee. The club won the Tooth Cup that year, but for me — I thought it was the end of the road. It appeared my coming back hadn't worked out. I was in my early 30s, with my leg in plaster, and I didn't think I had any future in the game.

"So I called it quits."

But no sooner had O'Reilly begun to enjoy the summer of 1980 than he received a phone call that would enable him to put the appropriate epitaph to his marathon career.

"Jack Gibson rang and said they'd lost a few front-rowers," O'Reilly recalls. "He said there was an opening there, and, if I was prepared to do the hard work, they'd be a place for me. I thought about it for a while and decided to have one last shot.

"The training was hard, but I knew we'd have a good chance at the title. Parramatta was really starting to come of age, with guys like Peter Sterling, Steve Ella, Eric Grothe and Brett Kenny coming through the grades. We had a reasonable pack of forwards and a backline that could do anything. I felt this could be my year."

Not long into 1981, O'Reilly chalked up his 200th first-grade game for

BOB O'REILLY

the club, which led to a bizarre presentation he will never forget.

"We were training at Granville one Saturday morning and, before the session, big Jack called all the players over and Mick Cronin made a speech. Mick explained that the boys had had a whip around and bought me this very expensive watch in appreciation of what I'd done for the club. He said it was one of the best watches money could buy, chosen by (coaching co-ordinator) Ron Massey, and gave it to me on behalf of everyone at Parramatta. I became overcome with emotion and responded with a speech saying how this would have to be one of the most touching moments of my career.

"Then we started training and, even as we were running around the paddock, I was still thanking each and every one of the boys. After training we had a barbeque and I was still shaking people's hands. But I started to notice Massey, who was a notorious practical joker, chuckling through his sausages and joking with a few of the boys whenever they looked in my direction. I walked up to Mass and said: 'What's going on here ... is there something wrong with this watch?'

"Well, Massey just exploded. 'You're an ungrateful bastard,' he yelled. 'These blokes have done this for you and you come around questioning them. You should be ashamed!'

"I sheepishly apologised and walked away feeling as low as a snake. But the laughter continued and I finally worked up the courage to go back to Mass. 'Look,' I said, 'there is something wrong with this watch, isn't there?'

"This time he gave me both barrels. 'You disgust me ... this is the second time you've come over and done this.'

"He then grabbed the watch off me, threw it on the ground and jumped on it. I picked it back up and the springs were all over the place, the face was smashed; it was a wreck. I cursed myself for my suspicious nature and opening my big mouth ... it was only later that they let on that they'd put a $2 watch in the case of a $200 one; they dined out on me for some time on that one."

With the experience of O'Reilly up front and the dynamic attacking skills of Sterling, Kenny and company out wide, the Eels swept all before them in the winter of 1981. Narrow semi-final victories over Newtown and Easts gained the club its third grand final berth (following losses to Manly in 1976 and Saints in 1977). In '81, the Eels faced stiff opposition in the improved Newtown side, but, after a stoic battle, the Eels won through, with the experience of O'Reilly up front a critical factor.

In an emotional moment after the match, O'Reilly and Jets skipper Tom Raudonikis, two of league's great warriors over the previous decade, embraced. Both knew it was there last chance at grand final glory; and fate had decreed it was The Bear who would have his moment in the sun.

"Without doubt that was the high point of my career," he says. "Parramatta had waited so long for this moment and I was honoured to be part of it. Playing for Australia was great, but it was something you do for a game here and there or a tour. But you work with your club for 10 or 11 months a year; you become like a family and there was nothing better than sharing victory with them. We celebrated long into the night and I'll never forget the reception we all got back at Parramatta Leagues Club."

The grand final champagne was especially sweet for O'Reilly, then approaching his 33rd birthday, as he had copped a bucketful of criticism throughout the '81 season. Many experts were convinced the Eels couldn't take the premiership with veterans O'Reilly and Kevin 'Stumpy' Stevens in their pack. Radio commentator Peter Peters was so certain the Eels wouldn't win the title he claimed he would walk from Wollongong to Palm Beach in thongs if the Eels were successful with the veteran duo in their side ... a bet he was forced to honour over the off-season.

"It was very satisfying to put some egg on the critics' faces as we'd copped plenty during the year," O'Reilly said.

O'Reilly batted on in 1982 and maintained his form, playing 17 top-grade games before damaging his knee late in the year.

"I was keen on back-to-back titles but did my knee again just a few weeks before the finals," he says. "This time I knew there was no coming back. I'd already made my mind up to retire that season no matter what, so it was finally the end of the road. Overall, I'd had a good run with injury over the years, and there were no tears; I knew it had to end sometime."

O'Reilly maintained his close friendship with Mick Cronin after retiring, and, when the Crow was appointed the Eels' coach in 1990, O'Reilly was the man he sought out as his deputy.

"I had four enjoyable years as reserves coach, even though they weren't all that successful," he says. "We came close to making the finals a couple of years but both the first grade and the reserves struggled in our time. I really felt for Mick; he was a good coach but didn't have the material to work with. The club didn't buy the players to support him and it was always going to be a struggle."

O'Reilly's sole association with football nowadays is with his 17-year-old son, Matthew, who was named in the Australian Schoolboys merit team in 1993.

"He's a member of Parramatta's Flegg side and has a bit of talent," O'Reilly says. "He's a second-rower and I won't push him.

"But if he wants some advice from a bloke who's played a few games up front, he won't have far to go."

HIT MEN

TERRY RANDALL

Aiming for the Rib-Cage

MANLY ironman Terry Randall is considered by some to be the hardest tackler rugby league has known. Built like a Greek god, and strong and tough to boot, Randall had all the credentials to become a rugby league great. And over 13 seasons with his beloved Manly club, NSW and Australia, Randall rattled the bones of opponents from Penrith to the northern beaches and beyond, unleashing his own special brand of terror with legal, but lethal tackles.

Randall's target was the rib-cage area — and he rarely missed his mark. Australian Rugby League boss Ken Arthurson, a father figure throughout Randall's years at Manly, credits the granite-like forward with the three hardest hits he has ever seen in rugby league.

"He is the finest defensive player the game has known and also ranks with the all-time greats of the Manly club," Arthurson says. "I'll never forget those three tackles. One was during a 1975 World Series match in Wales. He hit big Jim Mills so hard I thought he would break him in two. Mills is a giant of a man but Terry hammered him; the timing of that tackle was perfect. The other two tackles were in Sydney — one on Bob O'Reilly in a club match and the one I rate the best, which was on John Donnelly at the Sydney Cricket Ground."

Many critics who remember the tackle on Donnelly rate it as arguably the turning point in Manly's bold and successful premiership challenge in 1978. Playing in their fourth sudden-death game in 12 days, Manly looked down and out against the raw-boned Wests pack just before halftime. But then Randall let rip with *that* tackle, as Donnelly charged upfield with the ball under his arm. The impact drove the massive frame of Donnelly crashing back several metres, and the ball popped loose. Manly gained new inspiration from Randall's effort and rallied to win the game 14-7.

HIT MEN

"I remember the tackle well," Randall says today with a sly grin. "I came in from the blindside when Dallas (Donnelly) took the ball up. He had just caught the ball and his ribs were open — that's the best time to hit them, you know. I hit him pretty hard; from memory he was jolted back a couple of metres. It seemed to set the example. It gave our blokes the gee-up they needed."

Ironically for such a hard-hitting forward, Randall played virtually all his junior football out in the backs. He began playing at age 10, and scored plenty of tries out wide in the Manly juniors, starring in the Sea Eagles' Flegg and President's Cup sides. Once in his Flegg days he played in the second row for 40 minutes, tackling everything that moved. After he came from the field, Randall's coach patted him on the back and whispered in his ear: "That's where you're going to end up playing, son."

The words were soon to prove prophetic, even though Randall was graded as an 18-year-old three-quarter in 1969, playing for Manly during the latter stages of the season.

"It was all very new to me and a big step," he recalls. "My first game was in third grade against Souths at the Cricket Ground and I was as nervous as hell. It took me a long time to settle down."

Randall was given his first-grade spurs in 1970. During the following year, his coach, Ron Willey, told Randall the inevitable.

"He said: 'You're in the pack from now on.' It didn't really surprise me," Randall says. "I used to relish the tackling and often followed the ball across field. I'd be standing in the middle of the field with the forwards even though I was supposed to be playing out wide, so moving to the second row didn't take a lot of getting used to."

Randall had the perfect "minder" in his early days in the forwards in second-rower Allan Thomson, who had played three Tests for Australia and toured Britain with the 1967-68 Kangaroos.

"Allan was great and really looked after me," Randall says. "He was a real tough man and had been around for years — I looked up to him. He was a good talker on the field and would always be geeing me up. I'd make four tackles in a row and I'd hear him growl: 'C'mon Randall, do some work!'

In 1972, Randall and Thomson formed a not-to-be-messed with second-row pairing, with English enforcer Malcolm Reilly completing an awesome back-row at lock. The Sea Eagles were the team to beat throughout that season and celebrated for days after a 19-14 grand final win over Easts.

A year later, Manly made it back-to-back titles, with a bruising 10-7 defeat of Cronulla in the grand final. During that game, Sharks' captain-coach Tommy Bishop made it his business to "bait" several Manly forwards,

TERRY RANDALL

with Randall a chief target. After one stoush between the pair, referee Keith Page called out both Randall and Bishop for a caution. As they approached the referee, Bishop jostled Randall, prompting an immediate reaction from the Manly forward. Randall set off in pursuit of Bishop, who scooted off behind his forwards with the fear of God in his eyes.

"He was a trouble-maker, that bloke," Randall says. "It's probably just as well I didn't catch him."

Randall was rewarded for his consistent form throughout 1972 and '73 on the night of Manly's second premiership victory. Amid wild scenes back at Manly Leagues club, Randall's name was read out as a member of the 13th Kangaroos. But while the Roos went on a glory road through England and France — 17 wins from 19 games — the number 13 was to prove a jinx for Randall . The Manly ironman, who barely missed a game at club level, played just five matches on tour.

"It was such a thrill to be selected and go on tour, but once we got there it was one disaster after the next," he recalls. "In the very first game of the tour against Salford, I was tackled, but then a Pommie grabbed my ankle and did a cartwheel while he had hold of it. I could hear the crack as the ligaments went. That cost me six weeks. Then I came back and was in contention for the third Great Britain Test. But in the match before the team was selected, against Leigh, I went in to tackle a bloke and cracked my hand on his hard head. That was another four weeks and the tour was over for me."

But Randall did pick up one lasting memento of his lone Roo tour — his nickname.

"Tim Pickup was one of the real characters of the tour and had labels for everyone," Randall explains. "One day he just said to me 'You look like an Igor' and the name has stuck with me ever since."

Randall gave British fans a more lasting impression of his talents during the 1975 World Series. He played in seven of the eight Australian matches during the series, as Australia beat powerful international opposition to take the trophy. It was in the rugged encounter with Wales at Swansea, rated by Randall as perhaps the best game of his career, that he pulled off the crunching tackle on Jim Mills recalled so vividly by Ken Arthurson.

"I didn't actually start that game but got called into the action when our lock, John Quayle, was replaced after 10 minutes with a bad shoulder injury," Randall remembers. "I went into lock and straight into the frying pan against a very hot Welsh side. They had some good players in those days and Mills was the leader of a strong pack. I'd played against him when he was with Norths in Sydney and knew what to expect — he was a

HIT MEN

powerful man. But we managed to get on top of them and win in difficult conditions."

Two years later, Randall played in all four games as Australia retained its crown. With 11 World Series and World Cup games to his credit, Randall is third on the all-time list, behind only Manly club-mate Bob Fulton (15) and Arthur Beetson (14). Yet Randall never played Test football, a remarkable occurrence considering his lengthy and impressive service for his country.

"To be honest, I reckon I have played in a Test," he says "I've got a photo of me in a green-and-gold team in 1977 against New Zealand. I always considered it a Test, but apparently it was another World Series game. To me, it's six of one, half a dozen of the other. The record books may not show it, but I know I've played for Australia and that will do me."

Randall completed a quadrella of premierships with Manly in 1976 and 1978 and was a certainty to tour with the '78 Roos. But shortly before the touring team was named, Randall declared himself unavailable, saying he wanted to spend more time with his young family. Only now, years later, does he reveal the real reason behind his decision.

"Right at the start of that year I was knocked out cold in a trial match at Wyong," Randall explains. "It was a bad one. I was out for a couple of minutes and while I didn't make a fuss over it, I felt the effects all season. Every time I pulled off a big hit, I came up seeing stars. I was really worried but a brain scan showed nothing out of the ordinary, so I kept playing. But I was really shaky and nowhere near my best, especially late in the season when we had to win game after game to take the title.

"Once, against Wests, I realised just how bad a state I was in. I remember they kicked off after a try, the ball went up, and I called: 'Mine.' Our centre, Russel Gartner, who was standing near me, couldn't believe it. The ball sailed 10 metres over my head but because I was in a daze, I thought it was coming to me. I didn't tell him what was wrong and he shook his head and said: 'You're kidding, Igor.'

"I just didn't think I was up to a long Kangaroo tour, so I pulled out. I didn't even tell my wife the real reason; I didn't want to worry my family. It was a decision I regretted in later years, though — it would have been great to tour with such a great side."

Randall had the added problem of battling through Manly's courageous '78 premiership bid with a severe groin injury.

"I was getting painkilling needle after needle ... we all were," he says. "We knew we had to keep playing or we were gone. We played a few midweek games which made it even harder as we didn't have the normal time to get over our injuries. But we won the title and it was just super to

TERRY RANDALL

get there after such a hard road. The spirit in the club that year under Frank Stanton was fantastic. It was a very special team, full of goers. We were all mates and all drank together. It must have been the same in those great Souths sides a decade earlier. Harmony was the key."

Stanton later paid tribute to Randall's contribution to the Sea Eagles' triumph. "The whole series was a credit to the courage and determination of men like Terry Randall," Stanton stated. "I never saw Terry take a backward step in his career and his defence and no-holds-barred attitude instilled confidence in all around him."

Although one of Manly's most loyal sons, Randall admits he came within a whisker of quitting the Sea Eagles at the end of the 1979 season. Media entrepreneur John Singleton had just stunned the league world by luring Western Suburbs' favourite son, Tommy Raudonikis, away from the Magpies to join "battlers" Newtown. And Singleton still had other big fish to fry.

"One day Singo rang me out of the blue and said he wanted to pick me up in a helicopter in 20 minutes and fly me to Newtown Leagues Club, where he had a $50,000 contract waiting," Randall recalls. "I was stunned. I'd never met the bloke and here he was, offering me a deal of a lifetime. It was like winning the lottery, as I wasn't on great money with Manly at the time. I was tempted, all right. But I rang Arko (Ken Arthurson) straight away. He'd always looked after me and I felt I could confide in him. He was alarmed and just said: 'Don't sign, Igor, we'll work something out'.

"So I told Singo I was staying and Arko was good to his word, giving me an updated contract. That happened to a few other Manly blokes that year — we've got John Singleton to thank for us earning a lot more money from our own club."

A fitness fanatic, Randall still looks fit enough to be playing despite being in his early 40s. A landscape gardener, he has thrived on hard work throughout his life — on and off the field.

"I loved training and used to model myself on Allan Thomson and Bozo (Bob Fulton)," Randall says. "They were two of the most professional players I ever knew and really put a lot of thought into their training. I enjoyed training with the team, but also used to do a lot of private weights and endurance sessions to keep in top shape."

A resident of the Manly area all his life, Randall retains close links with his former team-mates. And while he was a quiet, unassuming man on the field, several ex-Sea Eagles revealed another side to the Manly workhorse.

"The thing I'll never forget about Igor is the performance he put on at a team barbeque we had in the late '70s," Paul "Fatty" Vautin remembers. "It was a real dull night and no-one was really enjoying themselves so when a big Gecko lizard ran across the patio, Igor decided to liven things up. 'Have a look at this, everyone,' he yelled.

"Igor picked up the lizard, held it up to his face ... and bit its head off. That really got things going. A couple of the girls screamed, they all left, and we blokes ended up having a good time. The following year we went on a pig-shooting holiday to Darwin with Bob Fulton and Max Krilich and I remember being in my room late one night when the three of them came barging in. Igor had this big grin on his face and I knew he was up to no good. As he entered the room, I saw he had something behind his back. It was a pig's head, freshly chopped off, and he just tossed it onto my bed. There was blood and bits of pig everywhere ... it was horrible.

"Igor was like that; he was a big kid at heart and loved to fool around. But on the field, he only knew one way — straight and hard. As a matter of fact, when I was breaking into the game, Terry Randall was my idol. I came into the Manly side as he was heading towards the end of his career and it was an honour to pack into the scrum with him. Every time we packed down, I felt like I was gaining strength from just putting my arm around him. He was the one for me.

"The secret of great tackling is timing, more than strength, and that was Igor's secret. His timing was just superb and he also had the strength to back it up."

Like Ken Arthurson, former Sea Eagles halfback John Gibbs has several Randall tackles burned forever into his memory. The one he rates as his favourite was also in Arthurson's top three — the hit on O'Reilly.

"It would have to be the most devastating tackle I've ever seen," Gibbs claims. "We were playing Easts at the old Sydney Sports Ground and The Bear was giving us plenty of trouble that day. Igor took it upon himself to fix that and just launched himself at O'Reilly's huge frame. The impact was massive and it looked like he'd driven the big bloke six rows back into the grandstand. He hammered him just under the rib-cage — his favourite spot — and I reckon every other player on both sides winced. To his credit, O'Reilly got back up again, but he was much quieter after that.

"Terry captained Manly a fair bit when I was in the side. He was by no means a captain who did a lot of talking, but you couldn't have had a finer skipper; he led by example and inspired his team-mates with his play. I also played a lot of touch football with Terry soon after we both retired and he took his same aggressive style into that game. More than once, I saw him crash-tackle an unsuspecting opponent. He was of tremendous psychological value in touch — you've never seen players pass the ball as quickly as when they saw Igor bearing down on them. He really put the fear of God into the opposition."

Randall was a central figure in the notorious, vicious Manly-Newtown

TERRY RANDALL

brawl that broke out soon after the start of the 1981 minor semi-final, and sees that match as the beginning of the end of his career.

"That was a spiteful game from the start and I remember the brawl that saw the infamous stoush between Newtown's Steve Bowden and our Mark Broadhurst," Randall recalls. "I kept out of it initially but then I saw what a hammering Broadie had copped from Bowden. I saw his face close up and he looked like the elephant man ... one eye was closed and his cheeks were all puffy. He was just a mess. I saw red and as Bowden went down in the melee, I kicked him. It was a stupid thing to do but it just happened. Bowden and I both got our marching orders and I copped a six-week suspension. Because we eventually lost that match and were therefore eliminated, I had to serve the six weeks the following year. That gave me a long break from the game, and I found I didn't miss it at all.

"Noel Kelly has been a mate of mine for some time and I remember asking him at the pub that summer when a player should retire. It must have been on my mind and I never forgot his answer. He told me: 'You'll know when to quit when you get dirty with the world. You'll be short-tempered with your friends, your family, your team-mates and your opponents. You'll start belting players for no reason and won't be enjoying the game any more. That's when you'll know.'

"It didn't take me long to find out what Ned meant. In one of my first games back we were playing Cronulla down at their home ground and I remember being really cranky that day. I was angry with my wife and just wasn't in the mood to play. We got on the field and I remember this young Cronulla kid making a bust down the blindside. I saw him and made up my mind to get him. I just about took his head off. I took out all my frustrations on him and ended up feeling really sorry for him later; I knew it was the wrong thing to do but at the time I just snapped. He got carried off on a stretcher and I was sent off. The judiciary gave me 10 weeks that time.

"I managed to get back into first grade for the grand final, playing in the front row. But when Parramatta beat us in the grand final I just hung up my boots on a peg at the old SCG dressing room ... I'd had enough."

While Randall was finished with rugby league, the game wasn't finished with him. Nearly two seasons later, Bob Fulton knocked on Randall's door. Manly was in trouble and needed Igor to make a comeback.

"I thought I'd give it a go as I respected Bozo's opinion. If he felt I still had something to offer, that was good enough for me. I really got stuck into the training again and pounded the tackle bags and the weights for a couple of days. But I remember waking up on the second day and I could barely move. My body was giving me a clear message — it wasn't up to it anymore. I knew if I went through with the comeback, I'd only make a fool of myself. I'd had a fair innings and didn't really have that strong desire to come back. So I rang Bozo and told him I couldn't help him."

However, Randall has never been far from the Manly club. He had two years as President's Cup coach and is currently on both the Leagues Club and Football Club boards.

"I guess I'll always be a Manly man. But I never really enjoyed the coaching as much as some other people. It was hard work and very stressful. I had a lot of raw young players and they weren't as professional in their outlook as I would have liked. I found myself in some cases having to be their nursemaid as well as their coach."

Randall remains a favourite of Manly fans even in retirement, as was evidenced during the Ron Gibbs controversy that surfaced during the 1987 season. Gibbs, who with Noel "Crusher" Cleal formed a lethal second-row pairing during that premiership-winning season, had upset the Manly faithful by signing a massive contract with the Gold Coast club mid-season, prompting a hostile reception the following Sunday. On the hill at Brookvale, as Gibbs ran out onto the field with the Sea Eagles first-grade team, a fan brandished a giant banner on which read the demand:

"Give back Randall's jumper".

As well as being a rebuke to Gibbs, the banner was a clear sign that although Randall's playing days were gone, he was never to be forgotten.

HIT MEN

JOHN DONNELLY

King of the Fibros

John "Dallas" Donnelly was the larger-than-life figure at the centre of the Western Suburbs legend that developed in the late '70s and early '80s. The Magpies were the most feared team in league during Donnelly's hey-day and opposing teams all dreaded the trip to their home ground, Lidcombe Oval, to face the fierce Wests pack.

Lidcombe Oval is now a rugby league ghost town, but little more than a decade ago it was the scene of many of the game's fiercest battles. Wests were the bad boys of rugby league and Lidcombe was the scene of face-slapping, sledging, all-in brawling and all-round mayhem. With coach Roy Masters and skipper Tom Raudonikis pulling the strings, Wests were a team not to be meddled with. Up front, they had the heavy artillery to smash any opposition, with Donnelly and heavyweight front-row partner Bruce Gibbs backed up by the likes of Les Boyd, Geoff Foster and Bob Cooper.

The infamous Manly-Wests 'Fibro-Silvertail' legend was born at Lidcombe, with John Donnelly one of its true believers. A simple boy from the bush, big Dallas revelled at the prospect of locking horns with the glamour Manly forwards. These were clashes that frequently saw two and three players given their marching orders.

Dallas Donnelly played for Wests for a decade which included some of the club's most successful seasons. While the Magpies didn't win the premiership during his time, they did win the mid-week Amco Cup, were frequent semi-finalists and usually were the team on everyone's lips. When Dallas drowned while frolicking in the surf early in 1986, a slice of the Western Suburbs spirit died with him.

Donnelly hailed from the northern NSW town of Gunnedah, a sleepy hamlet but a prolific breeding ground for front-rowers, and broke onto the league scene in 1973, when, as a raw young prop, he impressed for Country against City. His no-holds-barred approach in that match won him a NSW jumper — and a contract with Wests two years later.

Tom Raudonikis met Donnelly when he joined the NSW camp as an unknown in 1973 and vividly recalls his first impressions of the young prop from the country.

"He had just been picked to play for the state, but was very much an unknown quantity when we got together to prepare for the game," Raudonikis recalls. "This big guy wandered in with real long hair and a funny grin and we all looked at each other.

"'Who does this bloke think he is?' I remember saying to one of the other boys.

"But it didn't take long for Dallas to win us over. He settled in well and was everyone's mate. It was the same when he joined Wests. Even though he came from the bush and was totally new to Sydney life, his big heart was the thing that won everyone over. He was the classic case of a wild man on the field but a gentle, kind bloke off it.

"In that first series against Queensland in '73 he broke his arm in the opening game up in Brisbane. That was the worst thing for the rest of us. He just terrorised us for the rest of the week and gave us no peace."

Raudonikis says Dallas cherished the good life but denied he was a lazy trainer.

"The big fella loved a beer and his diet probably wouldn't have got Wayne Pearce's seal of approval," Raudonikis explains. "But a lot of people have told me over the years that they thought Dallas was a bludger. That couldn't have been further from the truth. Even though he did it tough sometimes, he always did the work and never whinged. I've known plenty of fitter blokes who couldn't go the distance like Dallas. There were plenty of times he played injured and did the right thing by his team-mates.

One well-known story backs up Raudonikis' view of Donnelly. The king-sized prop had suffered a fractured cheekbone in a match and was ordered to hospital. Never one to listen to sound medical advice, Donnelly was found hours later sitting in a corner of Wests' Leagues Club, sinking a schooner to dull the pain. Coach Roy Masters put him in a cab and sent him straight to St Vincent's Hospital, where he asked the doctor how long he would be in. When the doctor told the injured prop he'd be staying at least a few days, Donnelly replied: "In that case, you'd better have a look at my ribs and my knee. I think I broke a rib last week and this knee has been locking up for a month."

On another occasion Donnelly, who suffered from epilepsy, had a fit just moments before a torturous pre-season training run at Glenbrook, in the

JOHN DONNELLY

Blue Mountains, west of Sydney. All the players dreaded the run and several joked that Dallas would do anything to get out of it. But the following day, unbeknown to his team-mates, the giant prop ran it solo, returning to Masters' Penrith home upon completing the course. In searing heat, Donnelly collapsed in the backyard, turning a hose on himself to cool off.

Raudonikis says Donnelly revelled in the firestorm atmosphere of the Manly-Wests clashes in the late '70s and early '80s.

"They were the real Fibro v Silvertail days. It was the game everyone at Wests waited all season to play," he says. "Dallas, being a Fibro right down to his thongs, loved it more than most and I reckon the Manly blokes hated the sight of him. He'd come out all fired up and was a player not to be trifled with in that condition. The longer the game went, the better Dallas would get. He put the fear of God into them and played some of his best football in those great old days at Lidcombe.

"The Manly blokes were into sledging us in those days and I must admit some of our blokes didn't mind mouthing off either. But that was never Dallas. He'd do plenty of talking on the field, but it was to gee up his team-mates. He never bothered telling the opposition what he thought of them — he let his actions speak for him. League's always been a great game and still is, but there was something magical about those days and sadly we'll never see the like of them again. It's like Dallas. He was such a great character and there'll never be another one like him."

According to Raudonikis, Donnelly never needed the Masters-style face-slapping motivation to psych him up for a big game.

"That was the good thing about Dallas — you never had to worry about motivating him," he explains. "He was one of those rare blokes who never needed it. He always knew the job that had to be done and was always prepared to do it."

Raudonikis was Donnelly's "minder" throughout his career at Wests, ensuring the big man always received his medication when an epileptic fit came.

"The first time he had a turn, even though he'd warned me about them, it frightened the life out of me," he says. "I thought he was going to die right in front of me. But I got him through it and gradually I learned how to handle the situation. I remember once we had a training session with one of the representative teams. It was a tough session under George Daldry at Centennial Park and he had a fit there right in front of all the boys. They were all shocked — they were hard men but they'd never seen anything like that before. I had to tell one of them to whack a stick in Dallas' mouth as I ran to the car to get the medication. Being such a big bastard, he'd do dreadful damage to himself when he had a fit. Just think of it ... 18 stone

(114 kg) crashing to earth without his hands going out to protect him and then thrashing about. Dallas got a lot of his scars and bruises on the football field, but I reckon he got even more from those fits. His head copped a dreadful bashing sometimes. But after it was all over, Dallas would just brush himself off, get up and carry on with whatever he was doing. He never let it worry him and never once complained about having such a serious condition." Raudonikis captained the Combined Sydney side that toured New Zealand in 1975 and found his job as Donnelly's minder stretching him to the limit.

"I won't tell you what he got up to, but he gave me hell," Raudonikis says. "He had a couple of turns over there and I got in trouble later from the management for not telling them about what happened. But I was looking after him and wasn't about to give him up — I thought they may send him home if I did."

The Donnelly legend gained considerable impetus during that tour of New Zealand, with one performance in a plush hotel foyer stunning even the most battle-hardened players. After a night on the town, Dallas waddled up to a picturesque display fish tank, grabbed a couple of live goldfish with a giant hand ... and swallowed them.

Donnelly played for Australia in the World Series in 1975 and wore the green and gold in one Test match, against New Zealand in 1978. The Wests giant tore into the Kiwi forwards as Australia cantered to a 38-7 win in the second Test, at Lang Park, but still lost his place for the final Test to Saints prop Craig Young.

Donnelly may have had a longer representative career had it not been for his desire to live life to the fullest. Dallas was never one for self-discipline and Raudonikis recalls one day when he stretched the big man's tolerance to the limit.

"We used to drink up at the Railway Hotel at Lidcombe," Raudonikis remembers. "They'd close the bar at 10pm but that never worried Dallas. Just before closing time he'd buy four schooners and sit on them for the next half hour. Once, not long before a big Sunday game, the barman said: 'Last drinks, gents.'

"Dallas went up, ordered his usual, and came back with four schooners, two in each of those giant hands of his. But as Wests captain, I thought I'd better do the right thing, even if it meant putting my life in the balance. 'Dallas, remember we've got that big game coming up," I cautioned. "I wouldn't drink them if I was you."

"He just growled and emptied the first glass; I could tell I wasn't making much headway. So I picked up the other three full schooners and walked out of the pub and onto the footpath. Dallas followed me without saying a word and watched as I poured them into the gutter, one by one. He had this look in his eye as though he was about to kill me. There weren't many ways to rile a gentle man like Dallas, but I reckon I'd picked the worst. Here was a man who loved his beer. I knew I was tempting fate; his fist was clenched and I honestly thought he was going to belt me. But all he said was: 'Tommy, you're a bastard'.

"He turned around and went home. I didn't know if we were still mates or not. But on Sunday he turned up, was his old cheerful self, and played a blinder. I don't think Dallas knew how to hold a grudge; he was just too nice a bloke."

Donnelly was a frequent visitor to the NSW Rugby League's headquarters at Phillip Street. In fact, he was one of the first players to be cited and then suspended by video evidence following a premiership match. Donnelly and team-mate Boyd were among a group of players who found themselves summoned to judiciary hearings after a particularly brutal round of matches in 1978. Donnelly received a four-week "holiday" courtesy of the judiciary, one week more than Boyd, after being found guilty as charged after a match against, inevitably, Manly. But the Wests players thought so highly of Donnelly they gave him one thirteenth of their winning bonuses over the month he was sidelined.

A player from the "old" school, Donnelly had trouble adapting to the new order that judiciary chief Jim Comans brought to Sydney rugby league in the early 1980s. Comans had come to the job with a clear brief to clean up the game, and Dallas suffered from several appearances before Comans, the final one of which resulted in a 15-week suspension, for kneeing an opponent.

Popular former Magpies front-rower Bruce "Bruiser" Clark — similar to Donnelly in both build and attitude to life — fondly remembers his old team-mate.

"Dallas was always the life of the party," Clark recalls. "One year we went to Hawaii on an end-of-season tour and Dallas was whistling in this disco or nightclub which we used to hang out in. This massive bouncer came up to us and said Dallas' whistling was annoying the other patrons. He'd have to stop ... or else. Dallas just glared at him and replied: 'Look mate, I was thrown out of here in 1977, barred in 1978, and I've had enough. If you keep this up, I'm going to pick you up and put your head through that ceiling fan up there'.

"The bouncer could see it was no idle threat. 'Keep whistling, Dallas,' he said as he walked away."

Clark remembers how the imposing figure of Donnelly befriended him when he first joined the Magpies in the late '70s.

HIT MEN

"It was a bit intimidating for a young bloke coming into a club containing the likes of Tom Raudonikis, Les Boyd and Donnelly," he says. "But after one of my first training sessions, Dallas came up and introduced himself and said if there was anything he could do, just ask. It was my first introduction to Dallas and it really took me by surprise; he wasn't what I'd expected at all after seeing what he did on the field. As I came to know him I realised he was a Dr Jekyll-Mr Hyde-type character — a real gentleman to his mates but quite a different bloke when he put on the black-and-white jumper every Sunday. Then he just wanted to get out there and rip heads off."

Tales of Donnelly's appetite are as colourful as the man himself. Raudonikis recalls: "Once we were at Wests Leagues club and Roy Masters and I left at about 11pm, just before closing time. There was this little kid out the front of the club selling hot dogs, and it was a bitterly cold night. The wind was howling and the rain was starting, so Roy gave the kid a friendly tip. 'There's only a few blokes left in there son. Not much business for you. If I were you I'd pack up and call it a night'.

"Quick as a flash the kid replied: 'But I know John Donnelly's still in there and when he comes out, he'll buy half a dozen."

Terry Fearnley coached Wests for just one season in 1982 but, in that short time, gained life-long memories of Dallas.

"When I was appointed as Wests coach, I saw Dallas as a key man in our plans even though he was nearing the end of his career," Fearnley remembers. "Apparently there was some doubt about him playing that season so I thought I'd better go and sort it out. I remember driving to this house he was renting with some mates somewhere out west and it was a dump. The front yard was an absolute disgrace with grass knee high and weeds and rubbish everywhere. I had a battle on my hands just getting to the front door. He came to the door with a big grin on his face and I said something like: 'Nice lawn out here, Dallas, but don't you think it could use a mow?'

"'That's nothing ... you should see the back yard; we've got lions and tigers out there.' he replied.

"That was Dallas, always joking and never one for appearances. One night I'll never forget is when we had all the Wests blokes over to my house in Yowie Bay for a barbeque. I had an old pianola and Dallas spent the whole night there, surrounded by his team-mates, playing music and singing with a big smile on his face. He'd be pumping the pedals with those big feet of his and they all rocked the rafters until 2am. It was a funny thing about that Wests side — they were as rough and tough a bunch as you'll ever see but they all loved to sing. We'd be going somewhere on the team bus or would have just won a game and they'd break into song. I wouldn't say the Vienna Boys Choir were in any danger of losing their jobs, but the guys all put their hearts into it."

One of the highlights of Fearnley's short stint with the Magpies in 1982 was a win over premiers Parramatta before a packed house at Lidcombe.

"The scores were tied when Dallas put over a field goal. I thought the crowd were going to go mad," Fearnley says. "It wasn't in the game plan but it was effective and Dallas didn't let us forget it in a hurry. For weeks after that he was telling me how he used to play halfback and was more than just a big, bruising front-rower."

Fearnley says he could never complain about Donnelly's attitude at training. "He may have been a bit slower than the others, but he never shirked the hard work. There were no short cuts with Dallas; if you wanted 100 push-ups he'd give you them and he'd finish all the long road runs, even if he was a long way behind the field. He loved to play the game and his attitude was infectious."

Former Wests chief executive Rick Wayde, the man credited with saving Wests when the NSW Rugby League attempted to make the Magpie an extinct bird in 1983, remembers a story on Donnelly related to him by young hooker Mark Toomey after a reserve-grade match late in the big prop's career.

"We were playing St George at Kogarah and Dallas was up against an old hooker who he'd played against many times before," Wayde tells. "As they ran on the Saints bloke said something cheeky and Dallas replied along the lines of 'Here's us two old battlers up against each other ... it's a pity I'll see the game out and you won't.' Mark tells how the first scrum went down and then he heard a sickening thud. As the packs went their separate ways, the Saints man was lying there unconscious. He was stretchered off and took no further part in the game. Mark didn't know exactly what happened to him, but he had a pretty good idea."

Towards the end of his career, at a time when Wests were struggling for survival, Dallas did his bit to help the fundraising to keep the Magpies flying. At a fete in 1983, Dallas proved a big money-spinner as he manned the chocolate wheel, hounding passers-by for their last dollar. With tickets at 50 cents each, one man asked for two, handing Dallas a five-dollar note. The man was less than impressed when no change was forthcoming. He insisted on his change but Dallas would have nothing of it. He simply grinned and said: "Thanks for your special donation, sir".

Donnelly was awarded life membership for his services to the club he loved in 1986, and was given a special dinner to commemorate the occasion at Wests Leagues Club. But the first hurdle was getting Donnelly into the Ashfield premises — he'd been barred for life on more than one occasion.

HIT MEN

Rick Wayde vividly remembers Donnelly's speech at the dinner.

"It wasn't easy getting Dallas special dispensation to get into the club," Wayde says. "He'd been barred that many times we'd all lost count but they could hardly ban him from his own testimonial dinner. Former Wests president Bill Carson was dying of cancer at the time but made a very moving speech about Dallas and all he'd done for Wests. Bill spoke with the help of a series of cue cards he held in the palm of his hand. When it came time for Dallas to reply, he stood up and pulled a two-dollar bill from his pocket. 'I believe it's customary to use cue cards, but this is the best I've got,' he said.

"He then proceeded to make one of the funniest speeches I've ever heard, referring to his 'cue card' all the while. Midway through the speech, he turned the two-dollar note over as if to continue reading ... he had the whole crowd in stitches."

Donnelly played his last game at Lidcombe in reserve grade against Canterbury in 1984, leading the Magpies to a 24-20 win. After the match, he was driven around his former stamping ground on the back of a utility truck, to a standing ovation from the crowd. Following the lap of honour, Wests officials presented the long-serving front-rower with a huge oil painting of himself on the rampage with the ball in the black-and-white jumper. Although choked up with emotion, Dallas came up with one of his famous quips when handed the microphone.

"It's a great painting," he said. "But who's the good looking young bloke you got to pose for it?"

Despite spending the entire 1984 season in reserve-grade, Dallas was promoted to firsts for his final game in Sydney football, against Cronulla, the following week and the big man went out in with style, despite the final score. The Magpies, now very much struggling battlers, were thrashed 48-10 to end a season in which they won just one match. But Dallas lasted the distance — and was given a hero's reception as he left the field.

However, John Donnelly wasn't finished with rugby league yet and moved to England. Always one to cherish a challenge, he joined second division battlers Southend Invicta in 1985. Although the people of the seaside resort of Southend (located in England's south-east, faraway from the northern towns and cities where league is a way of life) barely knew their league team existed, Dallas soon became a cult figure around the town. Whether he was sinking pints at the local pub or jogging along the pier, the locals grew to know and love Dallas. But not even the imposing figure of Donnelly could save Southend — the club folded 12 months after his arrival.

Just as he was contemplating another English contract, Donnelly received a call from Australia. It was from the Byron Bay club, offering him the position of captain-coach for the 1986 season. Keen to return to Australia, Donnelly saw the offer as a godsend. He trained hard, got his weight down and received a warm welcome from the people of Byron Bay, on the NSW north coast.

However, less then a month before the season was due to kick off, Donnelly went surfing on one of Byron's lovely beaches. With his girlfriend, Tanya, in Sydney to sort out a legal matter, the big man was alone on the beach and when an epileptic fit came, he perished in knee-deep water. League fans from Sydney to Southend mourned the gentle giant as news broke of Donnelly's death, at just 31 years of age.

The entire town of Gunnedah virtually closed for his funeral, with local youngsters forming a guard of honour in their black-and-white uniforms. Wests hired a 60-seater plane for the occasion, but demand for seats was so high they would have been better off getting a jumbo jet. A fleet of buses from Sydney's west also made the long trek north for the sombre occasion. Draped over the coffin was Donnelly's cherished number-11 Magpies jumper — the armour he had worn into 142 first-grade games in his decade at Wests. The game had seen some better footballers than John Donnelly, but few had received a farewell to match Dallas' on that scorching hot day in Gunnedah.

As a mark of respect, the Magpies played the 1986 Winfield Cup opener without a player in the number-11 jumper. The number had special significance for Dallas on and off the field. The big man not only wore the number 11 throughout his career, but also saw it as his lucky number. A keen punter, Donnelly never let an opportunity pass to have something on number 11. In one of his biggest wins, he collected a handsome trifecta on the numbers four, seven and 11.

Tom Raudonikis is rarely allowed to forget his old mate even now, years after his death.

"His name and the things he got up to always seem to come up," he says. "Not long ago we had a 1973 Kangaroos reunion and, even though Dallas wasn't even on the tour, we found ourselves talking about him half the night. We'd remember some of the outrageous stories — the ones I'm not going to tell you — and we'd all fall about laughing. That was Dallas — he was fun while he was alive and his mates still get a smile out of him now he's gone."

HIT MEN

ROD REDDY

The Rockhampton Rocket

Lanky Rod Reddy was one of the game's most complete back-rowers in the 1970s. A brilliant attacking runner with outstanding ball skills, Reddy was also a crunching defender whose intimidatory play proved a key factor in St George's grand final wins in 1977 and 1979. Reddy played 204 first-grade games for the Saints before finishing his career at Illawarra, and had a distinguished international career for Australia, playing 16 Tests and making two Kangaroo tours. Off the field, "The Rockhampton Rocket" was one of the game's true characters — a joker who loved nothing more than having a good time at a team-mate's expense.

Born in Rockhampton in 1954, Reddy was the youngest of nine children. He started playing football at age 10 in an under-six-stone side, but in his final year of primary school was too heavy for that weight.

"So they made me play soccer for a couple of years," he recalls. "I mixed the two codes for a few years before concentrating on league at around 15. I played under-17s at that time but graduated to first grade in the local comp at 17. That was 1971. Late that year, a St George fan called Roy Cook, who had a sister in Rockhampton, got onto the club. Saints invited me to come down, and when they offered me $2000, I jumped at it. To me, at that time, it was a huge amount of money, particularly as they'd never seen me play.

"In September of '71, I sat in my lounge room in Rockhampton and watched the Sydney grand final between Saints and South Sydney. Soon after, I was in Sydney myself. It was a bit daunting training with guys I'd been watching on the telly only a few months earlier. But I was lucky to come to such a strong club, and the two senior players, Graeme Langlands and Billy Smith, really looked after me.

"I was mainly mates with the younger blokes, but Billy was great and really took me under his wing — both on and off the field. He gave me some good fatherly advice about how to behave ... the only problem was he didn't follow it himself. The main instruction I got in my first year was to follow Billy around the field and it worked perfectly. He was a very smart player and would invariably open a gap for me. In defence, I was told to do as little tackling as possible — to save myself for running the ball. Being a young bloke, I thought that was a great idea; unfortunately the game has changed now and you can't get away with that sort of thing today.

"Graeme Langlands was a great captain-coach who led by example. But he wasn't a big talker. I think he believed when players were in first grade, they didn't need to be told how to play. As a result, when he retired from playing to concentrate on coaching, he was pretty ordinary. I think even he'll admit that.

"Frank Facer, secretary of Saints at the time, was very helpful as I attempted to establish myself in the big city. He'd been at the job for years and made sure the new recruits settled in. Frank was a real father figure and one of the reasons Saints were so strong in the '60s and '70s.

"I adapted fairly well to Sydney and played eight games that first year. I made my debut against Parramatta and it proved the ideal start for me. Not only did we win 22-0, but I scored the final try and was named man of the match. But my main memory from that game is playing against two Test blokes in Bob O'Reilly and Keith Campbell. They were both big-name forwards and they worried the life out of me at the time. I remember at one stage coming in to tackle O'Reilly and seeing a big elbow flying my way. Luckily I was able to duck, get underneath it and complete the tackle. As we've both got back up he grinned and said: "If you tackle me high, that's what you can expect.'

"I didn't argue ... I tried avoiding him from that point.

"Saints didn't want to rush me and dropped me back to reserve grade after that. They only brought me back for the right games. One game I remember as a highlight of that year was playing against Souths at the SCG. Their pack had guys like John Sattler, Paul Sait, Bob McCarthy and George Piggins. These were guys I both idolised and feared, and the nerves really got to me on the day. I had a shocker. But the next day both teams got together for a barbeque at Dolls Point and it was a real thrill to get close to such greats. All the families came along and it was a social occasion.

"I continued to improve and in 1973 made the NSW team. Sattler had moved north to captain the Queensland team, but in those days, all the best Queenslanders were in the NSW team. In the three games, they didn't score a point. We beat them 26-0, 16-0 and 10-0. I remember in the first game I barged over the tryline but Langlands loomed beside me and screamed for the ball. I was that shocked at getting over the line I didn't know what to do ... so when the call came I passed it without thinking and "Chang" scored the try. At club level, I had a disappointing finish to that season. We were eventually knocked out of the finals by Newtown, but I missed the game with a bung shoulder. But I had some immediate consolation when the selectors named me in the Kangaroo train-on squad. I missed out on the tour but wasn't too disappointed. At that stage I was still concentrating on keeping a first-grade spot at Saints. To be honest, I never gave myself a chance of touring, but it was nice to at least know the selectors had me in the back of their minds.

"Australia had some excellent back-rowers at the time and I knew I would have to be patient. I actually went on holidays to England and watched a couple of Tests over there. I was one of only 9,000 people at Wembley for the first Test in the fog ... the place was like a ghost town. But I would still have killed to get out on the field."

In 1974, both Gary Stevens and John O'Neill were out injured, which led to Reddy's selection in the NSW team for the match against the touring Great Britain side — his first crack at the Poms.

"They moved Bob McCarthy up to the front row to fit me into the side," Reddy recalls. "I was really excited at playing in a fair dinkum international match. We beat them 13-9. However, my knees started playing up the following year. I did cartilage damage early on, and then came back and did it again. When Saints made the grand final I was on the sidelines, which in some ways was a good thing. Easts thrashed us 38-nil. I remember sitting on the SCG Hill with our five-eighth, Barry Hulbert, who was also out injured and watching Easts run in try after try, right in front of us, in the second half."

Reddy returned from injury in 1976 and considers that the year in which he really established himself as a force in the game.

"I played every game in first grade, played for NSW and got as far as the semi-finals with St George," he says. "But the year ended on a sour note when Canterbury beat us in the semi-finals and I got sent off after an altercation with their English import Mick Adams."

That match proved the start of a long-running feud between Adams and Reddy that was to erupt in both hemispheres in the following years.

"I jumped on his head," Reddy remembers sheepishly. "I split him open and from that day, we were at each other. In 1978 in England, Frank Stanton wouldn't even play me in the game against Widnes because he knew Adams was in their side. In the Test that followed that Widnes game, Adams and I watched each other all day. Then I got king-hit. I was certain when I turned around it would be Adams who I'd see facing me. But it was their centre, Eric Hughes, his mate who also played with him at Canterbury in 1976, who got me. He obviously didn't fancy me either and was getting one in for his friend.

"Adams then came out here in 1979 and I remember having a stink with him as we left the field after the second Test. I went up to him and put my hand out but he said something like: 'You couldn't lay a glove on me for 80 minutes; what makes you think you can do it now?'

"He was about to belt me and I backed off; I couldn't fight to save myself and he was a mean bastard. He kept coming, but eventually Steve Rogers came in and calmed things down."

Harry Bath took over from Langlands as St George coach in 1977 and quickly transformed the young Saints into premiership material.

"Harry was a wily old bloke and really got the best out of a raw side. We had a good blend of youth and skills and Harry knew how to make the most of it. Craig Young was in his first year with us and quickly adapted, John Jansen was in his second year, Bruce Starkey and Robert Stone were on the way up and I was at close to my peak at 23 years of age. It was a good pack and Harry knew just how to work us. He had a lot of experience and taught us to intimidate the opposition forwards. He'd pin-point one opposition player and we'd all rile him up. One bloke would pick on him, then another and then another. So in effect it was the whole pack against one opposition player and it worked very well.

"We drew 9-all in the grand final with Parramatta that year, but I always knew we'd beat them in the replay. We were a lot younger than them and they had quite a few players at the end of their careers. They had the experience but our youth was the difference. I remember all week in the lead-up to the replay we were so relaxed and in control. We didn't even train that much — we were as fit as we had to be and knew what to do. We'd just sit in the middle of Kogarah and listen to Harry's words of wisdom. We stretched the rules to the limit in the replay, but overwhelmed them, winning 22-nil."

Reddy led the way as Saints battered Parramatta into submission in the replay, but at the same time tested the patience of referee Gary Cook. But Reddy is quick to deny the popular story that he received five cautions in the game.

"There's no doubt I went a bit overboard. I remember Cook calling me over for my fourth caution and he was really pissed off. He made it clear that if I was in trouble again, I'd be straight off. A few minutes later there was another stink and I was tempted to get involved. But I'd been warned in no uncertain terms I'd be off and I could tell by Cook's tone he wasn't kidding. So, much as it hurt at the time, I actually broke that one up. The touch judge came on, I was called out and I thought my minutes on the field were numbered. But to my relief I heard him say to the referee: 'Player Reddy was breaking the fight up.'

"So I actually earned a few brownie points. But to this day, I know a lot of people believe I was getting another caution."

Reddy denied that he was sent out by Bath (who was known as the "Old Fox") with specific instructions to bash the Parramatta pack.

"Harry told us to just play it as we saw it. But we knew if we played aggressively, we'd win because we were fitter and younger than them. And that's the way it turned out.

"Harry was probably the best influence on my career. He really gave my game direction."

Reddy also made his Australian debut in 1977, being called into the national side for a World Series match after regular lock, Greg Pierce, was suspended.

"It was a small taste but I definitely enjoyed it," Reddy says. "It made me hungry for more. In 1978, I was selected for the three Tests against the Kiwis and then went on the Kangaroo tour. We had a good side, with guys like Bob Fulton, Greg Pierce, Steve Rogers, Tom Raudonikis and Graham Eadie veterans from the previous tour in 1973. They all played key roles on tour and, with Peter Moore the manager, Frank Stanton coach and Fulton the captain, we had a very tight ship. My only complaint was the amount of work we had to do. We trained twice and three times a day on some occasions and it was only later that I found out the reason for that.

"Apparently it was Peter Moore's idea. He reckoned if we trained that much we'd be too tired to go out and play up. But it made us a bit cranky and by the last leg of the tour we'd had enough. We didn't aim up well in France and lost the series there. I think 'Bullfrog' (Moore) learned his lesson from that. In 1982 we did a lot less work than we had '78 and were an even more successful side."

Reddy was named man of the match in a spiteful first Test against Great Britain on that tour, won by Australia 15-9. Rival halves, Tom Raudonikis and Steve Nash, were sent off after one scuffle and Reddy — not for the first time in his career — was accused of biting.

"But it wasn't me ... it was one of my team-mates," he says with a grin. "For the second Test the Poms brought back some old hard heads, including Jim Mills. I'd played against him early in my career, when he was at Norths. He was a brute of a man. I remembered facing him in my first season when I was still a lanky kid out of Rockhampton. He ran up with the ball and I waited until he was past me and jumped up on his back. I was trying to belt the hell out of him but couldn't even bruise him. He just kept carrying me. In the end the only way I could get him down was by tripping him.

ROD REDDY

"Maybe he hadn't forgotten, because in the second Test he put one of the best head butts on me I've ever seen. But he used a big wind-up and that's what saved me. I saw it coming and just managed to duck — he got the top of my head. But it was still like getting hit with a sledgehammer. The next day my neck and shoulders were still sore from the impact. I hate to think what a mess I would have been if he'd got me bang on target.

"The thing that made me really dirty was that the Pommy ref gave them the penalty — because Mills said I bit him!

"Their policy of bringing the old guys back worked in that match, and they won 18-14. Then I got injured, and I missed the third Test, which we won comfortably, 23-6, to retain the Ashes."

Heartened by the success of their "Dad's Army" side in that second Test of 1978, the Englishmen brought a team of veterans to Australia in 1979. But the old guard proved little short of cannon fodder for an Australian pack which included the likes of Reddy, Ray Price, Craig Young and the tearaway Les Boyd. The Australians romped to a 35-0 win in the first Test, in Brisbane, and followed that up with 24-16 and 28-2 wins in the final two matches of the series. Reddy scored tries in both the second and third Tests and his long-striding runs, clever offloads and aggressive approach made him the scourge of the Englishmen.

"They didn't fancy me and the feeling was mutual," he recalls. "They weren't a great team but there were some hard blokes in their side and I was always careful to avoid the likes of Mills and Mick Adams."

Reddy again used his tough, uncompromising style to help subdue a young Canterbury outfit in the 1979 grand final. The match was among the best grand finals of the era, between a brash, bruising St George side and the emerging talent of the Canterbury Bulldogs.

"The '79 grand final was far less brutal than in '77," Reddy remembers. "It was a grand final of two halves. We played smart football in the first half and charged to a 17-2 lead, and in the dressing room at halftime we thought all we had to do was hang on to win. But they charged back by playing some very enterprising football to reduce our lead to 17-13.

"I wouldn't say we were lucky to win. I thought we always had the edge on them but perhaps we made the mistake of closing the game down too early. Canterbury had come from fifth place on the competition table and had a lot of skill. They went on to win the comp the next year and deserved to do so."

Reddy toured New Zealand with the Australian side in 1980 and enjoyed a fine tour as the Aussies won both Tests.

"It was a very social tour and I enjoyed mixing with blokes from other clubs. There was a special chemistry between us and everyone got on famously. On the club scene, we couldn't repeat our success of the previous season and were knocked out by Wests in the finals. By this stage, I found the game was starting to change; it was definitely getting faster and a little less violent. The judiciary was laying down the law and coaches realised that foul play could have dire consequences."

One of the highlights of Reddy's career came during that 1980 season, when he wore the Queensland jumper in the inaugural State of Origin match.

"I'd played for NSW in the lead-up games against Queensland that season, and no-one was sure how fair dinkum the (Origin) game would be on the night," he says. "Our Queensland training was fairly low key; nobody was all that fired up. But then we arrived at Lang Park and saw the massive crowd. I think that was the moment we all decided to have a go. No-one said anything, but I think that is what really made us give our all. Queensland had copped a lot of hidings in the previous years, often from Queenslanders in the NSW side, and we all suddenly thought it was high time to reverse the trend.

"Early on, Arthur Beetson (who was captaining Queensland) came to blows with his then Parramatta team-mate (and NSW opponent) Mick Cronin in what's become a legendary incident. I was up against three of my Saints team-mates — Craig Young, Robert Stone and Graeme Wynn — which was a strange experience.

"We ripped into them a fair bit and I remember once when Tom Raudonikis scored a try for the Blues, I came in and tried to stop him putting down the ball. This started a bit of a flare-up and the first bloke to come in and give me one was Stone. He belted me on the back of the head. There was definitely no love lost that night. But the passion both teams showed proved that there was a place for Origin football — if it hadn't been such a raging success, they may well have abandoned the concept.

"It was an emotional night. Big Arthur was in his mid 30s and well past his best. They had dragged him out of reserve grade at Parramatta to wear the Queensland jumper for the first time and the crowd loved it. Mal Meninga turned 20 on the day of the game, and had a big influence on the outcome. I'm sure he's never forgotten the night."

Reddy was a controversial selection on the 1982 Kangaroo tour, having missed more than half the season through injury.

"Ernie Hammerton (the chairman of the Australian selectors) used to live around the corner from me," Reddy grins. "The word doing the rounds at the time was that I used to deliver his paper for him every day."

Reddy wasn't the only controversial selection in the touring party — fellow veterans Ian Schubert and Chris Anderson also won spots at the

ROD REDDY

expense of younger players. The team was roundly criticised and many scoffed at Ray Price's suggestion on the eve of the tour that the 15th Kangaroos wouldn't lose a game. Two months later, the Australians returned home triumphant. They were no longer the Kangaroos ... they were "The Invincibles", having won all 22 games on tour. And Reddy, the man who many believed should not have been on the plane in the first place, was among the men of the tour, playing in all five Tests.

It was on tour, both in 1978 and 1982, that Reddy earned his great reputation as a prankster. He shaved more than one eyebrow from unsuspecting team-mates, and generally ensured morale was kept at a high level. When the '82 tour began, a concerned coach Stanton pulled Krilich aside and said he had to room with Reddy. Krilich had his reservations but Stanton merely shrugged his shoulders and replied: "You'll have to room with him; I can't let him share with any of the young blokes."

Throughout the tour, the pair were constantly playing pranks on each other. At the Kangaroos' home base, the Dragonara Hotel in Leeds, Reddy gave restaurant staff strict instructions that skipper Max Krilich must *never* be served tea as the beverage brought on raging fits. The staff faithfully obeyed Reddy's orders for several days until Krilich finally exploded, demanding his morning cup of tea.

As the flustered waitress raced into the kitchen to get the Australian captain his tea, Reddy let Krilich in on the joke. Soon after, Krilich fell to the floor, following his first sip.

"You see ... I told you this would happen!" screamed the waitress.

"I was always into having a bit of harmless fun off the field," Reddy says. "I remember one of my favourite tricks was when we used to go away with St George for mid-week Cup matches and the like. We'd get our expense money on the plane and I'd make sure to be sitting next to one of the younger blokes. I'd open my envelope and if we got say $50, I'd slip another $100 in from my wallet when he wasn't looking. I'd count it out loud and say: 'Yep, 150 bucks, all there'.

"Then the young bloke would open his and find only $50. I'd immediately send him up to the manager to demand the rest of his money. That always got a laugh.

"I remember another time we were away for a mid-week night game in Brisbane. Harry Bath had called a meeting for 2pm in his room on the day of the game. I rung up a brothel and asked for a girl to be sent to (Saints five-eighth) Tony Trudgett's room, which was directly opposite Harry's, just before two.

"'Trudge' was lying in his room waiting for the meeting, while we all started to file into Harry's room. The girl lobbed and banged on Tony's door and, when he answered it, she said in full view of the team: 'I'm the girl you ordered from the escort service, Mr Trudgett.' You should have seen Harry ... he nearly hit the roof. He kicked her out quick smart.

"On the '78 Kangaroo tour, Max Krilich had his eyebrow shaved off while he was asleep by Bob Fulton. But Bozo was smart. He immediately woke Max up and said: 'Max, I swear it wasn't me ... it was Rocket.'

"So I copped the blame for that one. Max tried getting square for the rest of the tour, and on the plane on the way home he thought he had me. He was about to apply the razor when I opened my eye and gave him a big wink. But Steve Rogers eventually got me in 1982 after we won the third Test against the Poms. I'd fallen asleep under a chair after the celebrations and was gone to the world."

Reddy and Krilich remain the best of mates, although Rocket stretched the friendship one day at Kogarah the following season. As a scrum packed down early in the match, Reddy swung a short, vicious right hand into Krilich, opening up the Manly skipper's eye. As blood poured from the wound, and a stunned Krilich looked up to find the man responsible for the blow, Reddy yelled: "JJ — you shouldn't have done that — Max is a mate of mine."

For the rest of the game, the Manly forwards, who treated Krilich as a father figure, hammered the innocent John Jansen at every opportunity.

After the match, Krilich, Reddy and their wives went out to dinner at Saints Leagues Club. Throughout the night, Krilich kept commenting on what a low man Jansen was for belting him ... and Rocket just smiled in agreement.

Many Kangaroo players have bought old cars on tour, and Reddy, Steve Rogers and Craig Young had a bomb on their hands in 1982. At the end of the tour, they had to decide what to do with the vehicle.

"The car had just about had it. It was in such a state the hotel management wouldn't let us park it out the front of the hotel. We had to leave it out the back as they reckoned it gave the place a bad name. The day before we left we tipped it into the canal behind the hotel. As it started to go down, the water pressure must have forced the brake pedal down because the back lights came on. As it started sailing down the canal, and as we ran off, we yelled out: 'There's someone drowning in that car.'

"I think (Australian prop) Donny McKinnon got the blame for that one.

"Another time, on the tour of New Zealand in 1980, we were waiting at the airport in Hastings for a flight. There was a bit of a delay so to kill some time, I ducked behind the counter, grabbed a phone, crouched down and paged the manager of the team, Tom Bellew. When he picked up the phone on the other side of the counter I pretended I was the manager of the hotel

ROD REDDY

we had just left. I said in an indignant voice: "The room Mr Peponis (George Peponis, the Australian captain) was in is a disgrace. They've smashed the toilet, the whole place is flooded. You people promised you'd behave yourselves and now you've done this. Who's going to pay for all the damage?'

"Tom was stuttering and looking for excuses for about five minutes before I finally popped my head up on the other side of the counter with a cheeky grin. You should have seen the relief on his face."

After over a decade's service to the Dragons, Reddy decided it was time to move on at the end of the 1983 season.

"I was troubled by a foot injury for most of 1983," he says. "I hadn't play a lot of football and Saints were in a rebuilding stage. They didn't offer me much at the end of the season and the offer from Illawarra came. The Steelers had actually approached me in 1982 when they entered the premiership but I told them then that I was happy at Saints. But their timing was perfect the second time around — my time at Saints was up."

The move to Wollongong led to Reddy's first meeting with a young first-grade coach called Brian Smith, who was to have a profound influence on him over the next decade. A relative unknown at that time, but with a strong lower-grade coaching record, Smith inherited the Illawarra coaching hot seat for 1984 and saw the experienced Reddy as a key man in his plans.

"I felt I had something to prove that year and Brian and I clicked straight away," Reddy says. "He impressed me with his vast knowledge and his approach. It was a good year for us — we came into the last round knowing a win over Manly would get us into the finals.

"It didn't happen but it was still a mighty effort from a young club. I played every game that year, which was satisfying after having had a couple of pretty ordinary years with injury.

"I was actually going to retire at the end of '84, but was talked into playing again. In retrospect, that was a bit of a mistake. Even though I played 15 first-grade games, my body was starting to wear out and I often took the field carrying injuries.

"It was an easy decision to quit the big time after that. To begin my coaching career, I went up and took on a captain-coach job in Townsville in North Queensland. It was a learning experience. They didn't tell me until I got up there, but the team I took on had copped about five 60-point hidings the previous year. But in my first year we made the finals and found plenty of good young talent. I coached young Gorden Tallis, a player who now has a big future at Saints, when he was just 13 up there.

"In 1987 we won the Foley Shield for the first time in 20 years which was a real thrill."

HIT MEN

Reddy then moved to England, playing for second-division battlers Barrow in 1987-8.

"We had a mediocre season. I had gone over as a player but ended up being lumbered with the coaching job as well. At the end of that season, I finally retired, to concentrate on the coaching side of things. The following season we were promoted to the first division, which gave me a lot of satisfaction considering what I had to work with. We were just a young team of goers and did well to earn promotion. But once we got up to the first division, we were out of our depth, and won just one of our first 12 games. They then sacked me but I really felt the club was as much to blame as me because they didn't buy any players to handle the step up in class. We were going out to do battle every weekend with a pop-gun attack ... with the obvious result. I told them it was going to happen, but the club wouldn't listen."

After his departure from Barrow, Reddy had the unique experience of coaching a Russian side that toured Britain.

"Our team actually played in a curtain-raiser to the Australia-Great Britain Test at Wembley in 1990. I really enjoyed being with the Russian boys. It was like coaching 10 or 12-year-olds. We went right back to the fundamentals because they just knew nothing about the game. But they came up pretty well, and the side I coached became the national champions back in Russia. We also did a six-match tour of France and won five of the games. It wasn't easy getting through to them sometimes, but we had an interpreter with us full-time. I tried to learn some Russian but only managed to grasp one word ... 'vodka'."

Over the '70s and early '80s, Reddy faced many of league's toughest players.

"One bloke who always worried me was John Sattler. Luckily, by the time I came into the game, he was on the way out but he still packed some clout. Terry Randall was another hard man. His tackles would really hurt. I liked to consider myself smart enough to stay away from blokes like that. John Donnelly was tough, while Tom Raudonikis might not have been a big man but he was as hard as anyone. Rod Morris, the front-rower from Queensland, didn't get a lot of recognition when he played for Balmain but I respected him a lot.

"Of the Englishmen, Trevor Skerrett was a top player and probably could have even made the Australian side. Les Boyd was a hard player with the ball but was never really a big defender. Paul Sait was a hard man and he didn't mind niggling you.

"George Piggins was a real worry. The first thing Billy Smith told me when I played against him was not to rile him. If it was a hot day, Billy told me to say: 'Gee, it's a hot day. George. We really shouldn't be playing today.'

"If you called him an old man and tried to bash him, you'd live to regret it. I found the secret with a lot of these guys was not to let them know you were hurt. You had to grit your teeth and act like nothing had happened, even though you wanted to lie down and scream. If you showed them you were hurting, they knew they had you.

"Arthur Beetson was better known as a ball player but he was rugged. He never took a backward step. Charlie Frith of Souths didn't have a long career in Sydney but boy, could he hit. I remember once I took the ball up with my elbows cocked and he hammered me. It was a big collision and we were both waiting for each other to drop. In the same game we put on a move and because of Frith, we never used it again. The idea was to put Tony Trudgett into some space, but Jack Gibson, who was coaching Souths at the time, had obviously seen the move and alerted his players to it. Frith came through like an express train and cleaned Trudge up ... I reckon he landed four rows back in the grandstand at Redfern."

It was while coaching in England in 1990 that Reddy received a call out of the blue from St George chief executive Geoff Carr. Saints had just parted company with their first-grade coach, Craig Young, after two unsuccessful seasons, and were seeking a replacement.

"Geoff asked me if I was interested in the Saints job. I was flattered, but I turned him down. I told him: 'I'm not ready for it yet, but I'll tell you who is — Brian Smith.'

"Smith was the best coach in England at the time and was still getting better. Brian was coaching Hull, and getting some excellent results. Geoff rang him, but Brian actually turned him down the first time. But persistence paid off for Geoff and he eventually got his man. When Brian got the job, he invited me to join him and I jumped at the chance. He's as good a coach as I've known and is still getting better. I'm learning a lot as his reserve grade coach — it's been a real education.

"It's also been a bonus coming back to Saints. I've gone the full circle now. I started my career here and, after a lot of travelling, it feels great to be back home."

HIT MEN

LES BOYD

Toeing the Line

Les Boyd hit Sydney rugby league with the intensity and rage of a tornado in the late 1970s. A magnificent ball-running second-rower, Boyd was a key figure on both the 1978 and 1982 Kangaroo tours, where his fearless charges with the ball shattered the heart of the tackle-shy English defences.

Boyd was among Australia's trump cards in an era when the green-and-gold machine effortlessly outclassed all comers. On the club scene, he was part of the Western Suburbs team that won legendary status in league circles in the late '70s, before a much-publicised switch took him to Manly. But while Boyd was a brilliant attacking player, he will doubtless be remembered as a firebrand who earned two of the longest suspensions in league history and was eventually hounded out of Sydney, only to play his best football in England.

The game of rugby league has produced some controversial figures over the past 20 years, but none came close to having the impact of Lesley William Boyd.

A grazier's son, Boyd grew up in Nyngan and was interested in anything but football.

"I started playing at around 12 and was one of those kids who stood behind the pack and picked daisies," he recalls. "I wasn't that keen at first but gradually got into the swing of things. At 15 I got picked for the Australian Schoolboys to tour England. I was one of the youngest guys in the squad and we had a great time."

Boyd's selection in that tour was not without controversy. While playing for Western NSW in a trial for tour selection, Boyd was sent off for punching. A clear policy was in place that stated that any player dismissed from the field was ineligible for Australian selection. Only the timely

LES BOYD

intervention of coach Roy Masters swayed the selectors.

"I believed that Boyd had good grounds for retaliating and prevailed on the selectors to include him," Masters explains today.

Masters and Boyd were to build a close relationship on tour, and to have a profound influence on each other's future careers.

Boyd returned from the tour with a reputation as one of league's best up-and-comers. But he was happy to continue playing in the bush. In 1973, his family shifted to Cootamundra, in southern NSW, and he began a long and fruitful association with the local side.

"I played there for a few years," Boyd remembers. "Then in 1976 Wests lost their lock, Chris Wellman. Roy gave me a call and it was between me and I guy called David Howell for the spot. We both came down to trial in reserve grade against Cronulla. Roy drove me back to the airport after the game, and it wasn't until we were just about at the gate that he asked: 'Well, Les, what are you going to do?'

"I remember taking a deep breath and saying: 'Righto ... I'll come down ... for one year.'

"Roy was pleased, but all the way home I kept thinking I was a bloody idiot — I really didn't want to go. I still don't know why I said yes, as I had every intention of staying home."

Although only 19 years of age, Wests were convinced Boyd was ready to match it with the big men of Sydney football. He arrived back in town on the Thursday before the club's first trial match of the season — against reigning premiers Eastern Suburbs.

"I had one training run and then played on the Sunday," Boyd recalls. "Easts were the dominant team in the game at the time, and here I was lining up opposite my idol, Ron Coote. He scared the shit out of me. But we had a good game and beat them 6-0 — it was a great start for me. Then, the following week, we came up against Souths and it was a totally different story. I was up against Paul Sait and he bit me, gouged me, trod on me and then some. I just shook my head and thought: 'What in the bloody hell am I doing here?'"

At one stage, Sait and Boyd came to blows on the ground, as the young buck refused to give a centimetre against the old bull. After the pair were pulled apart by team-mates and the referee, Wests secretary Dudley Begar turned to Masters on the Wests bench and said: "I like the way he handled that; we'll give him a $4,000 contract."

"Wests were just starting to come good around then," Boyd says, "and midway through the season we were leading the comp. But then we fell apart a bit in the second round and just missed the finals. I was still satisfied with my progress, though, and decided to hang around and try making a go of it in 1977. But that year was a disaster. I was sent off three times for fighting and it was the only time in my career I played second grade. I also broke my thumb and I did some stupid things to get sent off. After having such a good first year in '76, it came as a blow. But it probably made me wake up to myself and the following year, 1978, I played some of my best football. I was the fittest I've ever been, at around 14 stone (100kg) and really felt good. I worked hard and we had a good year — we should have won the premiership in fact."

The Magpies won the minor premiership in 1978 but lost their momentum in the finals. First, Cronulla beat the Magpies 14-10 in the major semi-final, and the following week, Manly downed Wests 14-7 for the right to challenge Cronulla in the grand final. But the year was not without its rewards for Boyd, who won selection in the Kangaroo touring party at the end of the season.

Cyclone Boyd wasted no time wreaking havoc on British rugby league. The Roos opened their campaign at Blackpool, meeting a fiercely determined local side. Several nasty brawls interrupted the football, the most notable between Boyd and rival forward Jim Molyneux, who stood trading blows for what seemed an eternity. But Boyd also left his mark with his skills, scoring a try and creating several others as the Aussies romped home by the odd score of 39-1. Boyd was again on the warpath in the third tour game against Bradford. The Aussies won 21-11, with Bradford coach Peter Fox at one stage begging his players to: "Stop that bloody Boyd before he kills someone." Former Welsh hooker Tony Fisher attempted to follow his coach's instructions, elbowing Boyd in the face in an incident that only served to further motivate the fiery Aussie forward to tear apart the local defence.

Australia had taken an established pack to Britain, so Boyd, still a youngster on the way up, missed selection for the first Test, which the Kangaroos won 15-9. But his claims became too strong to ignore and by the second Test, he was on the reserves bench. Britain won that match 18-14 to square the series, and the Aussies lost star second-rower Rod Reddy through injury. But Reddy's misfortune opened the door for Boyd, who made his Test debut in the Ashes-decider at Headingley.

Boyd turned 22 the day before the Test but chose to do all his celebrating on the paddock. By halftime, Australia had taken a commanding 19-0 lead. And it was a typically barnstorming Boyd try, scored shortly before the break, that broke the Englishmen's spirit. The then ARL boss Kevin Humphreys said of Boyd's performance: "It was the most impressive Test debut I've ever seen."

With old hands like Jim Mills, Brian Lockwood and Fisher in their side,

LES BOYD

the British attempted to belt Australia out of the match. However, they found a willing adversity in Boyd.

"There was no doubting their tactics, but we accommodated them fairly well," he recalls modestly. "In the end we won 23-6 so it was pretty comprehensive."

Boyd returned from tour to what turned out to be his last season with the Magpies.

"We still had a good side," he says. "In fact, we didn't lose a game at Lidcombe in '78 or '79. We reached the finals in '79, but dipped out in the first semi and after that defeat I had to consider several offers to switch clubs. Manly had offered the same money as Easts — a lot more than what I was on at the time. Deep down I wanted to stay at Wests and went back to them and said: 'Look, I know you can't match these offers, but if you can come within eight or nine thousand of them I'll stay.'

"But they couldn't do it, so I went to Manly. It was a hard thing to do as I'd loved my days at Wests. But I knew eight or nine of the Manly players from the Kangaroo tour and it was a great opportunity for me. I settled in fairly well despite all the supposed 'Fibro-Silvertail' rivalry; to my mind footballers are the same everywhere. I was married by then and that fitted more into the Manly style. Wests tended to have a lot of young, single blokes who enjoyed a renegade lifestyle, whereas the Manly guys were a bit older and starting to settle down.

"I didn't have much luck at Manly even though the club made two grand finals while I was there.

In 1980 we missed the finals; in '81 we were knocked out in the semis; and in '82 we made the grand final but were beaten by Parramatta. The following year Manly again made the grand final but I'd been suspended mid-season for breaking (Queensland forward) Darryl Brohman's jaw in the State of Origin. I got 12 months for that. In the finals, I became the first bloke to get sent off the field without even playing. I was acting as a runner with the water bottle when the ref ordered me off. I came back to play in 1984 and then got an 18-month suspension (for allegedly gouging Canterbury's Billy Johnstone) and that was basically the end of my Sydney career."

Once that second suspension had been served, Boyd opted to continue his career in the northern hemisphere.

"I decided to go to the north of England to play with Warrington. I had five seasons there and it was without doubt the best time I ever had in my life."

As well as gaining Boyd, Warrington had signed two other uncompromising forwards — Bradford Northern's Allan Rathbone and Widnes' Kiwi

Test prop Kevin Tamati. When quizzed by journalists on whether his club was over-doing the aggressive approach perhaps a little, Warrington chairman Peter Higham replied, only half-joking, "Not really; at least one of them is likely to be suspended at any one time."

Boyd in fact had comparatively little trouble with authorities in Britain, despite arriving with a reputation second only to Jack the Ripper. He was sent off once in his first season, but subsequently exonerated on video evidence. He had clearly mellowed and became the leader of a young Warrington pack. With Boyd leading the way, Warrington won the premiership in his first season, and, in the final (a 38-10 destruction of Halifax), the Aussie import scored the first and last tries.

While Warrington never recaptured the success of Boyd's maiden season, they remained a force in the first division throughout his five-year stay.

"I enjoyed the lifestyle over there, the people and the football," he confesses. "The game suited me more over there but in 1985 I bought a distribution business back in Cootamundra and because it grew, I eventually had to come home. It was a hard decision to make, especially as I was offered the coaching job at Warrington for 1991, but I felt it was time to head back."

Boyd had a guest stint in Steve Rogers' Northern Territory team in 1991 and continued to play for Cootamundra for several years as captain-coach (he appeared in six games as late as 1993). At time of writing, he had just signed as coach of nearby Harden for 1994, after an association with Cootamundra that had stretched over 21 years.

Looking back over his career, Boyd admits he made mistakes.

"But I don't think I was as bad as people made out," he claims. "I got sent off three times in one year and I deserved it. I was a hot-headed dickhead and had it coming to me. I probably only got sent off a couple of other times. I got on fairly well with referees but it was the three citings that people really remember.

People think I was always off the field but it was only those three citings that saw me spend so much time on the sidelines. I was the first bloke ever to get cited (following a premiership match) after a Manly-Wests brawl in 1978 and I took them (the NSW Rugby League) to court over it. That was one time I was completely innocent and I beat them in court for denial of natural justice. But after the case they just tried me again and gave me the same suspension, which left a bitter taste. It's pretty hard to beat them — I learned that — but it did serve to make me more determined.

"When I broke Brohman's jaw in the State of Origin it was just a spur of the moment thing. I didn't mean to do that to him; I wouldn't do that deliberately to anyone. I deserved to get suspended for it, but whether I deserved to cop 12 months is another question. The second one, again I did it and I served my time without complaining too much. But I look on the bright side — if I hadn't have copped those two suspensions I would have never gone to England and so would have missed out on five of the best years of my life. The suspensions cost me a lot of money, but I wasn't bitter. Life always goes on."

Boyd's battle with judiciary chairman Jim Comans, the man handed the job of cleaning up rugby league's act in the 1980s, was one of league's most discussed feuds.

"He was a man who seemed to take a lot of pleasure out of handing out long suspensions," Boyd says. "It takes all sorts to make up the world and I think he saw this as a way to make a name for himself. I'm not beyond league or beyond anyone; I'm probably more dirty on myself than anyone because I was stupid at times. But I do think that Comans, and the League, let things get out of hand for a while. I think even the officials were shocked at a couple of those suspensions."

Boyd is convinced his decision to work as a promotions officer for the league and *The Sun* newspaper contributed to his downfall.

"It was a journalist at the *Sun's* rival, the *Mirror*, who first dubbed me 'The Baby Faced Assassin'," Boyd explains.

"It was obvious certain members of the media had it in for me. I didn't like it but I had to live with it. Overall, football was good to me but if I'd put a bit more time and effort in, I could have been a lot better. I was very lazy and didn't play to my potential very often."

Despite his reputation as a hot-head, Boyd was rarely baited by rival players.

"People often ask me that and a lot seem to have the misconception that blokes went out of their way to rile me. It's a myth. There's no time for that in football, particularly in the modern game. As for football now, I'm a bit disenchanted with the way it is played in Sydney. The rules have made it far too predictable and a lot of the excitement has gone. The players are all fitter, bigger and stronger, but they're just asking too much of them now. The hard, tough, physical games just don't seem to be around anymore."

The great paradox of Les Boyd's life is that while he was a ruthless competitor who took no prisoners on the field, he has always been a quiet, gentle family man off it.

"I suppose that's true. More than once, I've met people and once we've been talking for a while they'll say: 'Geez, you aren't mad after all'.

HIT MEN

"When I started back in '76, it was a tough initiation. I was a teenager playing for Wests and it was sink or swim. Remember what happened to me at the hands of Souths in only my second game. At that time, it was either adapt or become extinct. So I toed the line. If I'd come down to play as a young kid now, I've no doubt it would have been a completely different story."

HIT MEN

RON HILDITCH

Leading from the front

One courageous — some would sat insane — moment typified the approach to football of one of the modern game's great warriors, Ron Hilditch. Parramatta's "Hit Man" was the man at the centre of a unique attacking formation the Eels (who were trailing 13-10 at the time) used in the dramatic final moments of the 1976 grand final against Manly. The charge of the Eels' forwards, linked in pyramid formation with Hilditch leading the way, was called the "Wedge", and was league's equivalent of Custer's Last Stand.

For Hilditch, it was close to a choice of death or glory. In a ploy later banned by the NSW Rugby League, Hilditch took a tap inside the Manly quarter, and then, as the apex of a battering ram of five team-mates, was propelled towards the Sea Eagles line. The Parramatta move came within centimetres of winning Hilditch a place in grand-final folklore.

"There's one fallacy that I've had to correct time and again over the years about that move," Hilditch says. "For some reason, there are a lot of people convinced I volunteered for that role. Now I may have been a hooker, but I wasn't stupid. I got volunteered. It was Ray Price's idea, and came from his rugby union days. But he was smart enough to stay down the back out of harm's way. Ray Higgs was skipper and said he couldn't do the job either.

"The funny thing is, it almost worked. By the time Manly stopped our momentum, my eyes were actually on the tryline. But I had about a dozen bodies on top of me and there was no way I could get the ball out from under me and put it over the line. It was a classic case of so near, yet so far."

Determination and spirit were the trademarks of Ron Hilditch's game. The Hit Man wasn't the most gifted footballer of his era, but he was among the most respected. A fighter who often conceded opposition forwards many kilos, Hilditch more than made up for that with his tremendous drive and will to win.

An Eels man through and through, Ron Hilditch began his junior career with Parramatta City at the age of nine, before moving to the Hills District. His first position was at fullback, but he was moved fairly rapidly into hooker and played most of his career there before finishing up as a first-grade and international front-rower.

"I got graded in 1974 in under-23s and, after a few weeks on the bench, got a crack at it. We had a bit of a battle that year, though, and finished last in every grade. But it didn't take long for us to turn the corner. The first graders made the semis in '75 and the second grade, which I played in, won the comp. We beat Cronulla in the grand final and had a good side with guys like Tony Charlton, John Kolc and Graeme Atkins and myself who all went on to play first grade. We were down 13-2 at halftime in that grand final before we stormed home to take the match and I've always regarded that as one of the finest wins I ever had in my career.

"At the end of 1975, John McMartin, who'd been the first-grade hooker at Parra for years, left the club to go to Cronulla and that gave me my chance. I got the hooker's job in the pre-season and was lucky enough to hold it for most of the year. It was a hard initiation in those days, particularly in the hooking spot. There were plenty of old hard heads around and they weren't about to let some young kid step in on equal footing to them. I remember it took me quite a few weeks before I felt comfortable in first grade.

"We started the year inconsistently but then strung together 13 games without a loss to finish just behind Manly in the minor premiership. We then went all the way through to the grand final. Even though we lost to Manly, my memories of '76 are all delightful. It was the year I came into the top grade and went from being a nobody straight to the grand final. I achieved so much during the year and, while losing the grand final naturally hurt at the time, it didn't last long. It was Parramatta's first ever grand final and the people were fantastic about the whole thing. They were great times."

The Eels made it back-to-back grand finals in 1977 against St George, but once again that elusive first title slipped through their fingers.

"We drew 9-all in the grand final and I thought we played pretty well that day," Hilditch remembers. "We were down 9-nil but came back to level the scores. However, we had a few blokes carrying injuries in the replay and got hammered 22-0. But I'm not using that as an excuse -we were beaten by a younger and more enthusiastic team on the day."

Popular theory has it that the Eels were put off by the roughhouse tactics employed by Rod Reddy and his fellow St George forwards but Hilditch quickly dismisses this.

"They turned it on, no doubt, but I don't think it was what proved the difference," he claims. "We'd dealt with that sort of thing all year and I know personally it never worried me. Our two front-rowers, Graham Olling and John Baker, carried broken hands into the game so it was a bit hard to fight fire with fire. They are the sort of things people never realised at the time — we'd had a hard campaign and it caught up with us."

Hilditch bitterly recalls the circumstances behind the Eels' controversial departure from the following year's semi-finals. In an open premiership race, Parramatta, who had finished fourth on the ladder, once again looked capable of taking the title, but were held to a 13-all draw in the minor semi-final by Manly. When the match was replayed mid-week, several key decisions from referee Greg Hartley appeared to favour the Sea Eagles. It was one of the most controversial finals matches ever played; Parramatta's star lock forward Ray Price was sent off (and subsequently exonerated), while Hartley awarded Manly a try on the seventh tackle. A video-replay of the match showed he had also allowed Parramatta only five tackles on three occasions. Manly eventually won 17-11, and the Parramatta club took the unprecedented step of attempting to have the match declared null and void.

"You never really get over something like that and it still irks me," Hilditch admits. "The less said about it the better — I'm just lucky I finally managed to win a comp a few years later and that erased some of the pain. The other point is that Manly must feel a bit dirty about the whole thing because they had a great side and it was a real achievement winning the comp that year. But they have never got much credit because it has always been over-shadowed by the controversy. They didn't need any help to take the title."

A consolation for Hilditch was his selection as a member of the Kangaroo touring party that left for Britain and France after the finals series that year. The Parramatta forward was named as the third hooker behind George Peponis and Max Krilich, beating Queenslander Johnny Lang for the spot. In Brisbane, the reaction from QRL boss Ron McAuliffe was predictable — he slammed Hilditch's selection, putting the Parramatta forward under pressure even before the Roos' plane had had time to take off from Mascot airport.

"McAuliffe kicked up a stink," Hilditch remembers, "but I bumped into Lang later on and he's a terrific bloke. He congratulated me and we've never had a problem. I gave myself some chance of selection, even though many didn't. Looking back, I was probably the one 'outsider' in the whole team. Most of the other blokes had toured before and were seasoned internationals. I think the selectors saw me as a player who could cover several positions. That might have just tipped the scales in my favour."

Hilditch suffered a reaction to his post-tour inoculations and couldn't make his green-and-gold debut until the fourth tour game against Bradford. It was there that he was given a bizarre introduction to the harsh world of rugby league, English style.

"Before the game we all lined up at Odsal Stadium before a huge crowd and there was a lot of pomp and ceremony," Hilditch explains. "The Bradford players shook hands with us and gave each of us a pennant as a souvenir of the day. I'd never seen that sort of thing before a game but thought: 'Gee, this is nice'.

"Five minutes later, the game got underway and they were beating the daylights out of us. It turned out to be one of the most vicious games I ever played in. There were stinks from start to finish and only the experience of guys like Tommy Raudonikis and a few of the older guys got us through it. They really gave us a working over but we ended up winning 21-11."

It didn't take long for Hilditch to learn that the selectors did in fact see him as a utility forward. In a tour match against Leeds, he was named as a front-rower for the first time in his life.

"It was terrific to play there, but I was pretty daunted by the prospect when they first told me," he says. "I was terrified, in fact, and the first thing I did was knock on the door of (regular props) Ian Thomson and Craig Young in the hotel, who happened to be in the room right next door to me. 'Listen, these blokes think I can play front row,' I told them in a panic. 'I've never been there before. Give me a couple of tips.' Fortunately, they gave me some handy advice and I found it okay. It was a bit of a shock to the system at first but I was just busting my neck to play a game; I wasn't about to turn them down."

Hilditch had left Australia at long odds to play a Test on tour, but his tenacity saw him achieve his goal.

"We had some injuries and I got the call-up to play France in the last Test of the tour at Toulouse," he says. "I was rapt but my joy didn't last long. The Test itself was a dreadful game and they beat us 11-10."

Hilditch tried to be diplomatic about the home-town referee who played his part in the upset win.

"Put it this way — it was after that game that the international board decided to bring in neutral referees for Tests. It was an absolute joke. It wasn't just the penalties — this bloke was more subtle than that. He just wouldn't let us win a scrum and of course every marginal decision went their way. The defending team was never back more than three yards all day and that didn't help us either. It was very frustrating ... but I made the Test side against them again in 1981 and we belted them then."

Hilditch was a key man in the Eels' first premiership win in 1981, when the Parramatta machine overcame a dogged Newtown side.

"As a game it wasn't as tough as the '76 or '77 grand finals," he says. "But it was definitely still a hard game. There's something about grand finals; they just seem to be played at a slightly faster and more intense pace. Around that era we started getting freak players like Steve Ella, Eric Grothe and Brett Kenny. Easts were favourites to take out the comp in '81, but we beat them in extra time in the major semi and Newtown knocked them out in the final. We needed the week's break between the semi and the grand final, because we had some old blokes like 'The Bear' (Bob O'Reilly) and Kevin 'Stumpy' Stevens in the forwards. The Bear was a key man in our side — he was great to play with and we had lots of fun together. He wasn't just a hard player — he was smart with the football and never put you into a dead end if you ran off him. In the grand final, Newtown kept coming but we had a little more class in the backs and that's where we eventually got them. That win, as I said earlier, more than made up for the close misses and the disappointments of a few years earlier."

"I was just starting to really play my best in the early '80s but I also got some bad injuries late in my career to balance that out. I was playing great football in 1982 but ripped my groin. Then I got back for the semis but did my knee in the final against Easts. That year I rated myself a fair chance for the Roo tour until I was hurt. I decided to retire — due to the combination of the knee and groin injuries. But after a good break I asked for a game late in 1983 and Jack Gibson was good enough to give it to me. I played a few reserve-grade games and was feeling good. The time off playing had given the groin the chance to repair. I came back into first grade for the finals but did my shoulder badly in the final. That was the last straw ... I knew I was finished."

The shoulder injury was a legacy of the 'hit man' tag that Hilditch carried throughout his career.

"I never worried too much about the nickname and just went out there to tackle as hard and as much as I could. But I certainly rued it that day. I went to pull off a big hit, it all went wrong, and the shoulder was gone."

At his peak, Hilditch's power-tackling was among the game's big talking points. The Eels made maximum use of his fearsome style — and never more so than in a clash with arch-rivals Manly in the early 1980s. Manly had a pet move involving a "wall" that would see skipper Max Krilich emerge with the ball and pass it out to the backs. Coach Jack Gibson studied the move on video, showed the players, and arranged for Hilditch to give the Manly skipper a warm reception when he re-emerged after running behind the wall.

"Hilditch wiped him out — absolutely comprehensively," Eels teammate Peter Sterling recalls with admiration. "Max got up abusing his teammates -- I don't think he ever knew what hit him."

As one opponent once said: "When Hilditch hit you in a tackle, you felt as if the roof of your mouth had just caved in."

After retiring at the end of 1983, Hilditch sat out two years but the lure of playing one last season proved too strong. He signed up as captain-coach of Mudgee and led the team to the premiership.

"It took me a full two years to get over the shoulder problem. I was tossing up whether to play again. But I'm glad I did; it was a great way to go out and I really enjoyed myself out at Mudgee. We had a good young side and I was joined by former Parramatta team-mate Phil Mann. I was a shot duck by then, nothing like I used to be, but it was a great feeling to go out that way. I finished with a win in the bush and then said that's enough for me."

Hilditch made a point of trying not to take notice of players' reputations during his career.

"It was funny, I can remember on several occasions being told before I ran out onto the field: 'Oh, so-and-so isn't very good'. And just about every time that happened, the bloke would come out and belt me all around the park. It just goes to show what a hard competition it was back then and the number of good, tough players who were running around.

"Terry Randall was one bloke who lived up to his reputation and I must admit I always tried to avoid him on the field. He was among the most respected players at that time. I played a couple of games against John O'Neill and, even though he was at the tail end of his career, you could see he was a bloke not to be messed with."

"I always got on fairly well with the refs and the only time I got in hot water was in 1978 when I was cited, after a match against St George at Kogarah. The incident occurred on the same day as a Wests-Manly brawl, and the League, for the first time, cited players on video evidence after a premiership match. I thought the League's approach was inconsistent — they only seemed to cite blokes from certain games and I wasn't happy when they gave me two weeks. We appealed but got knocked back, so I had to cop it sweet."

Hilditch's short stint at Mudgee gave him a ticket to the competitive world of top-grade coaching, and he has held down a variety of jobs over the past decade.

"In 1987 I came back to Sydney and was assistant-coach to Tim Sheens at Penrith. The following year, I went to Illawarra and had their reserve-grade side before taking over first grade for 1989 and '90. The Steelers were a good club and I really enjoyed my time there. We did it tough for a while but when that great group of young guys came through together it was very satisfying. They really wanted to play the game and the club is still reaping the rewards down there.

"Then I took a bit of a break before coming back to Parramatta to coach the President's Cup in 1993. They asked me to take over first grade in '94 and that's my latest assignment. We're looking for the same good kids at Parra. We got them here a decade or so ago and the Steelers found them three or four years back. All you need is an Ella or a Kenny and things can turn around very quickly.

"I enjoy the coaching, particularly now I'm doing it fulltime, but the hardest part is the fact that you can't get out there and release your frustrations. And the pressure is enormous.

"Now I've done both (playing and coaching), I realise playing is just so much easier. It's harder physically, of course, but you're fit, strong and having a good time. Maybe I'm just saying that because I was lucky enough to be in a lot of winning teams, but playing is just one big ball. The trips away ... the mateship ...

"You just can't beat it."

HIT MEN

GEOFF ROBINSON

The Wild Colonial Boy

Canterbury's wild man Geoff Robinson will always be remembered as the player who destroyed Jack Gibson's "Parramatta Wall". The sight of Robinson charging full tilt into the opposition, long black hair and flowing beard in tow, remains one of league's most enduring images of the early and mid '80s.

Robinson never did more damage than against the rampaging Parramatta side that took out the premiership treble in 1981-82-83. The Eels had a pet tap move under Gibson whereby four forwards would turn their backs to the opposition, hiding the ball to confuse the defence. Until Robinson came along.

"It's a move I'd seen plenty of times before but what I did was really just a spur of the moment thing," Robinson recalls. "I thought ... I can't see the ball, so I'll bowl them all over. It was a stupid thing, head down, arse up, but it worked. I cleaned up a couple of the forwards and also gave Peter Sterling, who was working the move behind the wall, a shock as I charged through. Most players just stood back, watched the wall, and waited for the ball to become visible. My approach obviously stunned them. But it worked, as they dropped the ball.

"I did it a couple of times and I don't think they used the move nearly as much after that."

Robinson's destruction of the wall that Jack built was typical of his tornado-like approach that made him a favourite with fans at Belmore for 11 seasons.

"People used to say I was crazy doing everything at 100 miles an hour on the field, but that was the way I always played the game," Robinson says with a shrug. "That's the way I was taught and I enjoyed it. I probably wouldn't have known any other way."

GEOFF ROBINSON

A Canterbury junior, Robinson started his football days, at age 14, in the centres for the Villawood Sports club. He moved to Chester Hill, the club that produced renowned Bulldog Terry Lamb, and was graded in 1978 after playing in both the Jersey Flegg and S.G. Ball competitions in the Bulldogs' colours.

"I was only 18 at the time and had never played in the forwards, but that's where they decided to use me. Combining those two factors made it a big step and for a while I struggled. In fact, for a while after I was graded, I couldn't get a game. I sat there on the sidelines for a few weeks, and then went back to the juniors just so I could get a run.

"Finally, our coach, former Canterbury forward Geoff Connell, gave me a go in the second row after about 20 minutes of one game. I played the rest of the match. From then until the end of the season I never missed a game.

"I loved the feeling of playing up front rather than out in the centres. It gave me the chance to get more involved and I relished it."

Robinson continued to develop over the next 18 months, but, with internationals Bob McCarthy and Gary Stevens firmly entrenched in the first-grade second row, chances in the top grade were few.

"I finally got my spurs in an Amco Cup midweek game against Toowoomba up north in 1978, after Stevens pulled out through injury," he remembers. "I packed in the second row alongside Bob McCarthy — just doing that was one of the biggest thrills of my career. The adrenalin was pumping for the 80 minutes. Bob was a legend and a player I'd always admired so it was a special feeling packing into scrums alongside him. He gave me a lot of help throughout the game and I walked off with the man-of-the-match award, so it was a great start for me. But Stevens came straight back in the following week, which was fair enough — even though I'd gone well he was a Test player and I knew I had to wait my turn. It wasn't until the following year that I became a regular first grader."

While Canterbury's young side enjoyed a vintage season in 1979, it wasn't a scrapbook year for Robinson.

"Early in the season, I copped a high tackle playing against Newtown at Henson Park, and fractured my cheekbone ," he says. "And, when I came back from that, I did my medial ligament a fortnight before the finals. Our other prop, John Coveney, suffered the same injury and we both missed the semis. Canterbury won through to the grand final from fifth spot and I would have killed to be out there with them. Saints beat us 17-13 that year, but we knew our time would come."

The young Bulldogs, harder and stronger from the lessons learned in 1979, swept all before them the following season to take the title.

"We played Easts in the grand final and, from the opening moment, we were never going to lose the game," he says. "Easts came out all fired up and threw everything at us, but they overdid it and gave away stupid penalties. I think they had memories of the major semi-final a fortnight earlier, when we had an all-in brawl. Royce Ayliffe and I traded blows in that game and he was again the main instigator of their rough tactics in the grand final. I must admit I saw nothing wrong with their approach, though. In those days I thought the forwards were entitled to let off a bit of steam early, no-one would ever get hurt, and after the initial fireworks died down, you could all get on with the game and play footy. On grand final day, we kept our cool despite their aggressive approach, and in the end beat them easily.

"It was a great thrill doing the victory lap, and the party afterwards lasted for days. I've got a video of the game at home and watch it every six months or so ... it's great to relive the game again. I thought I had played well, but still asked my dad afterwards what he thought of my effort. All he told me was that every player knew, deep down, how he had played. And he was right.

"I was proud to be part of such a fine team."

The 1980 grand final will always be remembered for Steve Gearin's magical leap to score one of the game's great tries from a Greg Brentnall bomb ... and for the brand of football Ted Glossop's young Bulldogs played.

"There's no doubt there was something very special about that year," Robinson says. "When people want to talk to me about football, they don't talk about the premiership-winning Canterbury sides of 1984 or 1985 or 1988 ... it's always that game and that team they want to discuss. They never seem to tire of going back over it."

Former colleague Steve Mortimer will never forget Robinson's tremendous contribution towards the Bulldogs' success in 1980.

"The test for us came a fortnight before the grand final, in the major semi-final," Mortimer explains. "They obviously thought they could smash us up front and both their props, Royce Ayliffe and John Harvey, took it to us. But "Robbo" and John Coveney stood up and took everything they could dish out. Robbo in particular was great; he kept coming back for more and won the battle up front by a long margin. That was a tremendous psychological factor in our favour when we met Easts again in the grand final two weeks later. We knew we had their measure physically and all we had to do was stick to our natural game to take the title."

Mortimer, one of the code's finest halfbacks, played much of his football alongside Robinson and was always impressed by the bearded forward's courage.

"One day Robbo hobbled into the dressing room before a big game,

GEOFF ROBINSON

looking a mess. Somehow he'd damaged his back a couple of days earlier, but he wasn't about to let that stop him playing. I remember he looked in no shape to walk across Belmore Oval, let alone play 80 minutes of football. I was worried about him ... so I went up and asked if he was okay. He just waved me away.

"'Don't ask any questions ... I'll be right,' he said in a gruff voice.

"Once we got on the field, it was typical Robbo, charging into the opposition, showing no fear or favour. He was one of our best but was in agony after the match. A couple of days later he went off for tests and they showed he had a slipped disc in his back. That just shows the courage and toughness of the man. I played in the premiership for over a decade and in my time, he was as tough as they came."

Robinson had dreams of another title in 1981 but the Bulldogs were unable to build on their successes of the previous season.

"It didn't take us long to come back to earth after that great year," he recalls. "In '81 we had a disappointing year, finishing well down the ladder; we did even worse in 1982. But we came back well in '83 and got as far as the final. Then Ted Glossop was replaced by Warren Ryan for 1984, which led to a year of highs and lows for me.

"I played nearly every first-grade competition game before the semi-finals, but on the Tuesday night before the major semi (Canterbury had finished the regular season as minor premiers), Warren pulled me aside and said I was on the bench. Our regular hooker, Billy Johnstone, and I were both dumped, but I suppose I was a bit luckier than him; I got to come on for the last 10 minutes of the grand final, while he never got off the bench. It really hurt at the time, I can tell you, and the part that hurt most of all was that Warren never told us why we'd been axed. To this day I don't know why he did it. I'm sure he had his reasons and he had the last laugh as we won the game, but he was never a great communicator as a coach and I was just devastated. He did something similar to me in 1986 (Robinson was left out of the starting line-up after Canterbury won the major preliminary semi-final) when we got beaten by Parramatta in the grand final. I wanted to speak out, but I copped it on the chin."

One of Robinson's most cherished memories is of a stint with English club Halifax in 1985-86. Playing under current Bulldogs coach Chris Anderson, Robinson proved an instant hit with the Halifax fans. The English supporters warmed to his aggressive style of play and his total disregard for self-preservation, while the long jet-black hair and flowing beard helped his image as a wild colonial boy.

"The crowds really got behind us and helped the adrenalin pump," he says. "We won the championship and that was right up there with the grand final wins back in Sydney."

After 11 seasons with the Bulldogs, Robinson decided to hang up his boots following that disappointing finish to the 1986 Australian season. Although only 29 and still fit and strong, Robinson had had enough. Canterbury chief executive Peter Moore attempted to change Robinson's mind and even offered him a contract to come out of retirement 12 months later, but Robinson could not be swayed.

"I'd been there a long time and just lost interest in the game," he says. "I knew I couldn't give the game 100 per cent and that wouldn't have been fair on anyone. I was waking up after games feeling pretty sore and thought to myself: 'If I go on another year or two, how much worse am I going to feel?' I felt I owed the family some time and was tired of the training side of the game."

Robinson plays down the "wild man" tag that followed him throughout his career.

"It never really worried me," he says. "I didn't stop to think about it while I was playing. If people wanted to put a label on me then that was fine. I never went out looking for it — the beard and long hair were just me. I felt comfortable that way. People still call me 'Wild Man' now as a bit of a joke, even though the long hair and beard are gone."

Despite his fearsome appearance, Robinson felt he never received any extra attention from either the referees or rival players.

"I think I got a pretty good deal, really," he says. "I was only sent off once in my career — against Newtown in 1980. Tom Raudonikis was playing that day and was up to no good. He instigated a brawl, and me and their prop, Steve Blyth, came to blows. We both got marched, but he got four weeks while I only copped two, which I thought that was a bit of a moral victory.

"But I believe I hold the distinction of being the first bloke ever sin-binned in a premiership match. It was 1984, the sin-bin had just been introduced, and we were playing Illawarra in the opening round when I was put in the bin for fighting. It was nothing to be proud of, but it's a talking point. As for the players, I can't ever recall anyone sledging me. I don't think anyone even pulled my hair or beard. Occasionally I felt a bit of a tug but I think that was just an accident in the heat of battle. No-one ever touched it, although there were plenty of other things that went on. In those days, players weren't interested in hair pulling — that was sissy stuff. If they wanted to get their point across they'd just punch you in the mouth."

Robinson had just one taste of representative football — for City Firsts against Country in 1984.

GEOFF ROBINSON

"I enjoyed it and would certainly have liked to play some more rep football, but it didn't happen," he comments. "I played okay for City and everyone told me I'd be in the NSW side, but I never got my hopes up. Someone got injured and all the papers said I was the number-one choice as the replacement. But it never came about, though I must say it wasn't a major disappointment. There were a hell of a lot of good front-rowers around then and it was just a case of better players getting picked in front of me. I never lost any sleep over it. I used to say good luck to them and then got on with my own game. Good props seem a rarity nowadays, but in the '80s, they were a dime a dozen."

Taking on opposition hard men one-on-one was an aspect of the game in which Robinson revelled.

"There were plenty of tough players around and it was a challenge playing against them," he says. "John O'Neill, Arthur Beetson and Ron Coote all hit me hard but I tried never to show it.

"Terry Randall commanded a lot of respect because of the way he played the game. He hit me once in a legitimate tackle at Belmore Sports Ground and knocked me back 15 metres ... I don't think I've ever been hit as hard before or since. When I got back up I couldn't breathe, but I wasn't about to show it. I didn't want him to know the damage he'd caused. Not long after that Terry and I became quite good mates. We were both in hospital together having our knees operated on and I found him a very friendly bloke. But I still wouldn't tell him how much pain he caused me that day at Belmore! All in all, he was probably the hardest bloke I played against."

Although always a "no-nonsense" player, Robinson has some treasured memories of funny incidents in the heat of battle.

"We were playing South Sydney one day at Belmore Oval in 1978, and a mate of mine, Stuart Collis, was playing alongside me in the forwards. Stuart didn't play much first grade but he was a hard man and was all fired up on this occasion. Souths had a few Aboriginals in their side that day and Stuart liked to name-drop blokes. He called one of the Souths blokes a 'black bastard' after a tackle. None of us gave that a second thought, but Greg Hartley, who was referee that day, jumped in, glared at Stuart and gave him a stern lecture, finger-pointing and all.

"'If you do that again I'll send you off for racial discrimination,' Hartley warned.

"In the middle of a tough football game, we couldn't believe he'd say something like that. We cracked up laughing, so did Hartley ... and I think even the Souths blokes smirked at it.

"In another game, I was in the front row and Graeme Hughes was playing in the second row. As we packed down in a scrum, 'Heaps' tried to belt one of their front rowers, but all he succeeded in doing was getting me flush on the chin.

"I looked down at him in the scrum and said: 'Make sure you hit him, not me, next time. And make it harder, because I didn't feel a bloody thing.'

Robinson's fearsome charges doubtless caused many opposition forwards to feel trepidation but he maintains he never felt any fear for life and limb.

"You can't worry about being scared when you do something — on or off the field," he says simply. "My dad, Reg, taught me that when I was just a kid. He told me never to be afraid of anything and to be positive when you go into things . That's the way I've tried to live my life. He played a lot of footy in his time, although it was mainly rugby union, and he was the one who encouraged me to run as hard as I could.

"'If you do that you'll never get hurt,' he would say.

"Of course he wasn't 100 per cent right — I did get hurt plenty of times, but still not as much as some other blokes who never ran that hard. There were some tough times, but those 11 years were just great and I'd love to live them all again. It's always great to get together with the boys and talk about how the game was then and is now."

After retirement, Robinson switched to coaching, and achieved fine results with the Bulldogs' President's Cup side. He led the young Canterbury side to the finals in 1990 and then won the title in 1991 with a memorable defeat of favourites Parramatta.

"That was very satisfying because we had to win 13 games straight just to get to the grand final. Parra had a good side and we were down 14-4 at halftime and then 18-4 soon afterwards. But we fought back to win 26-18. I still feel a lot of pride about the way the boys played to win against such odds. We ended up winning 22 games straight, which was a Canterbury record. But they took a lot of players off me midway through 1992 and we crashed."

Robinson thought his results justified a promotion to reserve grade in 1993, but the club disagreed.

"I told them I wanted to step up or get out," he explains. "They wouldn't give me the reserves so I called it a day. Ironically, Ian Schubert, who had the reserve-grade job, ended up being stood down after only a few games because he had too much on his shoulders (he was also the marketing manager for the club). I told them all this six months earlier but they didn't listen."

The former Wild Man is still something of a celebrity out in Sydney's west and regularly relives his playing days for the patrons of Bass Hill's Twin Willows Hotel, where he works as manager.

"I must say I don't mind talking about the old days, although there are times I'd probably like to drop the subject," he says. "But I don't like doing that because then the people I'm talking to will think I'm a rude bastard. They all ask about the past ... the long hair ... the 1980 premiership ... how I broke the Parramatta Wall. It tends to be the same stories over and over again.

"But I still enjoy them."

HIT MEN

CRAIG YOUNG

As Tough as Concrete

In the late 1970s, St George's Craig Young inherited Arthur Beetson's mantle as the most dominant front-rower in league. Although a vastly different style of player to the attacking wizard Beetson, Young ruled league's engine room with an iron fist until the early '80s.

A first-year member of Harry Bath's "Babes" that won the 1977 premiership in breathtaking style, Young remained with the Dragons for 11 more winters as a player and two as a coach. But it was in England, during the 1978 and 1982 Kangaroo tours, that Young played arguably his best football. The rugged front-rower crunched the Great Britain forward pack with his aggressive defence and tore the heart out of their defence with powerful charges up the middle. There was nothing fancy about Craig Young's game — he played it hard, tight and in a no-nonsense style. But for over a decade, few players claimed to have scored a points victory over the man known as "Fat Albert".

Only one player — the immortal Norm Provan — has turned out in more first-grade games for the Dragons than Young, and since the days of Provan the St George club has had few more loyal sons. However, Young's sacking as Saints first-grade coach late in the 1990 season created a huge split between the great player and the great club. Sadly, the former front-row star has not set foot in Saints' Leagues club since the day of his dismissal.

Craig Young was born in the Illawarra in 1956 — the year Saints began their record-breaking 11-premiership run. In his early days, he looked certain to follow his father, Bob, by making a name for himself in soccer. Bob Young had played left-half for Corrimal Rangers, NSW and Australia. Craig's brother, Warwick, developed into a top-class goalkeeper in the Illawarra region, while Craig didn't even look at

CRAIG YOUNG

league for the first 10 years of his football life.

"I started playing soccer when I was around six years old," he recalls. "It just seemed the game for me to play. I grew up in a soccer family and dad was always there to lend support. I enjoyed it and never really thought about playing anything else. Then one day at Corrimal High they were looking for front-rowers to play in the school team. They took one look at me with my thick legs and stocky build and said: 'You're in.'

"I found I enjoyed the physical nature of the game, and, after just a handful of games, I somehow made the Combined High Schools side. We played in a tournament that turned out to be a selection trial for the first Australian Schoolboys side to tour England and I was lucky enough to gain selection."

Sydney talent scouts were quick to chase the likes of Young, Ian Schubert and Les Boyd after the schoolboys returned home with an imposing record. Coached by Roy Masters, who would later coach Wests and Saints in the Sydney premiership, the schoolboys won all 12 matches they played, and scored 402 points and conceded just 17.

"We had just one try scored against us the whole tour," Young says. "There were a lot of quality players there and many of us ended up playing with or against each other in Sydney. We handed out some hidings and generally had a great time. For a 16-year-old kid from Corrimal, it was just sensational. I'd been playing league for under 12 months and it was a great start to my career."

Young resisted the move to Sydney immediately after the tour, deciding to remain on the south coast.

"I played a few seasons with Thirroul and Corrimal and then made the Country Seconds side in 1976," he says. "Sydney thrashed us by 30 points but I must have made something of an impression because the late Frank Facer came down from Saints and offered me a contract. It was a good deal but I knocked them back at first. People were getting in my ear at home they wanted me to stay down the coast and play for Country again. But after saying no, I couldn't sleep all that night. My first instinct was to say yes and I should have stuck to it — it was an opportunity I knew I should take. I rang Frank back the next day to tell him I'd changed my mind and within an hour he was on my doorstep with a contract all ready to sign."

Saints were going through a period of transition when Young drove up the highway early in 1977 for his first training session with the Dragons. In 1975, Saints had been thrashed by Easts in the grand final; in '76, after finishing third on the competition table, they had gone straight out of the semi's race, courtesy of decisive defeats at the hands of Parramatta and then Canterbury. 1976 was also the year in which Graeme Langlands had finally retired, after a glorious career. Billy Smith, Saints' other link with the club's glory days of a decade before, was still in the club, but in the final year of his career.

"Billy was a great help," Young remembers. "And Rod Reddy had been around for a while. But, in the main, we were very young and raw. I went straight into first grade and, while the training was a lot harder than what I was used to, I didn't have too much trouble getting used to the pace of the game in Sydney.

"Even so, my first-grade debut was a bit of a shock. We played a pre-season match against Cronulla and it was like walking onto a battlefield. Cronulla-Saints games in those days were "little brother versus big brother" affairs. They came out all fired up, as if they had something to prove. I remember it was a pretty rugged start for me."

Young did it tough in those early years, working long hours as a coal miner in the Bulli pits, before travelling up the Princes Highway to Saints' training.

"It got to be a bit much," he says. "Eventually, I decided I should give football a real go so I tossed it in. I joined the police force and was with them for quite a few years. It (combining football and police work) was a good mix because it fitted in well with training, and wasn't so physically exhausting."

Harry Bath replaced Langlands as Saints coach in 1977, and, inevitably, Saints' youngsters, were quickly dubbed 'Bath's Babes' in the media. The side had a red-letter season that year, going from rank outsiders to premiers.

"We were very fortunate to have a wily old coach like Harry Bath in charge," Young admits. "He was just what we needed. He knew just how to handle a bunch of keen young blokes and he taught me plenty of tricks that first year that I used for for the rest of my career. Harry kept everyone on the boil. When the grand final came around, we were at our peak. No-one gave us much chance of getting that far; we weren't one of the more fancied teams, and, largely because of our inexperience, everyone thought we'd fall apart under the pressure of semi-final football.

"I didn't even rate us a grand-final chance. Parra were everyone's tip to win after coming close the previous year (when they scored two tries to one, but lost 13-10 to Manly). But once we got to the grand final, we were determined to win it. I'll always remember Harry telling us in one of our last training sessions before the game: 'A lot of players never get as far as a grand final; you might never get another chance so don't blow this one.'

"He made us realise that even though we were young and had a lot of football ahead of us, another chance like this may never come along.

CRAIG YOUNG

Parramatta had a lot more experience than us, but we hung in there and drew the first game 9-all. Then, in the replay, we crushed them 22-nil. I remember, late in the match, being almost in shock at just how big a margin we were winning by. I was still new to the whole Sydney scene and was still coming to terms with being in a grand final, let alone winning one."

The following year, Young, full of confidence after his dream debut season, began to cement his reputation as the finest front-rower of the time, and was selected to make his Test debut against the touring New Zealand side in the third Test, at the SCG. Australia had already won the first two Tests, but, despite the fact the series was decided, Young tore into the Kiwis with grim resolve. He played a key role in Australia's 33-16 win and wrapped up a berth in the Kangaroo team that would travel to Britain and France later that season.

Young was an immediate success on that tour. In fact, it was on the heavy grounds of England that he cemented his spot in Australia's Test squad for the next several years. He played 16 matches on tour, more than any other forward, including all five Tests against Great Britain and France.

"It was a great learning experience for me over there," he says. "Some of those smart Pommy forwards taught me a thing or two. We beat them in the first Test, but then they brought back all their old blokes in the second and turned on the biff. They just beat us, but we fought fire with fire in the decider and won fairly comfortably."

Early in 1979, coach Bath pulled him aside and hit him with a shock announcement.

"Harry called me over at training and just said: 'Albert, you're captain.'" Young remembers. "Steve Edge, our skipper through 1977, had been dropped to reserve grade in 1978, and our halfback Mark Shulman and then Rod Reddy (when Shulman had to retire because of injury) had had the job for the rest of that season. But in 1979, I was to be the man. I was shocked for a while, but because we were all about the same age, it worked out all right. I didn't have any old hard heads around to give me a tough time and everyone pitched in and helped me out. It ended up working out okay and, after a while, I started to enjoy the job."

After a fall from grace in 1978, Saints again won the title in 1979, giving Young his greatest success as a first-grade captain. Although only 23 years old and a league player for less than seven seasons, Young proved an inspirational leader as Saints downed Canterbury 17-13 in a thrilling grand final.

"We jumped to a big lead, then they gave us a scare," Young says. "But

HIT MEN

we hung on and it was one of my sweetest moments to hold up the shield after it was all over. Captaining the team to the title, especially at the Sydney Cricket Ground, was just great."

Players who experienced Young's captaincy confirm that Albert didn't use stirring rhetoric to get the best from his team-mates; here was a captain who led by example.

"He didn't say much, but he got his message across," one former team-mate explains. "And if you weren't doing you're job, he'd let you know it. He always led from the front and was very effective in getting other players in the team to follow."

Young was again a key man when Australia met the British down under in 1979, shattering the tourists' spirit with his power up front as the Aussies cruised to a 3-nil series whitewash. Three seasons later, on the 1982 Kangaroo tour, Young played arguably his best football as the Aussies again outclassed every side they met. The Invincibles' forward pack, with forwards like Young, Les Boyd and Ray Price at their peak, laid the foundations for brilliant backs Peter Sterling, Brett Kenny, Steve Rogers and Mal Meninga to finish the opposition off in emphatic style. The Roos won all 23 matches on tour, earning rave reviews wherever they played. And, while the wins over Great Britain were to be savoured, for Young and his fellow survivors of the 1978 tour, the two Test wins over France were just as satisfying. After suffering a shock series loss to the French under local referees in 1978, the Kangaroos reversed the result under neutral refs in 1982.

"We owed them one," Young recalls. "It was an honour to be a member of the first undefeated touring team. They'll all tell you that playing for Australia beats everything and that was certainly what I found. To be part of such a historic tour will always give me a buzz. They were the best team I ever played with and a great bunch of blokes as well. That was as good as it got as far as I was concerned."

Young had the dubious honour of marking Arthur Beetson in league's first State of Origin clash, at Lang Park in 1980. Although past his prime, Beetson rose to the occasion with a classic display. However, although the NSW front row of Young, Steve Edge (who had transferred to Parramatta that season) and Souths' Gary Hambly kept the Queensland forwards honest, the Maroons powered to a 20-10 win.

Roy Masters joined the Saints as first-grade coach in 1982, a decade after the pair's successful days with the Australian Schoolboys. In six seasons with St George, Masters achieved some excellent results and was desperately unlucky not to win a premiership. However, the pair had something of a rocky start to their association when Young was dropped for

CRAIG YOUNG

the only time in his career early in Masters' first season.

"I'd been playing with injury and it was a bit of a rude shock to go down," he says. "I only played a couple of games in reserves and it was a bit hard to take. But I got back quickly and it didn't do me any harm.

"Roy was a top coach and I really enjoyed our time together at Saints. In 1984 we had a great chance of taking the title but were beaten in the last couple of minutes by Parramatta in the final. In '85 we had a great year by winning the club championship and reaching the grand final in all three grades. We won the two minor grades but lost first grade by a point to Canterbury."

Young stood down from the representative scene after the 1984 season, in which he played in only one of the three Tests against Great Britain, his 20th appearance in a Test match.

"I'd been in representative teams for quite a few years and wanted to concentrate on my club football and spend a bit more time with my kids," he says. "I'd achieved what I wanted to at that level and there were plenty of good young players coming through."

Young's playing career concluded at the end of the 1988 season, but he went out in style, leading Saints to the mid-week Panasonic Cup during that year. The Dragons went into the Cup final against mid-week specialists Balmain as underdogs but pulled off a spirited upset. When the season closed, Young, with 13 seasons and 234 first-grade games to his credit, retired to take on a new challenge — coaching.

"It was a hard decision to make, but I'd done what I wanted to in the game so it was probably the right time," he says. "I thought it was no good hanging around and winding up in reserve grade — I wanted to choose the time to go out."

It was when he began coaching that Young's life at St George began to turn sour. Brought in to replace Ted Glossop, who had been sacked after one season by the Dragons' committee, Young had little time to settle in to the job. The rapid transition from player to coach didn't sit comfortably with Young and he believes he never received the full support of some senior players who had been team-mates not long before. Although he was able to lead by example as a captain, Young couldn't get the best out of his players from up in the grandstand. His side finished well down the ladder in both 1989 and 1990 and by the end of that second season, the knives were out.

"I learned about all the back-stabbing and intrigue that goes on," Young comments bitterly. "We hadn't gone well but I never saw it (his sacking) coming. Just before the second-last game of 1990 they called me in and told me I was finished. I was very dirty and still am. It was a low way to finish a long association with a club I'd never given anything but my fullest loyalty to for 14 years. I still keep in touch with a few of the players but I've never been back to the club — and probably never will. I now coach Wests in the local league in Wollongong and we made the grand final in my first year in 1993. There are some good young players down here and it's close to the hotel where I work."

Young now owns the Unanderra Hotel, 10 kilometres south of Wollongong, and has successfully established the business after some hard times early.

"It's a tough game, the pub business, but we're doing okay now," he says. "We had a fire at the start of 1994 that caused $300,000 damage. Later that day I was serving beers — the show always goes on."

Sadly, the rift between Saints and Craig Young, one of the finest forwards ever to wear the red and white, is unlikely to ever be healed. The hard, sometimes ruthless process of board-room decision making has left the former Test forward forever convinced he was hard done by. But in the hearts of Saints fans, Young remains a favourite son — a rugged competitor whose loyalty to the red-and-white cause could never be questioned.

There have been few more popular 'wild' men than Western Suburbs **John *'Dallas'* Donnelly** (right), who, perhaps more than any other player, captured his club's 'fibro' image of the late 1970s and early '80s.

Below: ***Donnelly*** argues with referee Kevin Roberts during a match against St George at Lidcombe Oval.

Below: ***Donnelly*** charges at the Canterbury defence that includes George Peponis (number 12) and Chris Mortimer (right) during the 1979 minor preliminary semi-final at the SCG.

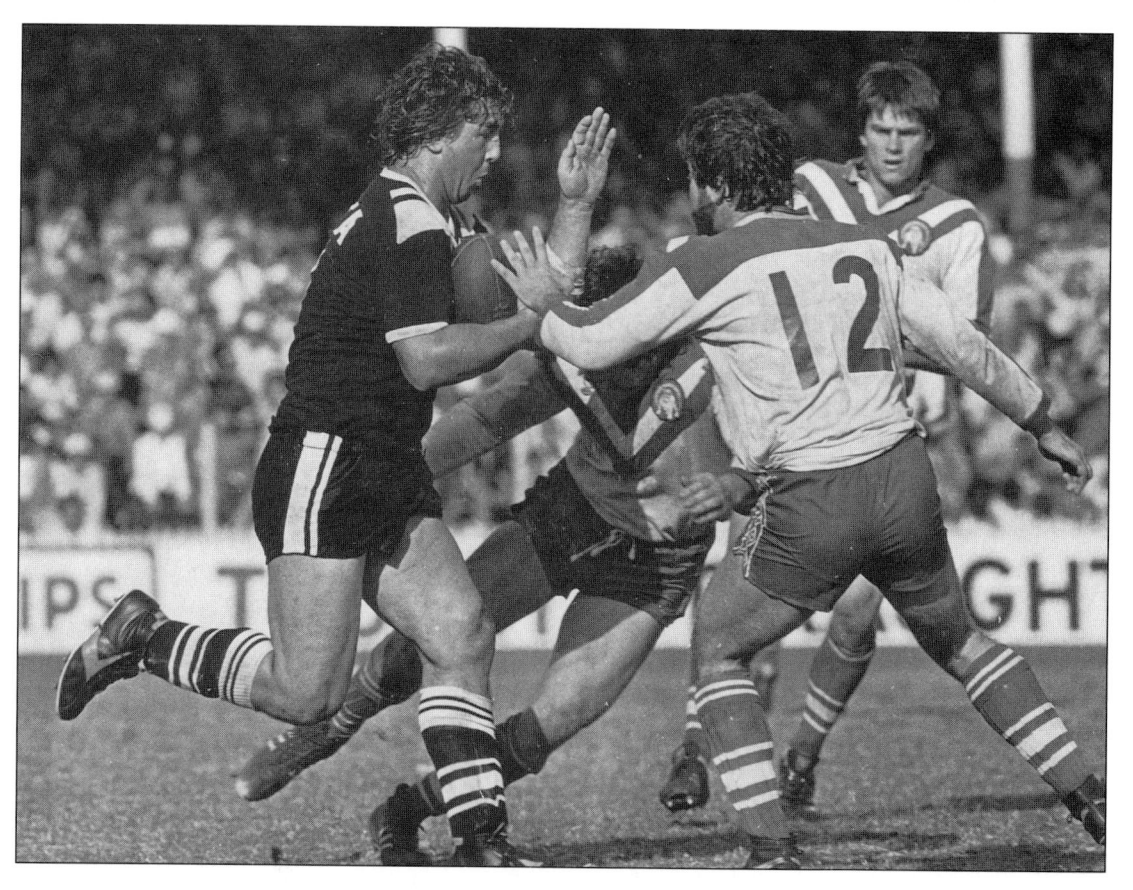

Right: A young **Rod *'Rocket'* Reddy** (right) grapples with Parramatta iron man Bob O'Reilly.

Left: *Reddy* attacking Parramatta's John Baker during the brutal opening to the 1977 Grand Final replay. Many critics considered Reddy lucky to stay on the field after he received four cautions for violent play. The other Saints defender is *Craig Young*, the Eels player immediately behind Baker is captain Ray Higgs.

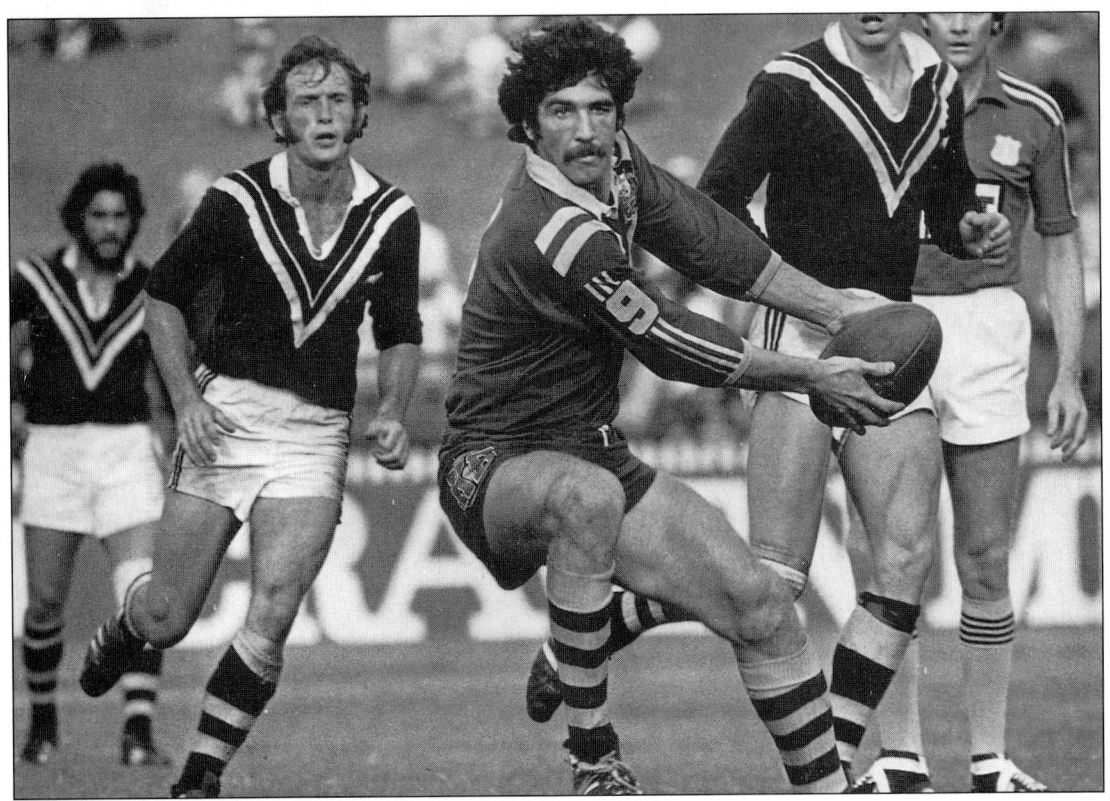

Reddy during his Test debut against New Zealand in 1978.

Above: Two of the late '70s and early '80s toughest men, **Reddy** and Manly's **Les Boyd**, settle their differences during a premiership match at Kogarah Oval early in 1983. Both players were sent to the sin bin, where they were captured by television cameras sharing a joke. But when the two returned to the field, they were soon brawling once again.

Boyd was once labelled by a Sydney journalist as 'the baby-faced killer'. In 1983 and 1984 he received lengthy suspensions that effectively drove him from the Sydney league scene.

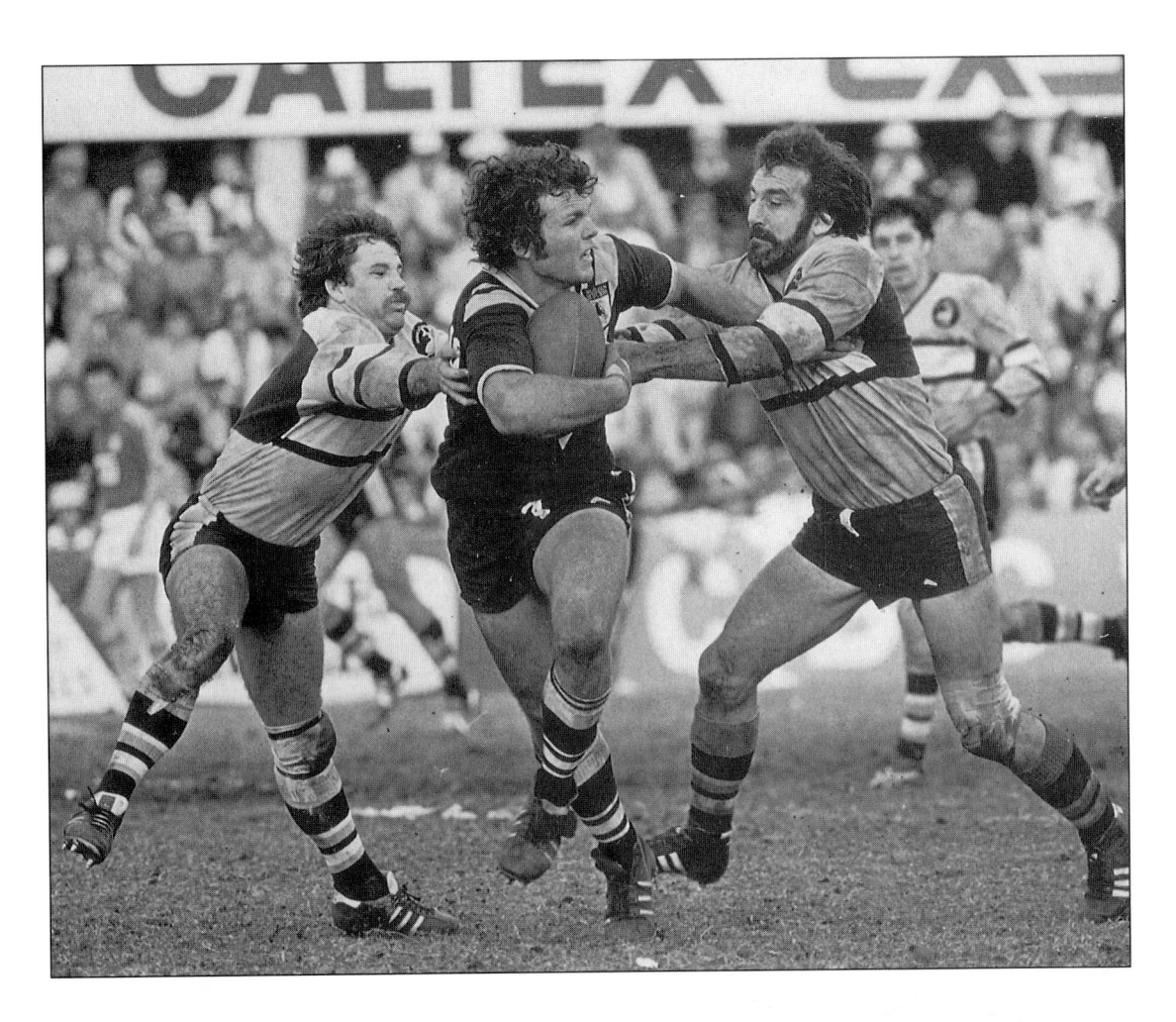

Above: **Boyd**, playing for Wests in 1978, charges between Cronulla's Steve Hansard (left) and John McMartin. Wests, coached by the controversial Roy Masters, won this final-round match 18-17, to win the minor premiership, but then lost in successive weeks in the finals, to miss a spot in the grand final. It was during 1978, arguably Boyd's finest season, that Masters first labelled Wests as the 'fibros', a symbol of the working-class suburbs they represented.

Right: **Boyd** wearing the colours of English club Warrington, where he resumed his career in 1985 and won a premiership winner's medal in 1986.

Above: **Ron Hilditch** playing hooker for Parramatta against St George in 1976, his first season in first grade, in the days before he earned the nickname 'Hit Man'.

Below: **Geoff Robinson**, Canterbury's 'wild man' of the early '80s, after a match against Cronulla.

Above: **Hilditch** in 1981, by now an international front-rower, shaping up to Steve Blyth of Newtown.

Left: **Robinson** challenged by Easts' centre Kerry Boustead during the 1980 Grand Final, which the Bulldogs won 18-4, their first premiership win since 1942.

Below: Canterbury missed the semis in 1981 and 1982, but came back in '83 to reach the preliminary final, where they were knocked out by eventual premiers Parramatta. **Robinson**, a key part of that side, is pictured fending off the Eels' tough front-rower Geoff Bugden. The other Bulldogs are second-rower Mick Pitman (at back) and lock Tas Baiteri.

Right: St George's *Craig Young*, one of the best of the many great props to pack down with the Dragons, cops a caution from referee Barry Barnes.

Left: *Young* pleads innocence after a play-the-ball fracas with one of his toughest rivals - Canterbury's *Peter Kelly*.

Below: *Kelly* establishes a record that may never be broken - sent off after the first tackle of the Bulldogs' Anzac Day 1986 clash with Souths at the SCG.

The other side of *Peter Kelly*, keeping the ball alive in a match against the Bulldogs' chief rivals of the mid '80s - Parramatta. The tackler (number one) is Paul Taylor, the Eel defender (at right) the great Ray Price.

A photo sequence from the early minutes of the 1989 grand final classic between Canberra and Balmain.

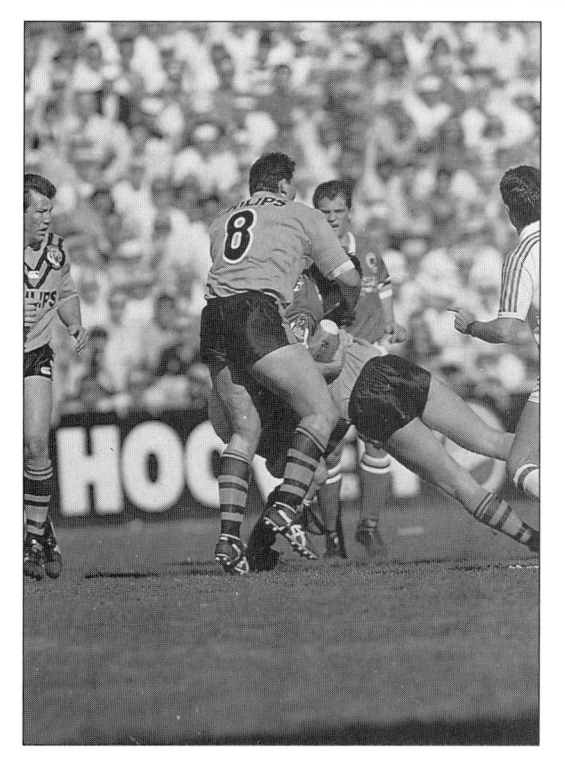

Top left: *Steve Roach (No.8) moves in to help team-mate Steve Edmed tackle Canberra lock Bradley Clyde.*

Top right: *The players react to the sound of referee Bill Harrigan's whistle.*

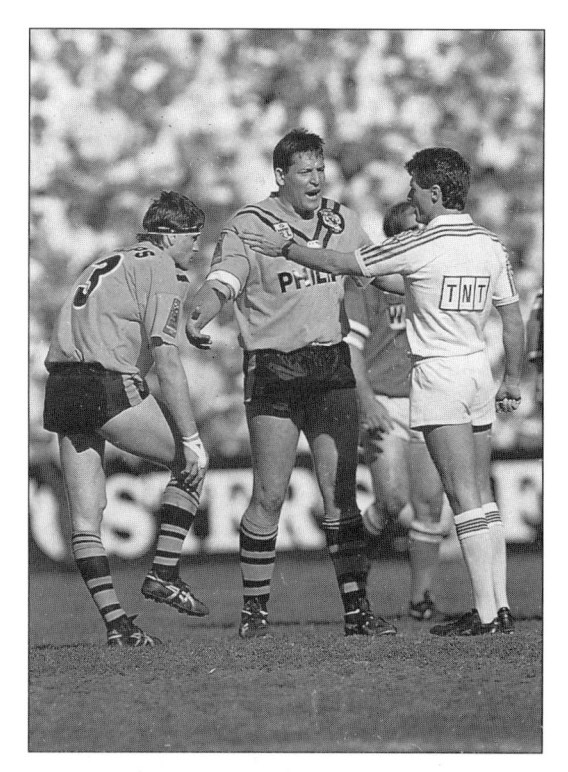

Bottom left: *As Clyde gets to his feet, Roach is called out for a caution.*

Bottom right: *Despite the protests of Roach, and the presence of Tigers captain Wayne Pearce, the penalty is going to the Raiders.*

Left: **Steve Roach** with his front-row partner from the 1990 Kangaroo tour, **Glenn Lazarus**.

Below: Balmain's *Roach* (right) and Canberra's *Lazarus* resume acquaintances during the 1991 Australian season.

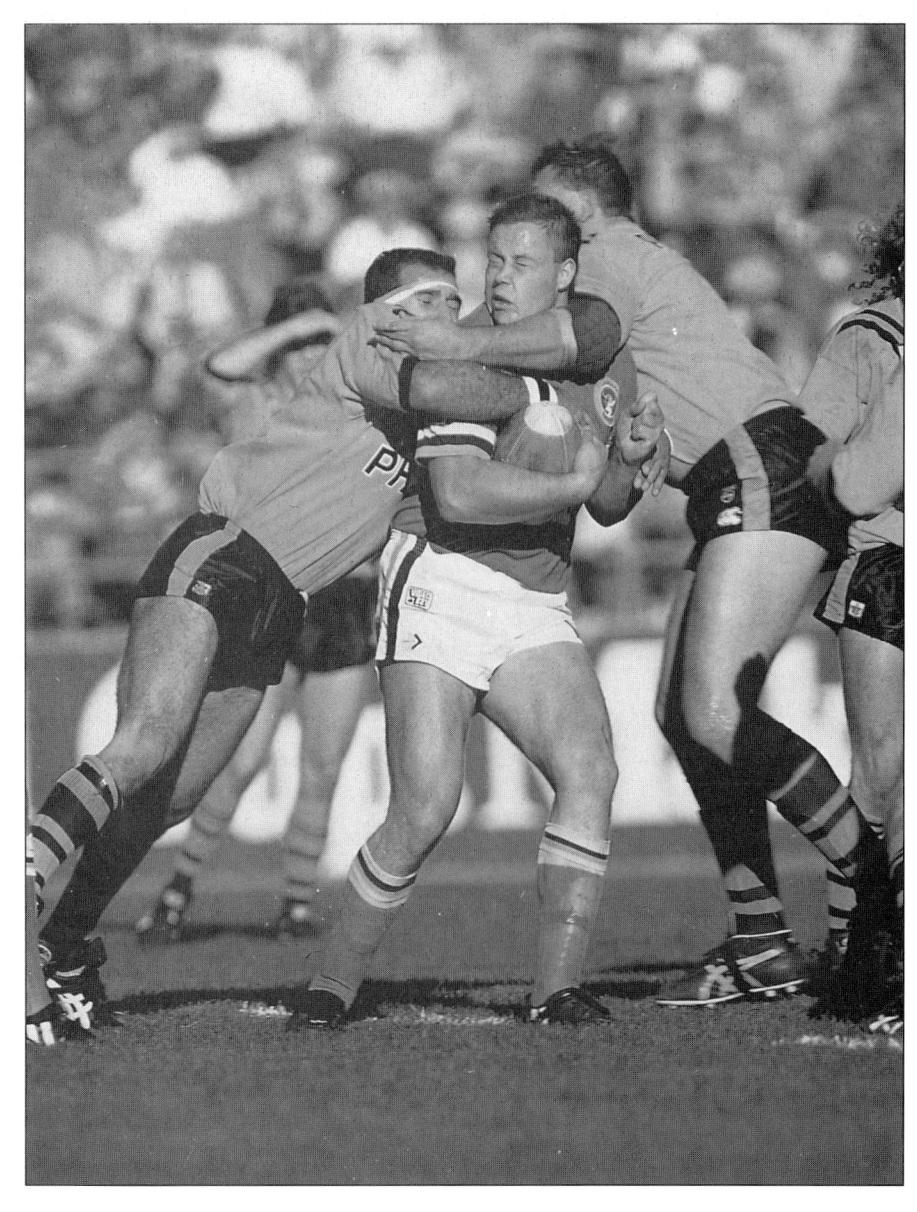

Lazarus playing for Brisbane in 1994.

Above: Penrith's John Cartwright (left) and *Mark Geyer*, with the Winfield Cup after the Panthers come-from-behind victory in the 1991 Grand Final. At this point in his career, Geyer was one of the game's most feared and respected players, and an integral part of the Australian Test team.

But by the 1994 pre-season (below), after a series of personal traumas and a much-publicised split with the Penrith club, Geyer was struggling to make an impact with Balmain. This shot was one of the last taken of Geyer in a Tigers jumper. After just two rounds of the '94 premiership, he was granted a release from the club.

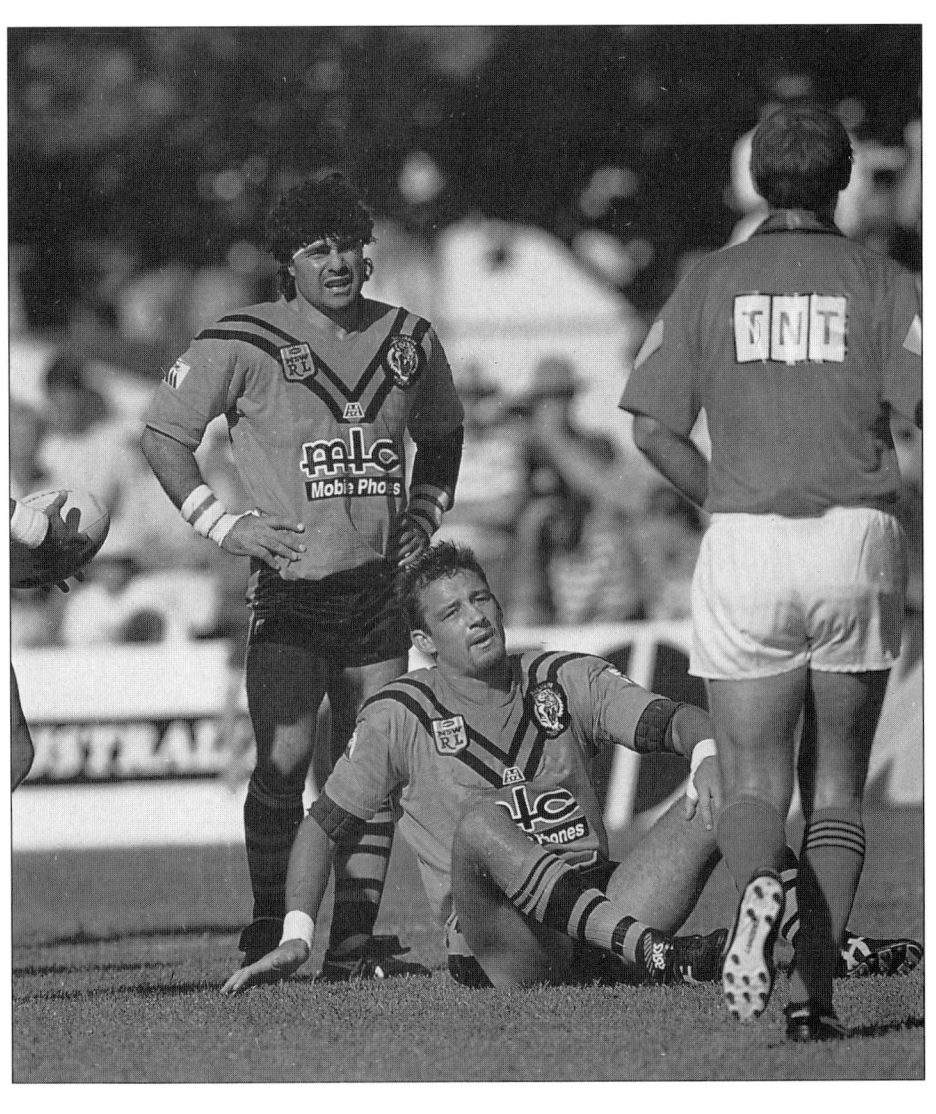

Geyer at his best - the imposing forward who made such an impact with the Panthers.

Below left *Craig Salvatori*, the ball distributor, showing some of the skills that remind people of another of Easts finest forwards - the legendary *Arthur Beetson* (above).

Above right: Easts *Salvatori*, in close contact with *Blocker Roach*.

Paul Harragon, of Newcastle, NSW and Australia, runs straight at Queenslands Bob Lindner during the 1993 State of Origin series.

Paul Harragon - the classic '21st century' hard man.

HIT MEN

PETER KELLY

Leader of the Gang

Peter Kelly breaks out in a sheepish grin whenever he refers to his unique entry in rugby league's book of records. Kelly holds the dubious distinction of being dismissed from the field in the quickest time recorded — just 16 seconds to be exact.

The former Newtown, Canterbury and Penrith enforcer, known simply as "Kel", believes it's a record that's unlikely to be beaten. "But the one consolation is that I still believe I'm innocent," Kelly says with a wry smile as he recalls the incident in question.

"We were playing South Sydney on Anzac Day at the SCG in 1986. We had this V-formation at the kick-off and, because I was the slowest player in the team, I was in the centre of the V. The formation made a player think he was making a good run ... and then I'd hammer him.

"Souths winger Ross Harrington brought the ball up, and I launched myself and hit him at what I thought was shoulder height. I absolutely creamed him.

"I still regard it as the best tackle I made in my career. He was knocked out by the impact. He was carted off on a stretcher and I was immediately given my marching orders.

"It's a funny feeling to have a world record. I'm not very proud of it, but it is a record I'll probably always have.

"All I can do is laugh about it now. The bugler had been out on the centre just before kick-off playing the last post. He was an old bloke — must have been 90 in the shade — and I beat him off the park. He was toddling off with our president Barry Nelson and as I ran past, I heard Barry say to the bugler: 'Oh, he must have forgotten his mouthguard.'

"The SCG was rock hard in those days and I'd put a gallon of vaseline on my legs. I didn't see a minute of the first half; I was too busy in the shower trying to get the bloody vaso off. I was all dressed up with nowhere to go."

Peter Kelly grew up in the quiet town of Eden on the NSW south coast. Being the third of five brothers, he quickly learned to stick up for himself. His earliest memories of football are of playing with all the kids in Bungo Street, Eden, with the "Kelly Gang" leading the charge.

"We played a lot of backyard games and most of us ended up being reasonably good sporting people." Kelly recalls today. "When Eden won premierships years later, the team had more than a few of the Bungo Street mob in it.

"My dad, Tom, was my first coach when I started playing fair dinkum stuff at around eight or nine. But I had trouble getting a game in those early days. To put it simply, I was too fat and mum and dad weren't keen for me to play. I spent a lot of time on the reserve bench. My best early memories are of the under 12-to-13s. We had some great battles against St Pats in Bega. They were from a bigger town and we liked giving it to them.

"My parents sent me to St Joseph's College in Sydney for two years when I was 13. It was a traditional rugby union boarding school, which I enjoyed, though I found, unfortunately, that I excelled at rugby but not at anything else. The experience toughened me up, mentally and physically, and, being a boarder with a lot of time on my hands, I learned how to train.

"I believe my strict Catholic upbringing was to help my football in later life. It taught me discipline ...

"When I went back to Eden they didn't have an under-16s side, so I was whacked straight into the under-18s. I was a bit worried but, after two games, was in the Group under-18s side.

"In my early days I was often playing against older blokes which helped mature me. It was a good apprenticeship and by 17, I was playing first grade for Eden."

The Kelly Gang remains well known on the NSW south coast for its footballing prowess and toughness, but Kel winces when he recalls one match that became a bit too much of a family affair.

"We were playing a team called Bombala-Delegate and they had a guy called Doug Cameron in their side. He was the group hard-man and used to have a lot of run-ins with my older brother Gerard. On this day, Doug and Gerard got stuck into each other. It started with punches but quickly degenerated to head butts and knees in the nuts. It was a good old blue with no rules and both gave as good as they got.

"I remember Doug Cameron's wife was eight months pregnant at the time and looked ready to drop the baby at any second. But that didn't stop her charging onto the field and getting stuck into Gerard. My mum was working behind the counter in the canteen and seeing this, she bolted on as

PETER KELLY

well and the two ladies had a stink. I didn't know which way to look but was determined not to get involved.

"It was a classic. A couple of years later, Doug and I had a set-to ourselves. He was a hard bastard."

Peter Kelly played in two grand finals for Eden, losing the first but winning the second. His reputation grew, and in 1979, at just 18, he received an offer to play for Lakes United in Newcastle. He was able to transfer his apprenticeship as a mechanic to Newcastle and travelled north to begin his life as a football journeyman.

In the Hunter he made a quick impression, winning selection in the Newcastle divisional side that won the NSW country championships. The following season he transferred to another Newcastle club, Waratah-Mayfield, where his reputation as an up-and-coming knuckleman resulted in more than one on-field battle.

"One day we were playing against North Newcastle," recalls Kelly, "and they had one of the toughest packs in the comp up there. Early in the game I was taking the ball up and accidentally elbowed in the head a bloke who was trying to tackle me. He went down in a screaming heap and had to be carried off.

"From that moment I was a marked man. The next time I took the ball up a bloke belted me from the left and then another came in from the right and king-hit me. The blow was one of the hardest I ever copped. I remember blowing my nose ... and snot came out of my temple. After the match, I found out the bloke who hit me had only been released from jail the previous week. I copped a broken skull, black eye and stitches, and he got a one-week suspension. The poor, stupid young fool that I was, I backed up the next week with my head all bandaged up ... trying to get myself killed."

Kelly's football career then took an entirely different direction when he headed to France in 1981, with three mates spending a season with the Entraigues club. For a country boy who had never been out of NSW, the experience was an eye-opener.

"The standard of football was average but the thing that appealed to us was that training was non-existent. It was too cold for that, so you didn't do much other than party. On the field, there were some hard men but in a different sense to what we're used to here.

"One day against Carcassone one of my mates gave a French player a hiding. So *three* of them got stuck into him and opened his head up with their studs. He was carried off on a stretcher. I wasn't impressed, and gave away a few penalties that day.

"In another match, we played a team called Le Pontet, the best team in France at the time. Seconds before halftime they scored a try, but, just as the referee was about to award the try, one of our players belted him. The ref composed himself, sent our bloke off, and was about to finally give the try when another of our blokes king-hit him and knocked him to the ground. The ref struggled to his feet and then called the game off as the crowd started spilling over the fence. As the ref was walking off, *another* of our blokes got into him, this time knocking him out cold. They had to carry the bloke back to the room. And then it was really on.

"When it all died down, all that happened was that we had two home games taken away from us. They're very emotional crowds over there. I've seen fans run onto the ground and kick players in the backside or poke them with an umbrella.

"It was a lot of fun, even though the club expected a bit more from us than they actually got. But I went back 10 years later and they threw me a civic reception, so I think they liked me. I remember I turned up in thongs and stubbies and they had a good laugh.

"'In ze 10 years, you have not changed, Peter,' the club president said."

Kelly returned to Eden in 1981 and realised it was time to go for the big league. Canberra and Illawarra were set to enter the premiership the following season and Kelly, technically a Canberra junior, was set to become a Raider. But it wasn't to be.

"Warren Ryan, who was coaching Newtown at the time, rang and said he wanted me to play for him. He offered me $2000, which seemed a fortune at the time.

"I said: 'Where do I sign?'

"I came to sign on the day of the infamous Manly-Newtown brawl in the '81 minor semi at the SCG. I walked into the leagues club that night and saw all the people cheering and yelling as they watched the players belting the crap out of each other on a big-screen TV. I thought to myself: 'Oh my God, what have I got myself into here?'

"But it turned out a good move, Newtown went on to make the grand final and then their big prop, Geoff Bugden (who had won the Rothmans Medal in 1980), joined Parramatta. I was one of the few people to walk straight into first grade from the bush. I never played a reserve-grade game at Newtown.

Kelly was a bundle of nerves in the months before he joined the Jets for pre-season training.

"Before I came up, I worked on a tuna boat for two months. I remember unloading fish and thinking about the great front-rowers like Craig Young and company that I'd be facing. I'd pretend the fish were them. I'd throw the big crates all around the boat. I was shit scared — trying to work up some courage for what lay ahead.

PETER KELLY

"Luckily, at Newtown I had a good team around me which made it a lot easier. Steve Bowden (who had been sent off in that Newtown-Manly stoush) was the hard man of Sydney then and he taught me a lot. He wasn't all that skilful but he was tough, mentally and physically. He had a reputation, and was well-respected.

"I wasn't a strong specimen at the time after spending eight months in France swilling red wine, but they quickly knocked me into shape. Warren ran a tight ship and we trained a lot with Johnny Lewis at his Newtown gym. Jeff Fenech was just a young pup on the way up at the time and would often join in our sessions. We did a lot of boxing, wrestling and strength work and it all taught me the body can go through a lot more than I had imagined.

"We had some top players — Phil Sigsworth, Mick Ryan, Mark Bugden, Col Murphy — blokes who'd been around. I was confident I could handle the game physically but big "Bowdo" gave me the mental toughness.

"'Just keep going no matter what happens,' he told me time and again. 'Never give up.'"

However, it wasn't all smooth sailing for Kelly with his new team-mates. In fact, his first training session almost became his last.

"I drove up on the Friday from Eden with my fiancee (now wife), Lorraine. We footballers went for a run around Coogee and then we all hit the pub.

"I was having a serious chat with Warren Ryan about the game and my future when Lorraine, who'd had a few by then, came up crying. She was complaining that one of my new team-mates was trying to crack onto her. I told her to leave me alone: 'You handle it ... can't you see I'm talking to the coach?'

"She came back a few minutes later hysterical at something her 'admirer' had said. I ended up leaving Warren and belting the bloke. I think they were trying to test me out at the time. From that day, they knew they had someone a bit different on their hands. The bloke I belted didn't seem to carry a grudge and, in the end, we became the best of mates."

The rough-and-ready world of Sydney football brought out the best in Kelly. In only his second season, 1983, he was made the Jets' skipper. He was just 23 at the time, making him one of the youngest captains in the game.

"It was a proud moment for me and we faced a real test , against Saints," he recalls. "They had a great pack including Young, Pat Jarvis, Robert Stone, Graeme Wynn and Graeme O'Grady. And they were just as good out wide, with guys like Michael O'Connor and Steve 'Slippery' Morris.

"I played opposite Craig Young and thought: 'Well, if he's the best, I've got to come up to his standard to make a success of this captaincy caper.'

"I got myself all fired up before the game. I used to build up a pretend anger. Not go off my head, but sort of meditate. Have a good think about what I was going to do. It put me in the right frame of mind for what lay ahead. In this game, in the second scrum, there was a flare-up and Craig and I stood eye to eye. We were going to give it to each other but the ref stepped in. There were no punches thrown but I could tell by just looking in his eye that I had his measure. In the front row you can sense these things and that gave me a hell of a lot of confidence. There was no stopping me from there. In the next few minutes I scored a try beside the posts and we won 7-6. I never mentioned it to anyone, but that was a big moment in my career — getting the respect of such a well-known international from one of Sydney's strongest clubs.

"A few games later I got picked in the first Country Origin team, which was a big break. City won a close game but I thought I held my own. As we left the field City's Geoff Bugden shook my hand and said: 'You were the best prop on the field today. You should get in the State team.' It was great to get that acknowledgement, but the blue jumper never eventuated at that time."

When the Jets "died" at the end of 1983, Kelly found himself in search of a new club. With Ryan moving to Canterbury, it seemed only natural that Kelly should follow.

"Their chief executive, Peter Moore, rang one day and said he'd like to meet me," Kelly explains. "He lobbed an hour later in his big Mercedes and we drove around the streets of Newtown. I threw a few numbers at him and he cut them in half, then divided them by four. I knew I was being conned but he got me to sign anyway ... for basically nothing. He was a very astute man that Peter Moore and I learned a lot about him that day.

"I'll never forget sitting with him in the back streets of Newtown in the Merc and being taken for a ride."

Kelly enjoyed four highly-successful years under Ryan at Belmore, playing in three grand finals.

"Warren was a great coach and he perfected playing league in the '80s under the rules of that time," Kelly says. "And I believe the people in Phillip Street who resented him changed the rules largely to thwart him.

"Being a school teacher, he could explain things very well and you always felt you could speak your mind to him. Rugby league is the sort of game where you can smell a weak character within five minutes. We didn't have any. That was our strength at Canterbury in that era. We were the Bullydogs rather than the Bulldogs. We were a strong, powerful side. Warren had hand-picked his personnel — blokes like Terry Lamb, Peter

PETER KELLY

Tunks, Dave Gillespie and myself came to the club. Steve O'Brien and Mick Potter were young blokes coming through. With old hands like Steve Mortimer and Steve Folkes it was a great blend and Warren brought it all together. He instilled a very disciplined approach that Canterbury had never had. Teams were scared of us — and we were so confident when we took the field we had a lot of teams beaten as soon as we kicked off.

"The media built us up as the Bullydogs and we thrived on it. All three grand finals were low-scoring games but in my opinion great matches. We beat Parramatta 6-4 in 1984 and Saints 7-6 the following year, before Parra got us 4-2 in '86.

"We were so well drilled. I remember in the '85 Grand Final against Saints how we just wore them down. We must have put up 20 bombs to Glenn Burgess, their fullback. He was a top player who should have played for Australia, but he was never the same after that game. We just hammered him; he copped a hiding. We never heard of him again. We did such a job on him he just faded into obscurity."

Like most players, Kelly's dream was always to win a grand final and he regards the 1984-5 double — and the man-of-the-match awards he won in both games — as the high-point of his career.

"Both games were such hard struggles and there was such a feeling of relief and joy when it was all over. My team-mates also gave me our players' award in both games, which made it even sweeter.

"But I thought I'd ruffled a few of their feathers in '85 against Saints. At halftime, Warren spoke his mind and then asked anyone else if they wanted to say anything. There was a long silence so I got up and just blasted the life out of some of my team-mates about not having the desire. I really gave it to them, because I didn't think we were playing to our best in the first half. I'm not saying it was all me, but that seemed to turn us around in the second half and we hung on to win."

However, after those heady days of 1984-85-86, the Bulldog team fell apart. Kelly blames much of that on Ryan.

"Warren's uncompromising approach that made us so successful proved the thing that destroyed the team in the long run," he says. "Warren was ruthless to the end and blokes dropped off, and started to back-stab each other. I didn't make a noise when I left (at the end of '87) but I thought the players had lost the desire to compete. I could smell it halfway through '87 — some of the blokes didn't have the determination and drive anymore. The hardness and discipline were gone.

"I had a few offers during that season and went to Penrith under Ron Willey. He never had the tactical genius of Warren but was also a hard, stubborn man. I tried to talk to Ron about a few aspects of forward play and he never really listened. As a result, I lost a lot of respect for him. Eventually Penrith got rid of him because he was just a bit out of touch. Don't get me wrong, he was a good bloke, but he didn't want to listen and I thought he was a bit past his best.

"Willey did, however, bring winning players to the club and he deserves plenty of the credit for Penrith's success in the late '80s and early '90s."

Kelly finally received the call-up to play for NSW while playing for Penrith in 1989. But he was surrounded in controversy after his first match against the Maroons.

"I was selected for the second match of the series and, just before running onto the field, was left with no illusions about why I was selected. Big Sam Backo and Martin Bella (the Queensland props) had run all over NSW in the first game. Two NSW Rugby League officials came up to me before I ran out and told me I was there for a reason — to sort out their forwards. They talked along the lines of: 'No player has ever been sent off in a State of Origin match. You've got an open book to do whatever you want. We'll stand by you no matter what.'

"So I went out and did my job. It was a tight game and a couple of their stars were either taken off or their ability to play the game to their best was effected. But in the aftermath, I got cited to appear before the judiciary for belting Mal Meninga in the eye, and copped a two-week suspension.

"I was filthy; they'd used me and then dumped me. But I've got to give a rap to Jack Gibson for sticking by me. He knew the whole story but, even so, I didn't think he'd pick me in the next game. But he did and his support was very heartening. He showed me everyone wasn't bad at a time when I was very disenchanted with the system.

"I felt that by 1989 my best football was behind me. Everyone gets older and in the front row, a year is like 10 years — your body takes so many knocks. I reckon they picked me at the wrong time; I could have done a much better job in my prime in the mid-1980s. But even so, I was grateful and proud to get a chance to represent my state."

Peter Kelly never wore the green and gold, but on more than one occasion, in his nine years in the Winfield Cup, had to watch front-rowers with less ability play Test football.

"I knew within myself that I had played all over Bella and Backo in my Origin debut. They won the game but when we got off the field, I sat in my corner and was satisfied. I could handle any front-rower on my day and know I could have played Test football.

"I believe success in this game is all mental and my ruthless approach often won me the day. There's a fine line in league between a great player and a dog. I've come up against better players in my time and got on top of them by just being relentless. If I didn't get on top of them one game, I'd be ready for them and get on top of them next time. Not many players suckered me more than once. I loved the game so much that I'd keep coming and coming. I would have loved to play for my country but I did a few things off the field, which I don't want to discuss, that harmed my image with Phillip Street."

Kelly had a love-hate relationship with referees over the years. "The truth of the matter is I never spoke to them," he says. "I totally ignored them. There was an element of risk in it but I tried to put them down through silence. I wouldn't even acknowledge they were there. I'd look down at my boots when they spoke to me. I used to walk away half way through their talks and they'd call me back as if I was a schoolboy. Then I knew I was getting on their goat. In retrospect, it wasn't a real smart thing to do because after a while, I think they started looking out for me.

"The refs did me no favours but I hold no grudges. Mick Stone sent me off about four times. Out of the blue a couple of months ago he walked into my pub and we had a few beers together. I got cited a few times but, I've got to admit, mostly it was warranted. That was the way I played the game and I accepted the consequences."

"But silence can be a useful weapon. I remember Steve Roach one day saying to me in a club game against Balmain: 'I'm gonna get you Kelly, you mongrel, you did this and you did that and you're going to pay.' I just nodded my head at him ... and proceeded to give it to him all day. I think we belted them by about 30 points."

While working as manager of the Lapstone Hotel at the foot of the Blue Mountains, Kelly is often asked to rate the toughest opponent he has faced.

"Anyone who plays league is tough," is always the lead-in to his answer. "There were plenty of good players I came up against over the years, but the hardest player I had to handle was the Englishman, Kevin Ward. I only played against him once, in 1988, when he was playing for Manly. We had to beat them at Penrith in a vital game and looking back, I took him too lightly, believing he was like other Poms — out here for a holiday. But this guy was strong, fit, and skilful. He was just a bit bigger than me and I found him a handful. I've got to say he played all over me that day. If I had played against him again, I'd have slowly nullified his game. But I never got the chance.

"Craig Young was a brick shithouse and if he didn't want to be moved, you couldn't budge him. Geoff Robinson just threw himself into the game and I respected his lack of fear. And I used to hate running at blokes like Dave Gillespie, because you knew your nose would get jammed two centimetres under the turf. Steve Bowden was one of the hardest blokes I knew.

HIT MEN

Then of course there was old Doug Cameron back in Eden ...

"But I also rated Terry Lamb a hard man. He would love to play and would do so every day if he could. He thrived on it and kept coming back for more. Ability-wise I'd rate Ward the best, while Bowden, physically, was the toughest player I knew. Luckily I never played against him."

A crippling back injury forced Kelly out of the game in 1990 but he has maintained contact with the code by coaching Penrith's reserve-grade side. "I try to help the players with the lessons I learned over the years," he says. "I tell them you must want to do it and be mentally tough to succeed.

"We had a bad year in 1993 and only retained about two of the 20 players in the squad for '94. They were losers and unprofessional. Many had the ability but wouldn't commit themselves. My expectations were higher than theirs ...

"I believe those that weren't mentally tough will struggle in life as well as on the football field."

HIT MEN

STEVE ROACH

Eye of the Tiger

No player in rugby league in the '80s had the ability to draw controversial headlines more consistently than Steve "Blocker" Roach. Roach's temper and antics found the Balmain giant in hot water time and again — but the big man weathered the storm to play 12 highly-successful seasons for the Tigers. A classy ball-player, with the ability to win games on his own, Roach was a marvellous front-rower who helped propel his club to two grand finals, although both ended in disappointment. He was also a key man in NSW State of Origin teams from 1984 to 1991 and played 19 Tests for his country.

However, Roach will be remembered as much for other things — his infamous head-patting incident with referee Eddie Ward, his feuds with Jack Gibson, his daring attempt to beat suspension from the 1988 grand final by flying to Britain, and his regular stoushes with many of league's toughest men of the past decade.

Roach's life has always been colourful and the Tiger stalwart makes no apologies for that, even if he did rub officials the wrong way more than once.

"I just did things on the spur of the moment," he claims. "If I had a minute to stop and think I probably wouldn't have done a lot of the them. That's just the way I was. But on the field I never gouged or bit or kicked anyone — I never did anything I was ashamed of."

Roach was always destined to be a front-rower. "I started there in the under-sevens for Wests in Wollongong and, even then, I knew I was there for good. There was only one other place to go — the bench. I was a big kid right from the start and it was the natural place to play."

Roach progressed through the grades at Wests, and found himself in the Illawarra and Country under-18 sides in 1979. It was around that time that

HIT MEN

a talent scout in the Wollongong area, Noel Yeomans, gave Balmain an early tip on the young front-rower's potential.

"Noel only sent three blokes to Sydney — Allan McMahon, Garry Jack and me and we all went on to play for Australia — so he's got a fair record," Roach says.

Roach, his father and Yeomans drove to Sydney and discussed the youngster's future with the Tigers chief executive, Keith Barnes, over some beers in a Balmain Leagues Club bar. Roach was only 16 at the time — little did anyone at the table that day know Blocker would break the rules many more times over the next decade.

"I was over the moon to get some interest from a big Sydney club. Barnsey signed me on a scholarship, and I played for a couple of years with the Balmain Police Boys club as well as in the Flegg and President's Cups for Balmain. I came to grade in 1982 and it was hard but I was that keen that nothing was going to stop me. I remember my first game in grade was in reserves against Parramatta and they had Kevin "Stumpy" Stevens in their pack. He was a tough old nut at that stage of his career, even though I didn't know who he was at the time. I'll never forget our coach Laurie Freier pulling me aside and saying to me: 'I want you to run at Stevens as hard as you can the first time you get the ball ... because then you'll know why I never want you to run at him again.' I was young and keen and obedient and I did what Laurie said — and Stumpy absolutely smashed me. But I learned from it. I was smart enough to keep away from him after that."

The following week Balmain met Souths at Leichhardt Oval and Roach found himself up against Peter Tunks, who in two years time would be playing State of Origin football with the young Balmain prop. Tunks decided to test the mettle of the new kid on the block ... and Roach wasted no time replying.

"We belted each other that many times the ref got sick of us and sent us both off. But it didn't stop there. I was so filthy I wanted to take him on behind the grandstand and settle the issue. We ended up trading blows in the tunnel. Funnily enough, Tunksy and I turned out to be good mates. We played Tests and State of Origin football together and have been out as a foursome with our girls. We've had a good laugh about that first meeting plenty of times."

Later that season, Roach made his first-grade debut, ironically against Illawarra.

"They all knew I was from the 'Gong and gave me plenty during the game," Roach recalls. "But we had a good side that day and just won it 17-16. The game I'll always remember came a couple of weeks later against St

STEVE ROACH

George. Kerry Hemsley and I were the Balmain front-rowers and we were just pups compared with the likes of Craig Young, Robert Stone and Rod Reddy. They bashed us, stomped on us — I finished with concussion and I ached for days. That was really my welcome to first grade."

It was in those early days in first grade that Roach was handed his nickname of Blocker. "But it actually started as 'Blockhead'," he reveals, "because of the way I'd charge into opposition forwards. Thankfully, it eventually became 'Blocker'. I could live with that."

Roach played for City in 1984 and was selected to play for New South Wales in his State of Origin debut that same season. Playing for the Blues held special significance for Roach, because alongside him in the front row was St George warhorse Craig Young.

"Craig was one of my heroes when I was a kid and the idea of packing down in the same front row as him tickled me pink," Roach remembers. "We'd played against each other a couple of times by then and even traded blows once or twice, but I still respected him immensely. On the flight up to Brisbane, 'Albert' turned to me and said: 'We've got to give it to those cane toad bastards'. With the look on Craig's face, I wasn't about to disagree with him. But when we got onto Lang Park, things didn't go exactly to plan. We'd barely kicked off when big Dave Brown (the Queensland prop) laid Albert out with a well-timed punch. I remember seeing poor Albert down there on the deck and thinking: 'Hey, we're the ones supposed to be getting into them.'

"We lost that series 2-1, but it was still a great introduction to Origin football for me. I've played the game at all levels and there's no doubt it's the hardest, toughest football there is."

A year later after starring at Origin level, Roach won his Test spurs for the series against New Zealand, which involved one match (the first Test) at Lang Park, and two matches in New Zealand.

"I was at my wife-to-be Cathy's house when the team for the first Test came across on the radio and I don't mind saying I cried — in fact I bawled my eyes out. The thing with me, I never had much else besides football. I wasn't a Rhodes Scholar and knew that footy was my path to success. Getting that green-and-gold jumper confirmed to me that I'd made it to the top. I just burst with pride and excitement.

"I was only 21 at the time and still fairly new to top-level football. The Kiwis had this hard man called Kevin Tamati and he took it upon himself to sort out both me and our other front-rower Greg Dowling. I was the appetiser and Greg was the main course. Tamati was a former boxer and, after we'd met each other early in the piece, I judged he must have been a fairly good one too. He belted me — I'd have to say it was the worst hiding I ever got on the field. To make matters worse, poor Cathy had flown all the way up from Sydney to see it. Then, after dealing with me, Tamati switched his attention to Dowling and the pair went at it like a couple of heavyweights. They were sent off but it didn't end there and as they left the field, they really got stuck into each other on the way back to the dressing room. We won the match 26-20, but they took most of the points in the fight."

Roach made the 1986 Kangaroo tour and played in the first Test win over Great Britain before a dislocated elbow put a big dent in his trip.

"It was sensational to win that first Test and I was a bit dirty I couldn't go on with the job," he says. "I came back in France but by then it was too late and I couldn't get back in the Test team."

However, Roach did get an opportunity to work off some of his frustration in a reunion with Tigers' soul-mate Kerry Hemsley in a French bar.

"We were having a quiet drink," Blocker recalls, "when in walked three or four blokes who'd beaten the crap out of 'Buckets' (Hemsley) in a club game a few weeks earlier. They'd given it to him boots and all then, and Buckets thought this was too good an opportunity to pass up. I was glad to help him even the score. The tour as a whole was great fun and everyone took great pride in the fact we didn't lose a game the whole way through, emulating the feats of the '82 Kangaroos. I made some lifetime mates and it was an experience I'll never forget."

Roach missed almost all of 1987 after suffering a serious knee injury in a trial against Wests. But the big fella still managed to grab some headlines. After an incident with the Balmain doorman was captured on film by a *Daily Mirror* photographer, Roach snapped. The Tigers star, frustrated at both his ruined season and the scrap with the doorman who refused to let him into the room, head-butted the photographer.

"It was a stupid thing to do," he admits, "and I regretted it the moment after it happened. The papers blew it up but I gave the photographer $1000 to give to the charity of his choice."

Roach defied the predictions of medical experts to get back on the paddock before the end of the '87 season, thanks to a series of sessions with boxing champions Jeff Fenech and Jeff Harding and their then trainer, Johnny Lewis. Roach made it back onto the field for the last four rounds and the finals but the Tigers didn't last long in the play-offs, being eliminated by Souths in the minor preliminary semi-final. After the season, Bill Anderson stepped down as Balmain coach and was replaced by Warren Ryan, opening the way for another stormy chapter in Roach's career.

The Tigers found immediate success under the iron-fisted discipline of Ryan, who revelled in the heavy artillery the likes of Roach, Paul Sironen, Bruce McGuire and Wayne Pearce provided up front.

STEVE ROACH

"A few blokes were dubious when Warren came to the club but I was looking forward to his arrival," Roach says. "And in that first season I wasn't disappointed. He taught us all heaps and I've had to say he's the best coach I've played under, although there's no doubting he was a difficult man at times. We had a good year in '88 and were boosted just before the finals by the arrival of Ellery Hanley from England. He was at his peak at that time and really added a new dimension to our attack."

Unfortunately, Roach's grand final plans fell apart in a play-off for fifth spot against Penrith at Parramatta Stadium. The Tigers easily won the match 28-8, but the fallout from a Roach tackle on the Panthers' Chris Mortimer was to last long after grand final day.

"That bloody tackle wrecked my year," Roach recalls ruefully.

The judiciary cited the Tigers international star, who swore Mortimer was on the way down when the pair came together and that the tackle was more a collision than anything else. But the judiciary was unmoved, and suspended Roach for four games — effectively forcing him out for the rest of the season, even if Balmain battled all the way through to the grand final, which they eventually did.

"It would have been my first grand final and I'm still filthy about it," he says. "The judiciary cost me that and I can't find it in me to forgive them."

Roach and the Tigers didn't accept the ramifications of the suspension easily. As the odds of the Tigers reaching the grand final shortened by the week, the club devised a daring scheme for Roach to sit out one of his four matches in England, while "playing" for the Warrington club, and then return home clear to play in the grand final. The star prop was secretly flown out of Australia and was en route to Britain when news of the strategy broke. However, when the NSW Rugby League caught wind of Roach's plans, it claimed the Tigers were playing dirty pool and Balmain reluctantly abandoned the scheme. Roach remained in England to play out his guest stint with Warrington, where he listened to every agonising moment of the Tigers' grand-final loss to Canterbury on a phone hook-up from Sydney.

While playing for Warrington, Roach became close friends with another player with a headline-grabbing habit — former Wests and Manly hard man Les Boyd. The pair were vital members of a strong Warrington pack that achieved considerable success in the season of 1988-9. One night, when the pair shared a drink in a pub after training, Boyd warned Roach: "I don't want to see them do the same things to you that they did to me back in Sydney. They'll chase you out of the game the same way they did me if you're not careful. You've got to have more discipline."

Roach took in the advice but wasn't overly concerned. "It came from the heart and I appreciated it, but I never felt I was losing control of the situation in Sydney. I'd been in plenty of strife in my time, but I was never ashamed of anything I'd done. I wasn't worried my career was on the line at any stage."

Les Davidson also played for Warrington that season and legend has it the club decided to sign he and Roach after viewing a video of a punch-up between the pair during a clash in a Sydney club match earlier that year.

"We'll have those two," a committeeman said. "A nice pair of ratbags."

Roach made a brief return to the southern hemisphere in October, 1988, to help Australia crush New Zealand in Auckland in the World Cup final, before completing his stint with Warrington. He then returned to Sydney for the 1989 season, keen to make up for the disappointments of 1988 and, after a year in which Balmain finished the 22 premiership rounds in second place, behind South Sydney, appeared set to erase all his frustrations as the Tigers stormed into the grand final.

Balmain went into the decider as hot favourites against a Canberra side that had fought its way into the big game from fourth spot on the ladder. For most of the match all seemed to be going well for the Tigers — they led 12-2 at halftime and had several chances to wrap up the title in the second half. But Canberra somehow hung on, and, midway through the second half, had pegged Balmain's lead back to 14-8. It was then that coach Ryan, in a move still hotly debated in Tiger territory, called Roach, and then another international forward, Paul Sironen, from the field. Ryan's theory was a sound one — he was replacing two tiring attacking players with two fresh defenders to protect the lead. But Roach has both publicly and privately expressed his anger over the move since that day, and has plenty of support among Balmain fans.

"If we'd hung on to win, Ryan would have been a genius and no-one would have said a word," he explains. "But Canberra levelled the scores with a 'Chicka' Ferguson try 90 seconds from fulltime and then won it in extra time. I'm dirty because I'm convinced that had Sirro and I have stayed on the field, we would have won the thing; even a couple of Canberra players told me that."

Although virtually a permanent fixture in NSW State of Origin teams throughout the 1980s, Roach found himself well and truly on the outer when Jack Gibson took over as Blues' coach in 1989. From the start, it was evident that Roach the free spirit and Gibson the strict disciplinarian had vastly different approaches to the game. Gibson never made his dislike of Roach's attitude to the game a secret.

"Roach's problem is with his ears," Gibson once said. "He never listens."

When Roach failed to make the Blues' team in 1989, he had no doubt it

STEVE ROACH

was Gibson's influence that cost him his place. However, after the Blues were thrashed 3-0 in that series, Roach found himself gaining a reprieve in 1990. But, although NSW took the first two games to clinch their first series since 1986, he was again embroiled in controversy. However, this time that turmoil was not of Blocker's making. In the days leading up to the third match, a press report revealed that Gibson had approached the selectors, asking that Roach be replaced in the Blues' starting line-up by Canberra's Glenn Lazarus.

"Jack pulled me aside a few days later and confirmed I was out of the starting side," Roach tells. "He said my discipline was no good. I was filthy; we'd won the series and suddenly I was out. But I got some satisfaction when I won a spot back in the Test team for the one-off clash with France in Parkes; at least Bob Fulton was sticking by me."

Despite his problems with Gibson, Roach retained his Test spot and was a strong performer on the 1990 Kangaroo tour. With that Ashes series locked at one-all, Roach played one of his finest games in the green and gold in the decider at Leeds.

"We stuck to our match plan beautifully that day and it was a great afternoon for us," he says. "They were never in the match and we beat them 14-nil. It was my last Test in England and I got a real kick out of it. On the whole, I enjoyed the '90 tour a lot more than four years earlier. By this stage I knew what to expect over there and felt far more comfortable; again I made a lot of mates and had a great time off the field."

Earlier in 1990, all hell had broken loose when Roach broke league's first commandment — never touch a referee. But the incident, although it drew a $5,000 fine and four-week suspension, was typical of Blocker's good-humoured and unabashed approach to the game. In a clash with Manly at Brookvale Oval, Roach was sin-binned by referee Eddie Ward for an off-the-ball foul.

"Patting the ref on the head was again a stupid thing to do but the thing I'll always maintain is that there was no malice in it," Roach insists. "It was a spur-of-the-moment thing; the ref sent me to the bin on a touch judge's report and I wanted him to know I wasn't dirty with him because he was only acting on what he'd been told. But didn't everyone give it to me over that one! The furore lasted for days and I now know how a mass murderer must feel when he picks up the papers."

Injuries finally caught up with Roach in the latter stages of his career.

"After my knee problems in 1987, I had more trouble with the other knee," he says. "I thought: 'That's it — I want to play with my boys when they're older.' I'd hit 30 and was happy enough to call it quits. My final home game was against St George and I went out with Garry Jack; we started together and it was good to go out together; it was an emotional day and I've got some great photos to remind me of it."

More than once in his career, Roach thought about leaving the Tigers.

"I got plenty of offers over the years, including a couple from Canberra and Penrith when they were right on top. Manly came to me once and I nearly went to them. But I thought Balmain gave me my opportunity in the game and I'd stick by them. If I had my time over again, maybe I'd go; I can't say for sure. But it would have been nice to win a competition, especially after coming so close. I've got a couple of silver medals sitting in the cupboard at home; what I wouldn't have done to change them for golds."

Since his retirement from the playing fields, Roach has made himself something of a celebrity with his media work, both as a television commentator and star of advertisements for the clothes store, Lowes.

"It's the type of work I really enjoy," he says, "but I don't get carried away because it can be here today, gone tomorrow. That's why I'm still involved in some other work in a sporting business and some other things. I know it's a tough business and people can disappear overnight. I was a bit rough on the TV at first but after a while I settled down and gained some confidence. I'm more relaxed now and enjoying it more."

Roach admits quitting Balmain at the end of 1993, after a year of coaching in the club's juniors, to join the coaching staff at South Sydney was a difficult decision.

"It was very hard after playing at Leichhardt for so long, but the simple thing is there was nothing there for me. I went to see them about a coaching job and there was just nothing available. So I had a choice — to wait 10 years for something to come up or to sew my own seed. When the Souths offer came up, I didn't have to think about it for long. I said: 'Well bugger this, I'll go where I'm wanted.' It was disappointing that after all those years, they couldn't find something for me. But I still love Balmain and I'll never close the door on them; who knows, I may even end up coaching there one day.

"Maybe I'll finally get that premiership trophy that way."

HIT MEN

GLENN LAZARUS

The Brick With Eyes

In rugby league's modern era of percentage football, Glenn Lazarus is the game's most potent yardage machine. Lazarus' ability to make ground up the middle of the ruck, with two and three defenders clinging to him, makes him one of league's richest commodities. Lazarus' record of five consecutive grand finals, for four wins, shows the value he has proved to both Canberra and Brisbane in recent years. A mountain of a man who takes a power of stopping, Lazarus has proved a formidable foe at club, state and international level. Apart from a brief fall from grace in 1991, when he lost form and confidence, "The Brick with Eyes" (as he was first tagged by Triple-J's H.G. Nelson and Roy Slaven and is now known by most league fans) has been the player opposition packs least wanted to tackle in the big games.

Although his name has foreign origins, Lazarus is as Australian as they come.

"To be honest, I'm not sure what our background is," he says. "Some people have told me the name is Jewish, others say it's Hungarian or German. But our family has lived in Australia as long as anyone can remember. My great grandfather was mayor of Queanbeyan, so the Lazaruses have been here for a while."

Lazarus played all his junior football for the Queanbeyan United club, starting at the age of six.

"They were my one and only club and I stuck with them right through until I joined the Raiders," he says. "I started in the centres and slowly but surely moved up. I went from five-eighth to lock and then second row.

"Canberra graded me in 1986, but I didn't actually move to the front row until the following year. One day, Don Furner, who was coaching the Raiders then, came up to me and said: 'Listen, if you want to make a go of it here, you're going to have to move up to the front row. We've got enough second-rowers in this club and there's no great future for you there. But we're a bit short on front-row talent and you're big enough to make a go of it'.

"So that was it — I've been up front ever since. I'm here for good now.

"I was never all that big in my early years, but I did a lot of swimming as a kid and that kept me in shape. It was at around 14 or 15 that I started to put on the pounds. I was what you'd call a 'good eater' and it really started to show."

Lazarus represented the Raiders' President's Cup side in 1986, when that competition was played over a month-long period.

"We made the grand final, but I just about broke my ankle and missed the game. Late in the season, I was graded and played a handful of third-grade games. I was expecting to go back down to Queanbeyan in '87, but Don Furner and Wayne Bennett (who shared the coaching duties at Canberra that season) signed me up. I was made captain of the under-23s. I also played around 10 reserve-grade games and ended up in the first-grade grand final squad. It was Canberra's first grand final and an honour to be part of it all, even though I never got on the field. I wasn't dirty at the time — I even managed to pick up a loser's medal which I've still got as a souvenir.

"I was just a young bloke, and they had some top forwards like Sam Backo and Brent Todd up front. Overall, it was a good learning experience. I made my first-grade debut early in 1988, after Todd broke his arm in a pre-season match against Parramatta. Brian Battese actually went into the side and I got my chance as a fresh reserve. I sat on the bench for the first two comp games, and then made my debut against Souths in round three. The Rabbitohs prop, Ian Roberts, tipped me on my head once during that game ... I knew this was the big time. But we won the game easily and I played every game for the rest of the year."

Lazarus made an immediate impression on the representative selectors and was named in the President's XIII that played the touring Englishmen during that season. The invitation side downed the tourists, with Lazarus revelling in his first taste of international football.

"I was so thrilled to be picked for an international match and I remember really giving it everything I had," he says. "We had a good team full of up-and-comers including guys like Mark Geyer. I think we surprised the Poms with our keenness. It wasn't their best side and we won fairly well on the day."

Glenn Lazarus hadn't even played in a grand final since he was six-years-old, let alone won one in his first 23 years. For that reason, 1989, when Canberra won their first first-grade premiership, will always be the most cherished year in the big front-rower's life.

"No matter what else I achieve in the game, nothing will beat the feeling of winning that first competition with Canberra," he says. "We were struggling to make the finals all season and I didn't help matters when I got sent off for the first time in my career in a match against Balmain. I'd had a stink with their prop Paul Clarke. The next time he took the ball up, I belted him high and copped four weeks. It wasn't a real smart thing to do, especially as it came at a time when we had six players in New Zealand on tour with the Australian side.

"We scraped into fourth spot after the preliminary rounds, but nobody really expected us to go any further. We were written off week after week during the finals, which was the best thing for us. Even when we got into the grand final, Balmain were the favourites.

"I get nervous before any game, but, with this being my first grand final, I was just about clawing the walls of the dressing room before we ran out. Balmain skipped away to a 12-2 lead but we came back to 14-all at the end of 80 minutes. As we entered extra time, I was so confident we'd win I would have put my house on it. We all knew we had them beat.

"When it was over, the feeling was unbelievable. I'd been there for the whole 100 minutes and was playing on sheer adrenalin by the end. I was exhausted, but the feeling was sensational and we partied long into the night. The reception when we got home with the trophy was brilliant. It was without doubt the pick of the grand finals I've played in. Winning the title again the next year with Canberra was great, and the two comps with Brisbane I'll always treasure, but nothing will beat the thrill of that first premiership.

"1989 was also a big year for me because it was during that season that I gained my first experience of State of Origin football, as a reserve in the opening game. Unfortunately, I was dropped after we lost. I didn't really do anything wrong but I think they were looking for scapegoats after that game."

Queensland dominated Origin football in the late 1980s, but, as the '90s began, NSW started to gain the ascendancy in the State of Origin arena. Lazarus' contribution was a major factor in this shift in the balance of power. The Canberra giant was again a "super sub" in the opening two games of the 1990 series. However, in the series decider at Lang Park, he made his starting debut and an immediate impact, barging over for the opening try of the game after a powerful burst from dummy-half. NSW never looked back and took the match 14-10 to clinch the series.

Lazarus made his Test debut in the one-off clash with New Zealand in

HIT MEN

1990. The Aussies went into the match with the established combination of Martin Bella and Steve Roach in the front row, with Lazarus on the bench, and cruised to a 24-6 win.

"I only got five minutes and didn't really do too much while I was out there," Lazarus recalls. "But it was a taste of Test football and I was over the moon — it's what I'd been dreaming about since I first started to play the game."

Lazarus went from strength to strength as the 1990 season unfolded.

"We won the minor premiership and then beat Penrith to make it back-to-back titles," he says. "After the grand final, as we were about to board the plane back to Canberra to celebrate the win, Tim Sheens came up with a list of the 28 players on the Kangaroo tour. We ended up getting five players on tour — myself, Ricky Stuart, Laurie Daley, Gary Belcher and Mal Meninga — but the thing I'll always remember about that moment when the team was read out was the disappointment we felt for Steve Walters. We'd all considered him a certainty to tour, but while his two brothers, Kevin and Kerrod, got the nod, he missed out.

"Because he played alongside me in the front row, I knew what a great player Steve was. I thought he should have been one of the first blokes chosen. Steve has since made the Australian hooking spot his own — he's a real champion."

Current Canberra coach Tim Sheens, who took over as the Raiders' chief in 1988, believes a secret pact between Lazarus and halfback Ricky Stuart, made even before the Kangaroos' plane had taken off from Sydney, proved the turning point in both players' careers.

"Glenn and Ricky both went away as second stringers and knew they'd have to do something exceptional to make the Test team," Sheens explains. "Even though the Roos did a lot of hard training on tour, the two boys got together and made a pact to do more in their own time. They were determined to break into the team and worked damn hard, over and above the call of duty."

Roach and Bella were Australia's props for the first Test, at Wembley, but Great Britain's shock win over the tourists in that match led to changes.

"I was on the bench for that one and got a run late in the game," Lazarus remembers. "But the Poms beat us 19-12, which really shook everyone up. I was in the starting line-up, in place of Bella, for the second Test, at Manchester, and Ricky was also in there, replacing Alfie Langer.

"We won 14-10 in the last minute when Ricky made that long break for Mal to score. I went well and loved the atmosphere — it was probably one of my best games on tour. I held my spot for the final Test, which we won to clinch the Ashes, and the Tests against France. Even though the score at

GLENN LAZARUS

Leeds was only 14-0 I thought we really flogged them. We'd copped a bit of flak after losing the first Test and scraping home in the second, but we put it all together in that one game. We outplayed them all over the park and the score could easily have been a lot bigger. It was a super feeling coming back on the plane with the Ashes ... and knowing I was now part of the Test team. They were my two aims when we went away, and to achieve them made the trip worthwhile."

It was in Britain that Lazarus first came up against the man he rates his toughest opponent — English prop Andy Platt.

"He has given us a hard time every time," Lazarus comments ruefully. "I'd have to say he's one of the main reasons English league has experienced a resurgence in the last few years. He has given them that authority up front that you've got to have in big-time football.

"There are plenty of hard blokes here in Australia too, and probably none tougher than Gavin Allen and Trevor Gillmeister. Luckily I've played plenty of football with them at the Broncos but I've also played against them at State of Origin level. They make every tackle hurt. I know with Gilly, players on the opposite team breathe a sigh of relief when he's not in the team. That's the highest praise you can get."

After establishing himself as a world-class forward on the Kangaroo tour, Lazarus came crashing to earth with a thud in 1991.

"It was a bad year for me personally, particularly after all the successes of the previous season," he admits. "I brought a shoulder injury that needed an operation back from the Roo tour so I was back-pedalling from the start. I missed the pre-season and didn't begin the premiership all that well. I probably wasn't as keen as in 1990 and I paid for that. The selectors gave me the chop for the Tests against New Zealand and I couldn't really argue — my form wasn't up to scratch.

"Then I damaged my sternum and missed eight weeks in the lead-up to the finals. The club also had problems and sort of stumbled into the finals. A few of the other blokes were also carrying injuries from the Roo tour and, by grand final day, we were a team of walking wounded. My sternum had recovered but I wasn't as match fit as I would have liked to have been. I'm not using that as an excuse — we led for much of the grand final but Penrith finished strongly and got the money."

Lazarus never made a song and dance about the sternum injury that plagued his season in 1991 and the Raiders kept the full extent of the injury quiet. But Tim Sheens knew the full extent of the problem.

"Most players just bruise their sternum and that is considered a serious enough injury. But Glenn cracked his. To repair it, they had to cut him right open. It was the closest a current player would come to having open heart surgery. The doctors really had a lot of work to do to repair the damage and we thought there was no way he could come back. He deserves plenty of credit for playing in the finals. Admittedly, he came back at a huge weight but that's only because he couldn't train. He was flat out playing every week and just didn't have the strength to train."

The one consolation to come out of 1991 for Lazarus was that the Australian selectors named him in the the squad to tour Papua New Guinea after the grand final.

"That made the pain of playing in the finals worthwhile," he says. "That enabled me to salvage something out of a pretty disastrous year."

Canberra's financial problems, which arose during 1991, ripped the heart out of the Raiders' side, with six members of the grand final team quitting the club. Although Lazarus had spent all his life in Canberra, for him the decision to leave wasn't a hard one.

"Canberra's strife co-incided with me getting some itchy feet," he says. "After my poor season in '91 and with the trouble Canberra was in, I found myself wondering what it would be like to play for another club. I was a bit filthy with Canberra cutting all our contracts by 20 per cent because of the drama. We played it as hard as we could, but we were the ones who had to pay for an administrative error. That didn't go down too well with me and a little voice inside me said it was time to move on.

"I started to look around and considered only a few clubs. Wayne Bennett was the coach at the Broncos and they had a few other former Canberra players as well, so to transfer there wasn't like a jump into the unknown. I felt it was fairly familiar territory and, luckily, it turned out to be the best possible move.

"When I got there, Wayne and his family were great and helped us settle in. (Chief Executive) John Ribot was also good. We got up early in November and found a house straight away so everything was in place for a big year."

But Lazarus started 1992 with the massive weight of the Brisbane public's expectations on his shoulders.

"Everyone up here was desperate for success," he explains, "and when I arrived they called me the great white hope and all that sort of thing. It was the last thing I needed, particularly as I was just trying to re-establish myself after not having the best of years in '91. It was pressure I didn't need. I knew if I failed, they'd come down on me like a ton of bricks. But, in the end, it worked out fine and we won the comp, but it's ridiculous to say it was just my coming to the club that made the difference. The Broncos went from seventh to first in 12 months — no one player is that good to make such a difference.

GLENN LAZARUS

"Performance-wise, I always rated 1990 as my best year, but I don't think I was far behind that in '92."

Lazarus came close to completing an individual grand slam in a remarkable personal season in 1992. He played for the Broncos in the final of the Nissan Sevens, Tooheys Challenge, grand final and World Club Challenge, for NSW Country Origin against City Origin, for NSW in the State of Origin series, and Australia in the Ashes series, the one-off Test against Papua New Guinea, and the World Cup final. In all but the first two of those matches, Lazarus emerged in triumph. Of 43 matches he was involved in, Lazarus won a staggering 35.

The barnstorming front-rower was again dominant as the Broncos took their second premiership in 1993, and played what he considers his two best-ever games that season.

"I thought I had the two strongest games I can remember in the club round against St George and then the second State of Origin game," he says. "The Saints game was straight after City-Country and I felt a fair bit of pressure on me to perform. I had copped a bit of flak in the rep game — the critics were saying the two City props had outplayed me. Brisbane were up against Saints at Kogarah, in replay of the 1992 Grand Final, and we all played very well. I was especially pleased with my contribution, which silenced the critics and ensured I retained my State of Origin spot. In the Origin series, we won the first game at Lang Park and came down to Sydney knowing a win before our home crowd would wrap up the series. We were down 6-0 early but stormed back with two tries just after halftime and went on to win 16-12. I was involved all the way and happy with my workload in that one."

Lazarus is smart enough to realise he has been fortunate to play in top sides under two of league's most astute coaches.

"I've been lucky to have great backlines at both Canberra and Brisbane," he says. "It's meant once I make the yards up the middle, the backs can make the most of the room that creates. Both Tim Sheens and Wayne Bennett have been strong influences on me, as was Mick Doyle, my first coach in the President's Cup at Canberra.

"I first met Wayne in 1987 at Canberra but didn't really get to know him then as I was in the minor grades. But he still took time out to tell me how he thought I was going and I really appreciated that at the time. Tim Sheens brought me into the top grade in 1988 and coached me for the next four years. He taught me so much about the game."

One of Lazarus' strengths — instilled into him by both Sheens and Bennett — is his discipline. Unlike many of the game's big men, he gives away few penalties and can rarely be rattled by opponents on the field.

HIT MEN

"I've always worked hard on my discipline and never been really worried by other players trying to niggle me," he says. "I like to stay focused on my own game. If someone has a go at me, I try not to retaliate. I just try to play harder and keep my cool."

Sheens, who, in a 20-year career as player and coach, has come up against many of league's hard men, believes Lazarus will be remembered as one of the game's greats. Yet ironically, Sheens almost sacked the youngster early in his career.

"There have been a lot of really good front-rowers and I'd probably rate Arthur Beetson as the best I've come across," Sheens suggests. "He started off in the old days and then adapted his game to the faster modern era.

"There aren't many blokes who could have handled themselves in both eras, but Glenn would be one. For a big man, he is very athletic, has plenty of skills and is one of the few big men you can rely on to play 80 minutes of football. When Canberra were at their peak, one of our real strengths was the stamina of Lazarus and (fellow prop) Brent Todd up front. As a coach, I knew that, barring injury, both men would be able to go the distance in any game, which made my life a lot easier. Glenn deserves the credit for that — he has worked hard on his fitness and kept himself in good shape for most of his career.

"When I came to the club in 1988, Glenn was still basically an unknown. We knew he had some ability, but we had plenty of talent right through the grades at that time. He carried a knee injury through the pre-season that prevented him from showing us his best and his weight ballooned a bit as a result. I can remember telling my training staff at the time: 'This kid's not going to make it.' He came close to missing the cut when we announced our gradings but toughed it out. When Todd broke his arm, it all fell into place for him. There was a hole there, and the guy we intended to be our back-up, Brian Battese, had just had knee surgery and wasn't fully fit. That left us in a dilemma but Glenn started to put some good games together in the trials and I just had that gut feeling that he might be the answer. He came in to partner Sam Backo in the front row and never looked back."

Sheens can reveal a side of Lazarus' virtually unknown to his fans in either Brisbane or Canberra.

"Having grown up in Canberra, Glenn played a lot of Australian rules as a kid. The same applied to most of the other Canberra players. Before the Raiders came along, league and rules were on a par in the ACT. Glenn was a very good rules player and has a fine kicking game. At one stage during his Canberra days, I even had Glenn kicking for line for me. He has a very good long punt and did the job well. His hands are also very good and I believe that's a legacy of his Aussie rules background."

GLENN LAZARUS

Sheens says the Raiders find playing against the Lazarus-charged Broncos a challenge since the big man moved to Brisbane.

"He always likes to play well against us but by the same token, our boys always remind him where he came from. It's a healthy rivalry and we'll all be mates after it's over."

Sheens believes Lazarus will continue to dominate the current game.

"The only danger is that boredom could get to him," Sheens says. "And by boredom I mean he runs out of things to achieve. He hit that flat spot after doing it all in 1990 and that is always a danger with top sportsmen. But he bounced back after his disappointments of 1991 and he's no doubt learned from that. He has kept himself in good shape since then and hasn't looked back. Take a look at what he's done and what he can still achieve and it's quite staggering. He's already played in five grand finals for four wins and has plenty more ahead of him. He could have the longest grand final run since the days of Norm Provan in the 1960s. John O'Neill had a similar record when he won comps with Souths and Manly.

"You'd have to say he's had a major bearing on the teams he's played with. We had a great backline at Canberra but he was still a big influence on us with his ability to gain yards up the middle. As for Brisbane, they were on the way to being a super side long before Glenn arrived. But he has added that strength and stability up front that was not there previously and you can see what a much more polished team they've been in 1992 and 1993.

"He'll go down as an all-time great and good luck to him. His ability and credentials stand for themselves. Judging football careers can be a very subjective thing. It all boils down to what you've got on paper and that's where his career will look so impressive in years to come. He's done it all at every level the game is played."

HIT MEN

MARK GEYER

Rebel with a Cause

Mark Geyer has had an annoying habit of attracting headlines for all the wrong reasons in his short but spectacular career. Although the public knows him as a wild and hot-headed player, Geyer has another side — he is also a private and determined individual who would love nothing more than to shed his image as one of the game's bad boys. However, 'MG' has a penchant for speaking his mind and a habit of exploding under pressure, traits that seem set to ensure that controversy will follow him throughout his career. Love him or hate him, there's no doubting Mark Geyer's football ability. The tall second-rower is a game-breaker in the true sense of the word, a player capable of changing the trend of a match with a big hit or a crashing run.

Geyer was born and bred in Sydney's west, in tough surroundings in Mount Druitt, where he began playing football at age five for the Whalan Warriors and then North Mount Druitt. He attended Whalan High, where his footballing talents quickly rose to the surface.

"We were a small battling school and didn't do too good when I was in Year 10, so I went back in Year 11 just to play footy," he says. "We got to the final of our group in the Commonwealth Bank Cup and played against John Paul II, a much bigger and richer school. The winner of that game got to appear on television in the next round — it was the biggest match I'd ever played. But we lost — and I was so filthy I quit school on the spot and never went back.

"I started an apprenticeship but that only lasted a couple of weeks. I was just over 16 and not sure what I wanted to do but then Penrith graded me. That gave my life some direction. In 1985 I started playing against blokes six or seven years older than me in the under-23s. It was tough for a while but good experience and I enjoyed it."

MARK GEYER

Geyer first hit the headlines the following season, during an explosive under-23 semi-final against Souths. The towering youngster tested the patience of referee Dennis Spagarino once too often and was given his marching orders. Graphic photos of the previously unknown Geyer, in tears as he left the SCG convinced he had blown his grand-final chance, featured in the Sydney papers the following day.

"Mr Spagarino and I never got on very well. He marched me for repeated shoulder charges," Geyer explains. "I could see my grand-final medal gone as he ordered me off and being the emotional bloke I am, I just started bawling. Luckily I got off with a warning at the judiciary on the Monday night and got to play in the grand final, again against Souths. But we got beaten. I thought we were better than them for most of the year but they stacked their team for the last few games and that proved the difference.

"The following year I went up to reserve grade," Geyer recalls. "After a few weeks, coach Tim Sheens selected me for my top-grade debut, against Canterbury. I can still remember their pack that day — Kelly, Bugden, Tunks, Dunn, Folkes and Langmack. I probably couldn't have picked six harder blokes to make my debut against. But Tim had faith in me, which counted for a lot and we had some good forwards too. (Captain and hooker) Roycie Simmons was a big help on the day. I was expecting them to have a go at me as they were quite well known for their intimidation at the time. But surprisingly, they didn't try too much to upset me, although Tunksie said a few things.

"We led for most of the match but they scored two late tries to take the game 16-10. Still, I wasn't too upset; we were a young side, I was still finding my feet and Canterbury had made the last three grand finals. We'd held our own. In a way, I found it easier than playing under-23s because even though the game was much quicker, I was playing with better players. They were able to look after me and put me through holes in the defence.

"Tim Sheens was a real gentleman and, even though he only coached me for a couple of years, he was probably the biggest influence on my career. He's a real players coach — they know they can trust him. He has the confidence of a lot of blokes at Penrith and Canberra."

While he survived his baptism of fire, Geyer found life in the big time to be anything but smooth sailing in his second game, against Wests at Orana Park in Campbelltown. The Penrith youngster had the crowd at boiling point after crash-tackling Wests forward John Elias out of the match in the early exchanges. Geyer creamed Elias in an awesome but legal hit — and the popular Magpie didn't wake up until several minutes later in the dressing room.

"I just lost the plot that day," Geyer remembers. "I was still trying to find my feet in first grade, their old hands, like 'Bruiser' Clark and Ian Schubert were baiting me, and I was copping heaps from the crowd. I hit Elias hard and, even though it wasn't an illegal tackle, they were all after my blood.

"At one stage I called Bruiser a fat old man and he chased me 20 metres across the field trying to belt me. Royce Simmons had bagged him earlier and I thought, if Royce can do it, so can I. I was just a kid at that stage and didn't realise you had to earn some respect before you could do things like that on the field. I was this 18-year-old kid who thought he was king of the heap. Tim Sheens ended up having to take me off early in the second half — I was just making a fool of myself. After the game all these Wests supporters wanted to beat the crap out of me behind the dressing room. So I hid in the bar. I wanted to make myself scarce but the first bloke I saw in there was Bruiser. I tried to walk past unnoticed but he shoved a schooner into my hand and said: 'I think you could use this, kid.'

"So I had a beer with him and he turned out to be a champion bloke. I felt a bit bad about what I said to him out there, but never got the chance to play against him again. I learned probably more that day than any other in football — Bruiser really knocked me down a peg or two."

Midway through the 1987 season, Geyer contracted pneumonia and missed eight weeks.

"I came back late in the season and ended up in the reserve-grade side that reached the grand final," he says. "This time we made amends for our loss the previous year by beating Manly. It was Penrith's first ever reserve-grade title and we whooped it up for days. It was a good way to finish a fairly big year for me."

Geyer became a regular first grader in 1988 and the representative selectors gave a pointer to things to come by naming him in the President's XIII that played the touring Great Britain side.

"We had a good team, with guys like Glenn Lazarus, Greg Florimo and Phil Blake," Geyer says. "It was a miserable day in Canberra — cold and wet with a howling wind. I think the Poms would have preferred to be somewhere else. But were were all super keen and beat them 24-16 — it was a match I really enjoyed."

Geyer climbed a step further up the representative ladder in 1989 when he was selected for his State of Origin debut for NSW. However, it was anything but a happy occasion for the young Penrith firebrand.

"Queensland had already won the first two games so when I was selected we were really in a no-win situation," he says. "I thought it strange that they had waited until the series was over to pick me. My form had been really good and I was hoping for a start in one of the earlier games. Plenty of people in the media were saying I deserved a go; maybe they just picked me in the end to shut them up ... We went to Lang Park and I was pretty nervous about what was to come. I was selected in the second row with Gavin Miller and, before we ran out, coach Jack Gibson just told me to trail him around the field. He assured me that if I did that, then the gaps would come. Well, I followed Jack's advice and I think I touched the ball once in that whole half. I didn't help matters by running around like a chook with my head cut off because I was so nervous. We ended up getting hammered, as Queensland made a white-wash of the series."

A nagging groin injury seemed certain to spoil Geyer's season in 1990. However, the lanky forward finally got back on the field, and played a major role in Penrith's surge to their first grand final.

"A month before the semis I was sitting in a groin brace doing nothing. I thought my year was over," he says. "But all of a sudden it came good and I got a run in a couple of the semi-finals to build up match fitness. By grand final day I was fully fit and all psyched up for a big day. Before the match, a Penrith official told me it was between me and my opposite number, Canberra's Gary Coyne, for a spot on the Kangaroo tour. That was all the motivation I needed — I went out there determined to take no prisoners. The Raiders beat us on the day, and a lot of that had to do with the emotion of the occasion. We had beaten them a fortnight earlier but they were far cooler on grand final day. We were so hyped up we didn't play the type of football that had got us that far. There were a lot of tears shed that night, but, at the end of it all, I realised that what many critics have been saying over the years was true — you often have to lose a grand final before you can win one.

"The big consolation for me was going on the Roo tour — it was a special time in my life. I wasn't in the Test side, but, while that was a bit disappointing, it had its advantages. The members of the 'B team' got to tour around a lot more. We saw a lot of the countryside and did more socialising. I played some good football over there and did manage to play in one of the Tests in France. We beat them 60-4 and it was all a bit embarrassing really. I don't think they'd beat some of the Metropolitan Cup teams back here in Sydney.

"It was a real 'good-time' tour. I remember one game against Halifax when we were beating them by around 30 points. But they scored a couple of tries and had the crowd all fired up because of their comeback. After one of their tries, we were all behind the goalposts, and I went berserk. I started to scream: 'Come on, we've got to do this ... for Australia.' It was a gee-up and guys like the Walters brothers and Alfie Langer, who always love having a laugh, pissed themselves. We were all in stitches. That was one of my most cherished memories of the tour. We made a lot of mates for life over there."

HIT MEN

Every footballer has one year in his career he treasures above all others and for Geyer, 1991 was that magical season.

"The Penrith blokes on the Kangaroo tour — Greg Alexander, Brad Fittler, John Cartwright and myself — all came back primed for a big year and we started in top form," he says. "I think the experience the Penrith guys gained on that tour really made the difference in 1991. We won our first seven games on the trot, and, even that early, I didn't think anyone could beat us for the title. We were just awesome."

But before Penrith's moment of glory, Geyer had other mountains to climb. He won selection in NSW's State of Origin side in the second row alongside another giant, Balmain's Paul Sironen. The Blues were now coached by Tim Sheens, the man who had brought Geyer to grade at Penrith. The Panther star felt far more at ease under such a familiar taskmaster.

Queensland won the opening game 6-4 in a typically tight encounter at Lang Park, before the teams returned to Sydney for one of the most controversial games in State of Origin history. On a rain-soaked night at the Sydney Football Stadium, a capacity crowd of over 40,000 saw a psyched up Geyer tear into the Queenslanders from the opening whistle.

"I was given the all clear by one of the NSW hierarchy before the game to get out there and get into them," he says. "So I went out and followed instructions. And I ended up copping a six-week suspension for it ... to say I was bitter wouldn't even begin to describe how I felt."

Geyer was cited for an elbow to the head of Broncos fullback Paul Hauff during the second half. However, it was his confrontation with Queensland skipper Wally Lewis in the seconds immediately after the halftime siren had sounded that made him the talk of the league world.

While most of the players were on their way to the dressing room for a much needed break, referee David Manson called out the pair for a caution. As the pair were given a tongue lashing by Manson, they began glaring at each other, then yelling, and eventually pushing. Only Manson's intervention prevented an ugly incident.

"I played right into Lewis' hands," Geyer recalls ruefully. "He's good at baiting blokes and I fell for it — hook, line and sinker. The referee called us out for a caution and next thing I knew he (Lewis) was getting stuck into me. I should have known better but I just exploded and started firing back at him.

"The Hauff tackle in the second half looked terrible but it was just a shoulder charge gone wrong; it really wasn't that bad even though on television it does look shocking.

"I'll admit plenty of what I did that night was premeditated. I went out there to get into them and that's what I did. But funnily enough, the Hauff tackle which they got me for wasn't intended to do any harm.

"While I was suspended, I went over to Perth for a couple of weeks to get away from it all, but even there I couldn't escape the controversy. Every second person I saw asked me what Lewis had said and what I had said back to him. Strangely enough, I can't even remember the exact words either of us used in the heat of that moment. All I remember is that there was plenty of threats and swearing, and that we both meant business."

While Geyer was under intense public and media pressure after the citing and suspension, he got his career back on track almost immediately after serving his time. In a major shock, Australia had lost the first Test to New Zealand 24-8. That result forced coach Bob Fulton and his selectors to do a rethink, and it didn't take them long for them to realise Mark Geyer was the man they needed. The Penrith forward was brought into the second Test side and played a key role as Australia produced a stunning turnaround to win 44-0 in Sydney.

"That was my first Test in Australia and I was desperate for a big one." he says, "as it was my debut and also to get the disappointment of the Origin business out of my system. In the end, we had a great win and I scored the opening try — it was a dream game in a dream year for me. Then we wrapped up the series in Brisbane in style, smacking them again, by 40-12."

Following the Test matches, Geyer set his sights on the finals and erasing another disappointment — the 1990 grand final.

"We won the minor premiership but then had to really struggle to beat Norths in the major semi," he recalls. "Canberra came through from fourth spot to meet us in the grand final. They were probably the last team we wanted to see there after what they had done to us the previous year.

"The grand final itself was one of the best games I've played in — and I'm not just saying that because we won. It was a high standard match which I've probably watched 1000 times on video since — it was such a thrill to play with and against such class players. Canberra led 12-6 at halftime and we were pretty worried. But then we came back to level the scores and went on to edge them out."

Geyer modestly plays down his own contribution to the win — two brilliant pieces of class that ultimately proved the difference between two closely-matched teams. After spending time in the sin bin for arguing with referee Bill Harrigan, Geyer resumed the battle. With the Panthers still down 12-6 and time running out, Geyer produced the pass of the season to put centre Brad Fittler into open space. Two Raiders had Geyer covered, but he somehow threw an "Arthur Beetson special" pass to the rampaging

HIT MEN

Fittler, who sent centre Brad Izzard over. Greg Alexander booted the conversion to level the scores and then potted a neat field goal moments later to edge the Panthers ahead.

Then Geyer produced the fairy-tale finale to Penrith's proudest day. With the final seconds ticking away, Canberra gambled on a short line drop-out towards several of their speed men standing out wide. The surprise tactic almost worked, but for Geyer's bold charge forward. After collecting the ball on the half-volley, he burst into open space, turned as he reached fullback Gary Belcher and found Royce Simmons (playing in his final match for the Panthers) lurking unmarked beside him. Geyer gave Simmons, who had also scored the game's opening try, the saloon passage to the line, and the premiership had a new home.

"I was so happy for Roycie," Geyer says. "He was what Penrith was all about, and for him to go out in that sort of style meant so much to all of us."

But Geyer had yet to exhaust his supply of headlines for 1991. A week after the grand final, it was revealed the controversial forward had tested positive to marijuana, earning him a eight-match suspension.

"I went from being on top of the world down to the gutter," he explains. "I never deny I took the pot, but the only reason I did it was that I thought I was out for the year. It happened a month before the semis while I had my leg in a cast because of a bad ankle injury. The only good thing was that it didn't come out until after the grand final. I really thought my year was over. I was at training, just sitting there with my leg in plaster, when these blokes came up and wanted a sample — they only tested one other player. I don't know who was behind it or why they chose to get me then.

"The whole thing really rocked me and probably made me wake up to myself. When it all came out my leg was again in a cast after an ankle reconstruction and I was stuck at home with nowhere to go. All hell broke loose — the phone rang every five minutes and I just couldn't get away. I lost weight and, even after the whole off season, I wasn't really ready to play again in 1992."

Little did Geyer realise much worse was to come ...

If 1991 was a dream year for the Penrith juggernaut, 1992 was a nightmare. For Geyer, the death of close friend and Panthers utility player, Ben Alexander, the Panthers' fall from premiers to also-rans, a dispute with Phil Gould after his sacking from the State of Origin team, an assault conviction, and a car crash all combined to make it nothing short of a horror year.

"It was always going to be tough defending our crown, but we never realised how tough until we actually started the season," he says. "Clubs were desperate to take us on every week and lifted themselves whenever they played us, no matter where they were on the ladder. We started okay but then things fell apart, especially after Ben's death. That just shattered the whole place and few of us were in the mood to play football again.

"I never thought I'd leave Penrith, particularly so soon after our premiership win. But the whole club just seemed to break down when Ben died. I'm sure if he was still alive, I'd still be playing for Penrith and everything would be sweet. I took it terribly hard; he was my best mate, he was gone and I couldn't even think about football. But I've learned that it's true that time heals all wounds and now I'm just starting to get over it."

When Geyer quit Penrith by mutual consent a month after Ben's death, he had no idea if he would ever play football again.

"I was just in limbo," he says. "It was the worst time of my life. I went on a drinking binge, I didn't care about anything or anyone."

Desperate to escape from the pressure and grief created by Ben's death in the close-knit Penrith community, Geyer fled to Greece with Greg Alexander and a couple of other mates.

"We thought getting away would be the best thing for us," Geyer explains. "We just wanted to escape. We picked this tiny, quiet Greek island which, before we left, had sounded like just what we needed. But when we got there, we found a heap of Aussies and Kiwis there. Every second person on the island recognised us. On the same day as we got there, Goldie Hawn and Kurt Russell also arrived. But I swear there were more people wanting to talk to us than them; it was unbelievable.

"When I came back, I didn't really care if I played in 1993 or not. I started looking around to see what was available, but most clubs turned their back on me. All they knew was that I'd left Penrith — I think they thought I was a bit of a troublemaker. But they didn't know the full story and they never will. But then (Balmain's then coach) Alan Jones stepped in and he was great. He told me there was a place for me at Balmain and gave me the urge to play again. He offered me a lifeline, so I became a Tiger.

"I started training well and was looking forward to the challenge in 1993, but luck didn't help me. For the first time in my career I found myself in an injury trot. I broke my thumb, then I cracked some ribs; it was one disaster after another. I must admit I'll have to take some of the blame; I now believe you are more liable to get injured when you're not fully fit and that was the case with me. I could have been fitter and I paid the penalty."

Geyer found himself in more hot water early in the season, when he was sacked from the City team for being late to training. To make matters worse, Geyer, never one to hide his feelings, exchanged angry words with City coach Phil Gould after being told of his sacking. And, much to Geyer's disgust, an allegedly verbatim report of their private feud appeared in a major newspaper the following day.

"A lot of that was my fault, but plenty of it was out of my hands as well. I left home well in time for training but got caught in traffic and got to Leichhardt Oval a few minutes late. The manager Geoff Carr then told me Gould had said I was out of the team. I couldn't believe it. I went into the empty dressing room and yelled and screamed at myself ... at Gould ... at everyone I could think of. I'd just won my way back into representative football after such a dreadful year and now I'd blown it.

"I should have left it at that but I didn't. I went and fronted Gould. I snapped, called him some names and asked him to come outside and sort it out. It's all very embarrassing when I look back at it, but I've never been able to hold back my emotions. I was stunned when the paper next day ran what was supposed to be the conversation between us. The story was by a journalist who is a mate of Gould's. It wasn't even close. In the story, Gould was supposed to have said, after I threatened to belt him: 'Don't let fear hold you back.'

"I can tell you, if fear was the only thing holding me back, I would have belted him. Paul Sironen pulled me aside and advised me to go home because I was so upset and emotional. But I couldn't even go home; it was like I was in a daze. I went over to Jonesy's house and stayed there for a couple of days to get my head back together. That weekend we played Parramatta and I came out like a man possessed; it was probably my best game for Balmain that year."

Alan Jones departed from Balmain after the 1993 season, to be replaced by Wayne Pearce. Unfortunately, the relationship between Geyer and his new coach got off to a rocky start, when Pearce dropped the fiery second-rower from the Tigers' top squad in January 1994, after Geyer failed to attend training. Geyer believed Balmain had breached his contract by failing to provide him with a car after Jones had arranged a vehicle for him the previous year.

"We sorted it out but again I was in the headlines for all the wrong reasons. Geyer commented at he time."I'm sick of looking like an idiot all the time. I think I bring a lot of it on myself. I worry too much and then do stupid things. If I could just get out there and play footy, I'd be fine. That's what I'm good at and if I can stay out of trouble for a while, things will turn around."

However, only a couple of months later, Geyer's career once more exploded in a mass of controversial headlines. Just two rounds into 1994, Geyer was called into the office of Tigers chief executive Keith Barnes. Less than an hour later, he walked out, with the club releasing a statement saying he had been 'granted a release' — league jargon for given the sack. Coach Pearce, a strict disciplinarian, had evidently come down heavily on Geyer for failing to attend training sessions and the club's first two premiership matches. Geyer angrily denied the charges, claiming he was struggling to overcome a groin injury and had been given permission to miss training.

Geyer is slowly but surely coming to terms with his wild man image.

"It used to worry me a lot when I was new to it all, but I'm older now and I'm starting to accept it. I can face facts — it's an image I'm never going to lose. There's no point even defending myself because of all the scandal I've been in. It's usually good to see your name in the paper, but not for hitting a bloke in a Leagues club. I've calmed down a fair bit, but I think I'll always be an emotional guy who over-reacts on occasions."

HIT MEN

CRAIG SALVATORI

In the footsteps of Big Artie

When Arthur Beetson first saw the burly figure of Craig Salvatori walk through the gates of the old Sydney Sports Ground almost a decade ago, he thought he was looking at a portrait of himself as a young man.

The similarities between front-row master and the man who became his pupil were nothing short of remarkable. Beetson and Salvatori share the same birthday, have Aboriginal blood in their veins, and both love food, wine and the good times. Both started their football days in the centres before their mobility and size saw them progress to the second row and ultimately the front row. Both were maligned by the critics early in their careers yet managed to go on and play for Australia. And both had their fiery on-field temperaments quelled when awarded the captaincy of the Eastern Suburbs team.

"I looked at this big, green kid and it was like looking back into a time tunnel," Beetson remembers. "He was the mirror image of me — a big kid with talent, ball skills, and he was very mobile for a bloke his size. He got into a bit of strife and enjoyed life. Sal was a happy-go-lucky character who never looked like living up to his potential in the early days. But he got fair dinkum and played for his country, and has developed into one of the best forwards around. The captaincy brought about a change in him, just as it did with me at Easts in the mid '70s. It was a similar gamble to the one Easts took giving the job to me but in both instances, I'd like to think it paid off. He's also had the tendency to put on weight at times in his career so you can see, it's more than a passing similarity. I remember when he came to first grade in 1987 I used him mainly as a shock trooper. He handled that role very well. I never knew whether he'd make it, but he's been around for a long time now and deserves full credit for what he's done."

Salvatori only became a regular top grader after Beetson left Easts in

CRAIG SALVATORI

the late '80s, but still gained plenty from the big man's influence.

"I really regret not playing more under Arthur because he could have taught me so much," Salvatori says. "Whenever I was in his team, I'd always learn something. As a front-rower he was up there with the best of them, and he read the game so well as a coach. When I was young and raw, he gave me some valuable insights into front-row play. I lapped it all up because, even then, I knew I was getting advice from the best."

Born in Sydney, Salvatori's background is an intriguing mix of Italian, English and Aboriginal cultures.

"I've got all sorts of blood in me and one day I'd love to go to Italy to have a look around at where my ancestors came from," he says.

Salvatori moved down the south coast to Corrimal, in the Illawarra, with his mother and sister at an early age, before returning to the eastern suburbs of Sydney when aged seven.

"That was when I started playing for Marist Brothers Pagewood and then Maroubra," he says. "I spent virtually all my early years in the Souths juniors before moving over to the Dunbar Hotel, at Paddington in the Easts area, when I was 16. Easts saw me and graded me from there in 1985. I started playing under-23s and, while it took a while to adjust, I thought I was lucky not having to play third grade where you could come up against some old hard head who'd been around for years. But there were still some experienced 22 years olds, while I was 18 and very green, so I learned a few things."

Two years later, Salvatori made his first-grade debut against Cronulla.

"It was a Saturday television game and a big deal for a kid who'd never played in top company before," he says. "I was packing it before the start but surprised myself by how well I did. I just ran off Tony Melrose all day. He was a talented ball player who'd been around and looked after me. He kept finding the holes and I'd run straight and hard. He made it easy for me. I scored one try, set up another and we won, so I was pleased. When I came off, they told me I'd won a couple of man-of-the-match awards and that really made the day for me. I ended up playing a handful of first-grade games that year which was a good grounding for what was to follow."

However, Salvatori's hopes of cementing a regular top-grade spot in 1988 were dashed by injury. He started the season in reserve grade and broke his collarbone, an injury which forced him out for half the year.

"But it wasn't a total loss," he remembers. "I came back in time for the reserve-grade finals and we made the grand final, which was the biggest game of my career to that point. It was great to be involved on grand final day, but we lost to a very strong Manly side. Despite the setbacks, I was happy with my form that year, but just couldn't crack the top side again."

HIT MEN

In 1989, Russell Fairfax, who had coached Salvatori in both the under-23s and reserve grade, graduated to the top job at Easts, replacing Beetson. Fairfax knew Salvatori's game better than anyone and had confidence in the giant front-rower's ability to handle the pressure of top-grade football on a regular basis. Salvatori rates the often maligned Fairfax as the major influence on his career.

"I came right through the grades with Russell. He coached me for five years. A lot of people are quick to bag Russell because he never had much success in first grade. But the thing they forget is that he did extremely well in the lower grades and to me, that showed he had the ability. He made the finals four years in a row and that's a fine record. If he had a failing, it's that he wasn't much older than some of our senior players. That wasn't his fault but I think it led to some of them not respecting him as much as they should have."

Salvatori was a major attacking force in Fairfax's side, playing 16 first-grade games in '89. But the Roosters finished well down the ladder, in 11th spot, and, by the start of the following season, the knives were out for Fairfax.

One notorious match early in 1990 all but sealed Fairfax's fate. The Roosters travelled to Bruce Stadium in Canberra to take on the Raiders, at a time when the the Green Machine were at the height of their powers. Canberra won the match 66-4 — the worst defeat in over 80 years of football for the Eastern Suburbs club. The Raiders shattered a host of records, with Mal Meninga posting an astonishing 38 points. Salvatori recalls the match with dread.

"You know, I'm the only survivor in the whole Easts club from that day," he says ruefully. "The rest have either retired, left of their own accord, or been sent packing. (Five-eighth) Brendan Hall was with the club but, luckily for him, was out injured. I reckon Mal had funnel web spiders on him that day ... none of our blokes would go near him. That game was an embarrassment. We tried ... in fact, I don't even think we were all that bad. There was just nothing we could do to stop them. It was one of those days when the likes of Meninga, Laurie Daley, Gary Belcher, Ricky Stuart and Bradley Clyde all had unbelievable games. But if you think the match was bad, you should have seen the bus trip home. We've got on the bus and Russell was fuming. He not only banned us from drinking beer, he made us watch the entire video of the game. We had to sit through try after try. With a minute to go and the score at 66-0, Tim Dwyer scored for us and the whole bus erupted. Everyone was screaming and clapping and whistling ... it was a funny moment. The cruel part was there was a blatant knock-on in the try and it happened right in front of the ref. I'm sure he saw it ... I reckon he just felt sorry for us. The following week we salvaged some pride in Townsville and drew 12-all with Canterbury, who were premiers at the time. Then in the same match the following season in Canberra, we beat the Raiders, which was very satisfying."

But Fairfax wasn't around to savour Easts revenge, having been dumped by Easts supremo Ron Jones before the end of that 1990 season. In his place, Jones appointed Jack Gibson as football manager, and from the start, Gibson, and the man he named first-grade coach for 1991, Mark Murray, took the hard-line approach needed to get the best out of Salvatori. They worked on the big man, concentrating on both his mental and physical approach to the game. But it was sometimes far from smooth sailing.

"I was looking forward to playing under them, but got sent off in the very opening game of 1991, against Souths," Salvatori says. "It was hardly the start I wanted and Jack and Mark rightly gave it to me."

Salvatori was marched in the opening 10 minutes for what he believed was a justified action in helping a team-mate who was copping a hammering from a Souths player in a brawl. He was the only player waved from the field, despite the messy fight, and Souths went on to win the game. Salvatori's career reached its lowest point on that day — sent off in the premiership opener for an impetuous act, which cost his team a win and earned the wrath of coach, team-mates and fans. No one could have imagined as Salvatori walked from the Sydney Football Stadium, head bowed and hands on hips, that this was to be the turning point of his career. Or that less than four months later he would be making his Australian debut on the same ground.

The judiciary let Salvatori off with a caution, but he knew that wasn't the end of his troubles. Soon after, Jack Gibson called the big front-rower in for a "chat" and laid it on the line.

"Jack didn't beat around the bush," Salvatori recalls. "He did a lot of talking but the basic message was: 'Cool it or you won't get a game.' He's always been strong on the discipline side of the game. He told me to keep it under control if I wanted to go places. Otherwise, I could pack my bags and leave. Looking back, it was probably the best thing that could have happened to me. I had to take a long, hard look at myself. I'd like to think I got the message."

The change in Salvatori's game was immediate — he suddenly worried less about the niggling from opposition players and problems with referees, and concentrated instead on letting his natural talents emerge. For the rest of the first round of the 1991 premiership, as Easts charged up the ladder, he played the best football of his career. With new halfback Gary Freeman and Salvatori calling the shots, the Roosters emerged as shock finals contenders. And the representative selectors were quick to take notice. Salvatori was selected as a fresh reserve for the third State of Origin game.

"It was a huge thrill to gain the recognition from the selectors and make it to Origin level," he says. "I got 55 minutes and managed to make an impact. It was a great experience — the atmosphere was unreal. The blokes really made me feel at home which was a big thing. Most of the blokes had been there for years and they accepted me as the new boy straight away. I think Wally Lewis tried me out a bit and kept running at me. But I didn't let him through so I was happy. It was Wally's last Origin game and the Queenslanders rode high on the emotion of the occasion at Lang Park. They pipped us 14-12 to take the series, which was a bit of a downer in my first rep game."

Salvatori thought that brief taste of representative football would not lead to anything more that season, even with Test jumpers up for grabs against the Kiwis. The Easts forward wasn't even considered for the first Test, in Melbourne, nor did he expect to be. However, things in rugby league can sometimes change extremely quickly. Salvatori clearly remembers the odd circumstances that led to his selection for the second Test of that Kiwi series.

"It was funny ... I was watching the first Test down at the pub and naturally cheering for the Aussies. Mid-way through the game they were only leading 8-6, but I thought they were going to finish strongly so I went home. But the Kiwis turned it all around and won the game 24-8 in a major upset. I wasn't to know it at the time, but that was the best thing that could have happened to me. Had we won, I've no doubt the selectors would have stuck to the same team and I wouldn't have got a look-in.

"My one regret is that Blocker Roach got dropped to make way for me. I suppose everyone's time comes at some stage."

In winning a green-and-gold jumper, Salvatori became the first Easts front-row junior since the legendary Ray Stehr to win Test selection.

"It was an honour for both me and the club, and was beyond my wildest dreams," he says. "Mark Geyer also made his debut in the second Test, at the SFS, and it was heaven on earth for the pair of us. It was particularly great for me running out on my home track. There were a lot of Easts fans there and they really spurred me on. I'll never forget the feeling in the dressing room as the touch judge banged on the door and said: 'Come on Australia let's go."

Easts fans lined the tunnel as Salvatori charged onto the field, chanting his name and holding up a massive banner bearing the words 'Sal's Army'.

"It was enough to bring a tear to my eye, running out to such a reception," he says. "It's a feeling you can't really describe to anyone who hasn't

CRAIG SALVATORI

been there ... a mixture of pride, excitement and nerves. But it was sensational. I was really nervy the first time I touched the ball. And I remember at one stage early on I was taking a breather behind play when the Kiwis toed through a loose ball — I just froze. I didn't know whether to fall on it or pick it up ... it was scary. There were some fireworks early on which thankfully I kept well clear of. The Pommy referee sent off both Peter Jackson (Australia) and Jarrod McCracken (New Zealand) after one stink. But things settled down after that and it was a memorable night. We won 44-0 and I was happy with my form. But I felt far more relaxed in Brisbane for the third Test. We gave them another hiding 40-12 and I was just more comfortable. The nerves from my debut were gone and it was great to help Australia come back and win the series."

Salvatori was rewarded for his fine form with a spot on the Australian tour of Papua New Guinea at the end of the 1991 season. But the trip provided a sour ending to the best year of the big front-rower's life.

"Late in the season, I did the posterior cruciate ligament in my knee against Newcastle," he explains. "It wasn't too bad but I found it's the sort of injury you never completely get over. They can't operate — you have to learn how to run with it and how to fall without doing further damage. I probably wasn't 100 per cent fit for the PNG tour but got through the medical and was convinced in my own mind I'd be right. But it wasn't to be. I fell awkwardly in the first game and did it again. That was the end of my tour and it was very frustrating. I would have loved another couple of Tests under my belt.

"PNG was a fascinating place, even though I only saw it briefly. I remember against Lae — we were leading 24-0 when Ian Roberts made two of the biggest hits I've ever seen in quick succession. How the little blokes got back up was beyond me. The crowd went mad after both hits and in the end we had to tell Ian to quieten down. If he'd kept it up, there would have been a riot for sure. I needn't have worried. A few minutes later I ruptured the knee and was on the first plane back home for an operation."

Easts awarded Salvatori the first-grade captaincy in 1992, after the retirement of respected Kiwi Hugh McGahan. Easts again started the year well, and Salvatori revelled in his new role ... before disaster struck in a vital match against Penrith at Penrith Park.

"They had been niggling me and I got all worked up," Salvatori recalls. "I stood up in a tackle and led forward angrily with my head, without really looking. But I got the marker right on the chin and was sent straight off. That put a bit of a strain on the captaincy, to say the least.

"When I got a five-week suspension I realised I should have fought the judiciary back in '91, when they gave me that caution after I was marched against Souths. I'm sure I could have fought the judiciary then and cleared my name. When I got the five weeks, I think that was partly because of my previous conviction. But if I'd had a clean slate, which I believe I could have, they might have only given me a fortnight. At the time of the caution against Souths, I was just happy not to get suspended. I wasn't in the wrong. The bloke who refereed that game had over-reacted a bit. He's not in first grade any more so enough said."

Once again, Salvatori's problems didn't end when he left the judiciary room. The Easts hierarchy, fuming at the way his actions had cost the team a vital game, told Salvatori he wasn't welcome at training.

"Mark and Jack didn't take the episode well, understandably, and I went through some hard times. But a two-week suspension from my own club ... that hurt. I ended up going to New Zealand for a week just to escape everyone. I came back and stayed low key; then Jack rang me and invited me back. But I'd like to think I learned a lot from it; particularly how to keep my cool. I lost it that day and it cost both me and the club dearly."

Salvatori struggled from the start in his bid to retain his Test spot in 1992.

"At the end of 1991, I underwent a groin operation and, because of that, wasn't all that fit for the start of '92," he says. "Then I didn't have a real good game in the City-Country Origin and couldn't make the starting side for the State of Origin. I was a bit dirty the selectors didn't stick with me. Country won for the first time in years and obviously there was a big push for their players to get into the state side. Being a current Test player, I thought I deserved to keep my spot. Being named on the bench virtually destroyed any chance of me regaining my Test jumper. I thought they should have given me the chance to perform at the Origin level before dumping me. I never really got the chance but you just have to live with those things. The selectors have stuck with other players on reputation, but for some reason they didn't do that for me."

The selectors attempted to soften the blow by singing the praises of Salvatori as an impact player who could turn matches from the bench. And their words proved prophetic, as Salvatori scored the second of NSW's two tries to wrap up the opening game of the '92 series. But Salvatori was unimpressed.

"I don't picture myself as a great bench player." he contends. "What is an impact player? Calling me that was an excuse for not being able to find a spot for me in the side. It's a bit of a let-down when you're not in the starting side. I'll always do my best when I get on, but give me a spot in the top 13 any time."

The Easts enforcer started 1993 injury free and played a starring role

CRAIG SALVATORI

for City Origin against Country. But both Salvatori and Norths second-rower David Fairleigh, regarded as two of the best players on the field in that match, couldn't crack the NSW starting 13 for the first match of the '93 series. The Blues took that opening encounter, and Salvatori made his presence felt, playing strongly enough to raise hopes of a Test recall. But a premiership match, played on the rock-hard WACA strip in Perth, for Easts against Canberra the following week brought a premature end to Salvatori's season.

"It was an embarrassing way to go because no-one was near me when it happened. I was running down the blindside when I thought I spotted a gap just outside Mal Meninga. I stopped, and pivoted to go for the gap. My whole body came to a halt except my knee. It kept going and I heard this loud snap. I went down in a crumpled heap and Mal just patted me on the back and asked how I was. He'd heard it too and knew I was gone.

"To make matters worse, the paramedics ran on with a neck brace — they thought I'd snapped my spine. I just told them to get away. They finally brought out the stretcher and carted me off and that was that. In the same game, our young five-eighth, Scott Murray, suffered a similar injury to put him out for the year. It was a tragic night for the Roosters. There was a lot of talk at the time that the hard surface caused the injuries but I don't think so."

Salvatori didn't go in for surgery immediately, hoping against hope that building the knee up for six weeks would enable him to return for the latter stages of the season.

"I knew it was a long shot but Easts were still alive and I was desperate to get back. An arthroscope showed I'd snapped my anterior cruciate ligament, and the doctors gave me the option of rebuilding the knee to last the year out. Easts put no pressure on me whatsoever, but I thought I owed it to them to try. I gave it a go but I could feel it wasn't quite right. Easts were also on the slide and once they bowed out, I went under the knife."

Salvatori's much-discussed temper has been quelled by the persistent influence of the Easts coaching staff, although there are those who believe the Easts enforcer should retain his aggressive approach.

"Jack Gibson and Mark Murray have really taken the rough edges off my game. They have taught me to control my temper even though Blocker Roach reckons I should keep the aggro. He's told me I shouldn't mellow, but, in the modern game, you just can't afford to get into strife. I suppose it's still there in a way, just more controlled. What I'm trying to do is harness it and use it to my advantage. But I worry about snapping again all the time. People niggle me and I keep having to tell myself not to retaliate. I try to channel the aggression into other areas. I do a lot of talking on the field and I think that helps keep my cool. I don't shout at players to bag them — I'm just trying to keep the boys on edge and their minds on the day."

Salvatori's booming voice carries so much clout that team-mates once nick-named him "Foghorn" because of his incessant yelling. But the Easts skipper sees his booming voice as one of his most valuable assets.

"When I'm not playing, I think the boys miss it," he suggests. "I think that's my biggest influence on the team. It gets the other blokes talking and that's a good sign on the field. To my mind, players are like sheep — if they're told to do something, they do it. If they're not, they don't."

While the trend for modern forwards is to stay in tight, gain the hard yards and make the big hits, Salvatori prefers to stick to his own game.

"I'm not a David Gillespie or Paul Harragon who goes in there and does the big hits in defence," he says. "I pull one off now and then but it's not really my go. I'm more a running style of player and I like to attack with the ball out wide. I'm a safe defender and don't miss many tackles, but have never put fear into the opposition like some of these blokes. Maybe that's why they haven't been picking me for the Origin games ... who knows? It's something I may have to develop in the future. I know some old time front-rowers have criticised me for roaming out wide rather than staying in tight. But I'm convinced my way is the right one for me. It's what I do best and I think that, at club level at least, it's the right thing for the side. We've got players at Easts like Jason Lowrie and Bruce Sinclair who like hitting the ball up and do the job well. They enjoy it and it gives me more freedom to play their own game. In the City or NSW side, if (coach) Phil Gould wants me to play in tight, I'll be only too pleased to do it. But I really think the best part of my game is running off the five-eighth at the outside backs. Frankly, I can't see the sense in running at brick walls all day up the middle of the ruck. It's further out that most breaks are made and that's where I like to aim my runs. My game has evolved over the years — I started off just running the ball up but now I pick my mark and run wider. At Easts, I'm given a fairly free reign in attack; Mark Murray doesn't insist on me doing a lot early and that enables me to pick my time. I just like to go where the gaps are ... I've even scored tries on the wing. I tend to stand back for the first couple of tackles, looking for a hole to open before I make my move."

Salvatori is signed with Easts until the end of 1995 and will have played 11 seasons with the club by that time — not bad for a young firebrand few thought would go the distance.

"I'll be 29 in 1995. If Easts don't want me again at that stage, I'll think about playing in England," he says.

CRAIG SALVATORI

Salvatori and Brendan Hall are to be honoured with a testimonial for 10 years service in 1994. Easts, the club known as the transit lounge throughout the '80s because of its vast player turnover, has had few more loyal clubmen in recent years.

"The last blokes to get a testimonial were Kevin Hastings and John Tobin," Salvatori says. "That was 10 years ago and they came through the ranks together just like Brendan and I, so the precedent is there. I've never thought much about leaving; I've always been happy to sign well ahead of time and so other clubs haven't had much of a look-in. I've had a few nibbles, but nothing more than that. What it boils down to is that Easts have looked after me and I've never felt like playing elsewhere. I grew up here and feel very comfortable."

Salvatori is an occasional goalkicker and his style has often been the source of amusement for his team-mates.

"In 1991, Fatty Vautin bagged me all week saying: 'You're kidding; how can a big boofhead like you kick goals?' On the Sunday, in the game against Souths, we scored our first try right in the corner. Fatty then said to me: 'Let's see how you go with this one.'

"I hit it beautifully ... and the ball sailed right between the posts. I've come back with a big grin on my face and, as I ran past him, said: 'Get that one up ya, Fatty."

"He had a good laugh too but the coach wanted to know what we were doing giggling in the middle of the field. Luckily we won the game but if we hadn't, we might have had some explaining to do. Fatty was a fun guy. He could work himself up and get really motivated, but he was always ready for a laugh. I enjoyed his two years at Easts."

Fitness has posed some problems for Salvatori, but over the years he has learned to keep himself in good shape, and has firm views on training and its rewards.

"I put on a stone (seven kilos) every off season and it's hard work taking it off," he says. "But I don't think I'll put five stone on when I retire. Come March, I'm usually at the right playing weight. Easts have got me seeing a dietitian now to make sure I eat properly. I like my fast food and beer and that's probably brought me undone a bit. But I've been playing 10 years now ... that's longer than most blokes and it's too late to change. These 'new age' players, who train four hours a day and eat all the right stuff, worry me; I could never be like them. I believe you only have to be fit enough to play 80 minutes of football. Some of these blokes could play two games straight but it doesn't make them better players. You've just got to steel yourself for the 80 minutes and that's what I do."

After he retires, Salvatori hopes to break into coaching. "I've played under some good coaches and learned a lot from them," he comments. "It would be nice to get a start in the country or somewhere. To learn the ropes, I've become involved with a local C-grade team in the Eastern Suburbs in 1994. Ultimately I'd love to own a pub."

That last thought, perhaps as much as any other, would make Arthur Beetson proud.

HIT MEN

PAUL HARRAGON

Towards the 21st Century

Newcastle Knights colossus Paul Harragon is rugby league's lethal weapon of the '90s. Tall, muscular and athletic, Harragon is the prototype of the footballer of the 21st century. A gentle giant off the field, Harragon becomes a ruthless ground-gaining and opposition-crunching gladiator when he runs onto the paddock each winter weekend.

Dedicated to the cause, and with an intensity and professionalism akin to Balmain's remarkable local hero of the '80s, Wayne Pearce, Harragon is unlike the heavyweight forwards of the past. There isn't an ounce of fat on his massive frame — it's all muscle on muscle. And both sports scientists and rival forwards agree that muscle causes a lot more damage in a crunching tackle than fat. But it is Harragon's devastating tackling style that has found him unwittingly placed in the spotlight of controversy throughout his short but spectacular career. Harragon's uncompromising defence has more than once raised eyebrows in the NSWRL's headquarters in Phillip Street, as well as among opposition forwards. A quiet, indeed shy man by nature, Harragon, known to all as "The Chief", has worked hard to shed himself of the spectre of controversy. Mention his much-discussed tackling style and you feel the frustration build within Paul Harragon.

"People may not believe this, but I'm not naturally a tough guy," he says, almost pleading. "I don't know ... I just try to run hard and tackle hard. That's the nature of the game and the way I've always played it. You've got to do those things to be successful in league. I've had some nightmares over the past two years with the pressure people have been putting on my tackling. (Former Manly captain) Michael O'Connor was one, and there were many others. I was going into the game conscious of the way I was tackling. But I had less problems in 1993 than 1992. Maybe that means I'm past the worst of it ... I'd like to think that's the case. I'm not stupid and could see the writing on the wall. I have made some minor adjustments to my tackling style and 99 out of every 100 tackles I make, no-one could ever complain about."

While he may be a controversial figure outside the Hunter Valley coalfields, The Chief is nothing short of a superstar in the Newcastle region. The talented forward has the charisma and class of a winner, on and off the field, and has quickly endeared himself to the masses. He is a local boy made good; an honest toiler who has overcome adversity to wear the colours of Newcastle, NSW and Australia with pride.

Harragon's football pedigree is impressive, hailing from the town of Kurri Kurri — home of nearly a dozen internationals over the years — where he was born in 1968. Young Paul moved to the Lakes area in his early years and because of his size and speed, found himself starting his football days as a centre. He played for Valentine-Eleebana before moving up to Lakes United in the under-15s.

"I was tall and skinny ... built like a minute to six," he says. "I loved playing in the centres in those days and enjoyed roaming out wide." Yet Harragon's most vivid memories of his early football days are of his time as a ballboy. "Mate, I used to ballboy for anybody I could find. I loved to be close to the action and to watch the big boys go around. When my elder brother Mark was playing seniors for Lakes, I would just watch him and marvel. He was hot and it was a privilege for me to be ballboy for his team."

Mark Harragon made the move to Sydney in the early '80s and played with Newtown and Norths, before a broken leg brought a premature end to his career.

"That was a tragedy," Paul says. "Mark had as much potential as anyone and I really expected him to make it big in Sydney. That injury was a bad one and prevented him from going on with it, but I still have great respect for his ability and knowledge as a footballer. Come State of Origin time, I still ring him every day — that's how highly I rate his advice and help with my preparation. When I was a kid, I used to idolise him. We're still good mates. We're a real close family in general and my parents, Harold and Judy, have been a big help to me throughout my life, both in and out of football."

Lakes decided Harragon was ready for first grade at 18, and the move proved an instant success, with the Harragon-charged Lakes winning the Newcastle premiership in his maiden season. Ironically, club officials had to twist the Chief's arm to play football that year.

"After some disappointments in the previous season, I was a bit hesitant about playing at the start of that year," he remembers. "We'd only made the (second-grade) final after winning the comp in '85 and I really felt it. I was

PAUL HARRAGON

a bit disenchanted with the game and was thinking of quitting, at least for a while. But at the start of '87 I made the Newcastle rep side even though I hadn't played a game in first grade. That really blew me out of the water and gave me the drive to play again. I played for Newcastle in the NSW Country under-19 championships and we won it for the first time in yonks. That was a huge deal for us at the time and proved my stepping stone to the Knights. A couple of others blokes from the team, including Ashley Gordon, also signed up. When the Knights approached me, I jumped at it, even though it was for fiddlesticks ... I'd have played for no money at all. The prospect of playing for the club in its first year was a rare honour and I had had a great lead-up by playing in that winning Lakes team in the '87 grand final."

It was in his days at Lakes that a team-mate dubbed Harragon "The Chief", after the character in the '70s hit movie, *One Flew Over the Cuckoo's Nest*.

"It stuck and, to be honest, I quite like it," Harragon muses. "I've been called a lot worse in my time. It's got a nice ring to it. The guy in the movie was a big, silent type whose action spoke louder than his words, and he had long hair as I did at the time. So, I guess there are similarities."

In 1989, when Harragon initially burst onto the first-grade scene, a journalist at Knights training asked experienced forward Tony Butterfield why the players called the new young giant The Chief.

"Because he tells us to," Butterfield replied dryly.

The Knights recognised they had a rare talent in Harragon from the start, but were content to bring the youngster along slowly in their maiden season in 1988.

"I mainly played in the under-21s, although I did get eight reserve-grade games," he says. "I was also named in the NSW under-21 side and that was a thrill because we were coached by Jack Gibson. I'd heard so much about him and enjoyed getting to meet the man."

Harragon admits he didn't take kindly to biding his time in the lower grades.

"I thought I was ready to play first grade that year and to me, playing President's Cup was a bit of a backward step. The Newcastle comp was strong and we regularly played in front of big crowds so I was looking forward to making it straight away with the Knights. I was a big kid by then, there were no problems with size. But because I was still only 20, they wanted to bring me along slowly. They kept me down a little bit and told me to be patient."

At the beginning of 1989 Harragon was back in the President's Cup, yet by mid-season had forced his way into first grade.

HIT MEN

"I was again in the NSW under-21 side," he recalls," and, straight after I came back, (Newcastle's then first-grade coach) Allan McMahon named me in his team. At the time, we had several Kiwis in the Newcastle side and they were away on Test duty against Australia. That gave me my chance. I remember making my debut against Balmain in a Saturday game at home. The Tigers were a strong side that year, and went on to make the grand final, and we were given little hope of beating them. But we went out and belted them. I had a fair game and there was no turning back. Being my first game, I played like my life depended on it. I was ready for a big one and was desperate to make an impression. There was a big crowd there backing us and that lifted me. I had the drive, had the chance, and was determined to make the most of it."

Harragon was determined to build on his success in 1989. He trained harder than ever during the 1989-90 off-season and looked set for a memorable year ... before it all went wrong.

"I remember starting '90 like a train," he says. "After hitting the weights over the summer, I was 116kg. I then trimmed down to 110 by the time the season started. I was feeling confident within myself and played great football in the first five games. My immediate goal was to make the Country side and I knew I was a good show. But two games before the Country team was named I did my knee against Penrith. I was ecstatic at being named in the team, but when my name was read out I knew I had next to no chance of playing. Somehow I got through the medical but it was just delaying the inevitable. Being a Kangaroo year, I was desperate to play in the first rep game of the season and then possibly go on to NSW and Australian selection. But the cartilage was torn to smithereens. I tried to train but it was just a joke, and I reluctantly pulled out the day before the City-Country game. Soon after, I went under the knife and was out six weeks.

"I came back midway through the second round and thought I could still salvage something out of the season. But, in my second game back, I did my hamstring badly against Canterbury. That set me back again but I was still determined to make the Roo tour. I came back again, against Wests late in the season, and did the hammy again. And once I did that, my back started to play up. I had injections ... the knee and hamstring were still bad ... I felt like I was falling apart. At one stage I thought I'd never be the same again. Our club doctor, Neil Halpin, was great and helped me a lot.

"Eventually it was some advice from Mal Cochrane, who used to play for Manly, that put me on the road to recovery. He'd had a similar injury and had the same problem finding a cure. Eventually, he found that walking up a hill every day for an hour enabled him to gradually get back on track. I

PAUL HARRAGON

was desperate by this stage and ready to try anything. So every day for two or three weeks my dad and I would go up this hill. After that, I jogged up it for two or three weeks, and finally I sprinted up for another few weeks. I missed the first five games of 1991 but I knew the treatment was working. And, once I got back, there were no further problems."

The year 1991 was one of turmoil for the Knights. The team failed to perform to expectations, leading to McMahon rocking the coal city by quitting midway through the second round. David Waite took over the hot seat.

"We had a lot of problems that year but I was coming off contract and knew I needed to go well to get a decent deal for the future," Harragon says. "I started to hit my straps again late in the season, after Waite took over, and the Knights came to the party, giving me a good contract."

That strong finish to 1991 proved the impetus for the coming of age of both Paul Harragon and the Newcastle Knights in 1992. The Knights reached the semi-finals for the first time, while Harragon won both NSW and Australian honours.

"It was a vintage year and really put me on the map," he says. "One reason why things went so well is that I started the season injury free. I made the Country side and we beat Sydney for the first time since 1975. I scored a couple of tries and then made the NSW side.

"Playing with the Blues was a real learning experience. Their preparation for the State of Origin matches was great — we left nothing to chance.

"Looking back, you don't realise how important it all is until it's over. I was just so involved that I didn't take a wider perspective at the time. Now I can look back and take pride in it all. In the opening game at the Sydney Football Stadium I came out all pumped up but was quickly given an old-fashioned State of Origin welcome. I got knocked senseless in a heavy hit by Gavin Allen and Trevor Gillmeister. They just snotted me in the first five minutes. I stayed on although my legs were pretty rubbery for quite a while."

Harragon also found himself the subject of bitter feelings from the Queensland camp for a strong tackle that KO'd Maroon forward Gary Larson during a frantic first half.

"There was a lot of ill-feeling over that, but what people don't realise is that I was knocked out not long beforehand. I can't remember that whole first half. After the match blokes came up to me and said: 'Geez, you hit that Larson with a beauty'. The first I knew of it was when I saw it on video. Fortunately we won that game, before Queensland squared the series with a last-minute Alfie Langer field goal up at Lang Park.

"Even though I was again knocked out — and again by Trevor Gillmeister

HIT MEN

— in the third game, it will go down as easily the best day of my life. The game was back in Sydney, which was a huge advantage to us because of all the fantastic home crowd support. As well as trying to help the Blues with the series, I was concentrating on making the Test side. The team was to be named after the game and I knew I was close. I felt I had to play just one more big game to get the nod from the selectors. Although I once again went down for the count, we won the game convincingly, 16-4, to take the trophy. NSW haven't won that many series over the years and it was a superb feeling. To cap it off, the Blues coach, Phil Gould, gave me his man-of-the-series award when we got back to the dressing room. To get such a seal of approval from the State coach was magical.

"Then we wandered over to the Members Bar at the old SCG, where ARL chief Ken Arthurson announced the team to take on the Poms. To hear my name get called out was just sensational. It was a long time coming, and the first thing I did was hug my dad, who was standing beside me. I knew it meant as much to him as it did to me."

The fierce Anglo-Australian Test arena proved to Harragon's liking as the home side defended the Ashes against the traditional enemy. The Australians picked a tried-and-tested combination for the first Test at the SFS, with Harragon the lone new cap. The young forward went into the match knowing the Englishmen were certain to test his mettle.

"Being in the dressing room before kick-off ... wearing the green and gold ... staring at all my team-mates and knowing we were about to do battle with the enemy ... it was an enormous feeling. They (the Lions) were dirty buggers and there's no doubt they targeted me as the new kid on the block. In the first scrum, Kelvin Skerrett and Ian Lucas gave me a hard time, sledging me. I didn't say anything back. 'They'll keep,' I thought, and concentrated on the game. Soon afterwards, Lucas came at me and I hit him with a hard tackle which people later tried to get me in trouble over. But it was a legal tackle. I hit him around the chest and then his head hit me right on the hip and that stuffed him up."

Lucas was never the same player after that tackle. He returned home soon afterwards and retired within 12 months, citing the tackle from The Chief as the one that finished his career.

"When we got to England for the World Cup later that year, the Poms really gave me a bagging over the Lucas incident. But I didn't even hit him with my arm; it was his head hitting my hip that did all the damage."

Australia won the opening Test in decisive style 22-6, with Mal Meninga stealing the limelight, scoring two tries. The Lions hit back with a shock 33-10 win in Melbourne, before Australia took the series in the Lang Park decider, 16-10. The Englishmen showed a distinct dislike for Harragon's bit

PAUL HARRAGON

hitting and straight running, with the Knights forward prominent throughout the series.

Harragon then set his sights on the one-off Test against the Papua New Guinea Kumuls in Townsville. The match represented a major stepping stone to another crack at the Great Britain side in the World Cup final, which was to be played in October, at Wembley Stadium.

But fate stepped in. After having the football world at his massive feet only weeks earlier, Harragon found himself on the outside, looking in. The Chief was selected for the Kumul Test but was then promptly cited for a tackle on State of Origin team-mate David Fairleigh, in a club match against North Sydney. In a controversial decision, the judiciary suspended the Test prop.

However, the ultimate penalty proved far harsher — the suspension ended up costing Harragon his place in the World Cup final.

"I can't tell you how demoralised I was," he says. "All the time it took me to get there ... I'd climbed the mountain and done all these great things. It was a bullshit tackle really and I reckon they were catching up with me for the Larson tackle in the first State of Origin clash and the one on Lucas. They didn't cite me for either one but I'm certain the word was out to get me. In the end they got me for a nothing tackle on Fairleigh. It was just a joke. They pulled me off the plane to Townsville, and I was shattered. That ended me as far as rep football went that season. I went away with the World Cup side but couldn't get a game. It was horrible watching it all from the sideline. I was spewing ... there was nothing worse than going all that way and not getting a game. Wembley Stadium ... I'd dreamed about it and it would have been great to get on there. I'd gone the full circle that season. I reached the top but no-one told me what to do next. I'd achieved my goals but then was lost for a while. All I could do was start climbing again."

The one saving grace for Harragon late in 1992 was Newcastle's charge into the finals. Buoyed by a convoy of fans that travelled to Sydney with the team, the Knights took the SFS by storm. With Harragon and Mark Sargent calling the shots up front, the Knights boasted the most feared pack in the finals. Even so, they went into the minor preliminary semi against an experienced Western Suburbs side as underdogs, and started shakily. But a fierce Harragon hit midway through the first half proved a turning point, inspiring the Knights to hit their straps. It was a tackle Harragon had waited over two years to make.

Back in 1990, the Magpies player had decked Harragon with a high tackle during a club match. Harragon was unconscious even before he hit the ground that day and took eight minutes to come back around in the dressing room. The case went to judiciary but the tackler was found not

HIT MEN

guilty because the video evidence was inconclusive. Harragon obviously did not forget the incident. As Wests swung the ball out, he picked his mark and launched a 116-kilo missile at the Magpie's sternum. The tackle was perfectly legal, and brutal in its intensity. The Wests forward staggered to his feet, but played little further part in the game.

Newcastle won the match 21-2, but the following weekend were unlucky to go down to St George 3-2. Cruelly for Harragon, he was penalised for a play-the-ball indiscretion against Saints in the desperate last few minutes as the Knights attempted to keep their premiership dream alive. After that ruling, Saints worked play downfield and were able to hang on for a dour win. But the Knights had done Newcastle proud, though Harragon and his team-mates left the SFS that night convinced they could have easily taken the game and moved a step closer to the grand final.

The disappointing finish to 1992 left Harragon determined to regain lost ground the following year.

"I reasoned that 1993 was the time where I had to decide between being a one-year wonder or really setting myself up," he says. "It was a real make-or-break situation in my own mind I was starting from scratch. I was hungry and happy with my early season form — I thought I was playing as well as the previous year, but Newcastle weren't winning as many games. Even so, the critics jumped up and said: 'The Knights are losing ... Harragon and Sargent aren't playing that well.'

"To my mind, I was playing great and the stats on stuff like work rate confirmed that. But when the City-Country match came around, the Country selectors only named me on the bench. That to me was the lowest of the low. Just a year earlier I'd helped them to beat Sydney for the first time in memory, scored two tries, yet they didn't even give me the courtesy of letting me try to do it again. To me, I was left with nothing. I didn't know if I'd get five minutes, 20 minutes or half a game. I thought my Origin chances were washed away. But, thankfully, I got plenty of game time. I did okay for Country and then got into the NSW side and it all fell into place."

The Blues again won the series against Queensland, taking the opening two games, at Lang Park and the SFS, before Queensland salvaged some pride in the final match back on their home turf. Harragon's powerhouse play was among the Blues' trump cards, with his toe-to-toe stoush with Queensland opposite Martin Bella one of the talking points of the series. The two big men traded blows for over 30 seconds, with Harragon taking a clear points decision. The Chief's effort made such an impact that a leading boxing promoter approached him to fight professionally. But Harragon had other things on his mind and was delighted at winning a green-and-gold recall for the Tests against New Zealand.

PAUL HARRAGON

"It was a new experience playing the Kiwis and I was very happy with the way I went," he says. "We drew the first Test, in Auckland, but then won the second in trying conditions at Palmerston North. I was lucky enough to win the man-of-the-match award in that game, and then we finished them off with a win at Lang Park in the third Test."

An astute reader of the psychology of rugby league, Harragon is intent on not resting on his laurels in coming years.

"I'll play the game for another five years and I haven't given a thought as to what I'll do after that," he reveals. "I'm pretty good as far as work off the field goes. But I'm realistic enough to know that whatever I do after football will be linked to how well I play the game. If I can really make a name for myself, it will be that much easier in later life. If I do my best here, hopefully I will have set myself up when I finish. I've still got a lot to prove. That I'm not a half flash in the pan and that sort of thing. It comes down to how badly I want things and if I'm prepared to make sacrifices. At the moment, I've still got the hunger to succeed."

Harragon has become a celebrity in Newcastle, and is occasionally embarrassed by his sudden rise to fame. Modest by nature, he remains one of the boys and hasn't let the adoration of the fans get to his head.

"You've got to put it in perspective," he says. "In Newcastle and the Hunter Valley there are 500,000 people and they are all mad keen on rugby league. It's a big area — easily the second biggest market, after Sydney, in NSW. It can be a bit hard sometimes, but overall it's great. Generally all the boys enjoy it and it's a good kickalong to have so much support."

Sponsors have been quick to latch on to Harragon's immense popularity, with the Chief endorsing a health fund, a brewery and a radio station, as well as car and tyre companies in the Newcastle area. Indications are it won't be long before Harragon is used in national advertising campaigns alongside the likes of Andrew Ettingshausen and Allan Langer. Knights marketing manager Leigh Maughan regards Harragon as commercial dynamite.

"He could well be described as the most promotable forward in the game," Maughan claims. "We've found that the Chief is the pin-up boy of the four-year-olds and the 84-year-olds. He has the size, the good looks and the personality to really win over a crowd.

"I'll never forget when the Newcastle contingent arrived at the Sheraton Hotel in Sydney for the Rothmans Medal presentation in 1993". There were photographers everywhere but when we walked in, they all surged on Paul. The rest of us looked at each other and agreed ...

"Chief had arrived."

Bibliography

BOOKS

Malcolm Andrews, The ABC of Rugby League, ABC Enterprises, Sydney 1992
Geoff Armstrong (editor), The Greatest Game, Ironbark Press, Sydney, 1991
Jack Gibson, Winning Starts on Monday, Lester-Townsend, Sydney, 1989
David Hadfield, Playing Away: Australians in British Rugby League, Kingswood Press, London, 1992
Ian Heads, The History of Souths, Hoffman-Smith, Sydney, 1985
Ian Heads, Sterlo: The Story of a Champion, Lester-Townsend, Sydney, 1989
Ian Heads, The March of the Dragons, Lester-Townsend, Sydney, 1989
Ian Heads, The Kangaroos, Lester-Townsend, Sydney, 1990
Ian Heads, True Blue: The Story of the NSW Rugby League, Ironbark Press, Sydney, 1992
Gary Lester, The Sun Book of Rugby League, Fairfax Press, Sydney, 1984
Gary Lester, The Story of Australian Rugby League, Lester-Townsend, Sydney, 1988
Roy Masters, Inside League, Pan, Sydney, 1990
Jack Pollard (editor), Rugby League The Australian Way, Summit Books, Sydney, 1981
Steve Roach, Doing My Block, Ironbark Press, Sydney, 1993
Alan Whiticker, Grand Finals of the NSW Rugby League, Gary Allen, Sydney, 1992
Alan Whiticker, The Encyclopedia of Rugby League Players, Gary Allen, Sydney, 1993

NEWSPAPERS & MAGAZINES

The Daily Telegraph Mirror; Rugby League Week; League's Top 40; Rugby League Week's Top 100 Players